W9-BQL-417

A HISTORY OF
IBERIAN CIVILIZATION

A HISTORY OF
IBERIAN CIVILIZATION

BY

J. P. DE OLIVEIRA MARTINS

TRANSLATED BY

AUBREY F. G. BELL

WITH A PREFACE BY

S. DE MADARIAGA

COOPER SQUARE PUBLISHERS, INC.
NEW YORK
1969

Originally Published and Copyright © 1930
by the Oxford University Press
Reprinted by arrangement with The Oxford University Press

Published 1969 by
Cooper Square Publishers, Inc.
59 Fourth Avenue, New York, N. Y. 10003
Library of Congress Catalog Card No. 71-81778
Standard Book Number 8154-0300-3

Printed in the United States of America
by Noble Offset Printers, Inc.   New York, N. Y. 10003

PREFACE

ON Oliveira Martins as a historian and on the place which his *History of the Iberian Civilization* must be assigned in Iberian Literature, the reader will be enlightened by the introduction which Mr. Aubrey Bell has written for his translation of this remarkable work. Why such a translation should be one of the first books to appear under the auspices of the Oxford Chair of Spanish Studies will be obvious to all readers of the work and of Mr. Bell's introduction. 'History seen through a temperament' is Mr Bell's definition of Oliveira Martins' work. But is not all history 'as she is written' seen through a temperament ? The antithesis implied in contrasting scientific with temperamental history overlooks the fact that scientific history is but history seen through the scientific—or rather through a scientific—temperament, and, furthermore, that the qualities which go to the making of scientific temperaments imply features which determine the treatment of the historian's material and his vision of history, not always to the advantage of that immanent truth which lurks behind scientific truths and delights in eluding the searcher.

Oliveira Martins and his work afford an admirable subject for observation in this respect. An intuitive historian with the gift of vision, he lived in an age which believed in science 'with both feet together' as the Spanish saying goes. Yet, when he fails, it is in the use of scientific methods, not in his intuition. True that his scientific methods are defective, so that his failure is but a vindication of science. But it is doubtful whether a better scientific method and a severer discipline would have improved his brilliant, penetrating analysis of the Iberian fact. It certainly would have removed blemishes of detail, some of them, it must be

owned, of important detail, such as those which Mr.
Bell has brought out in his introduction. Oliveira
Martins is moreover, as his translator rightly says,
somewhat prejudiced in favour of his native Portugal.
But, leaving aside the fact that such a failing is wellnigh
universal in historians, what is admirable in Oliveira
Martins is his capacity for seeing right through a maze
of errors as well as his courage in putting before the
Iberian peoples the general lines of a civilization and a
culture which most of them had proved unable to see
as one harmonious whole.

The *History of the Iberian Civilization* is not of
course the last word on the subject. The last word in
history is never said, for history must be re-written
periodically through every age's temperament, to adopt
Mr. Bell's telling expression. But it is the first word.
For the first time an Iberian looks at Iberia as Iberia
and reports to the world what the world has received
and may still expect to receive from the peoples of the
Peninsula. It is a singular good fortune that this bold
Iberian should have been a Portuguese. For under his
free and ardently patriotic pen, the Peninsular vision
which animates his work can never be interpreted as
impairing even by a shadow of a doubt the independent
nationhood of Portugal. With that prophetic gift
which his translator has discerned in him, Oliveira
Martins saw the truth which our present age is beginning to realize, mostly by the example of the
British Empire: that spiritual unity may underlie
political variety and give it strength without depriving
it of liberty.

S. DE M.

CONTENTS

TRANSLATOR'S INTRODUCTION

THE most brilliant and original of Portuguese historians, one of the most interesting literary figures of nineteenth-century Europe, Joaquim Pedro de Oliveira Martins (1845–94), was born of poor parents at Lisbon in the year 1845. His education was broken short at the age of twelve by his father's death, and for the next twelve years he worked in an office in Lisbon and supported his mother and brothers and sisters. He was already married and a writer, author of a novel and some literary criticism, when he accepted a post in a mining company near Córdoba. Here the literary and practical sides of his character manifested themselves in the books he wrote: a study of the poet Camões and a study of the theory of Socialism. In 1874 he returned to Portugal and was employed as engineer on the railway then building between Oporto and Povoa, of which subsequently he became director. These years, 1874–84, were years also of fervent literary activity, and saw the publication of such well-known works as *O Hellenismo e a Civilisação Cristã* (1878), *Historia da Civilisação Iberica* (1879), *Historia de Portugal* (1879), *Portugal Contemporaneo* (1881), besides several important works on early myths and races and economic subjects. The *Historia da Republica Romana* followed in 1885.

In politics Oliveira Martins had begun by being a Socialist of a revolutionary type, and throughout his work we find him opposed to private ownership of land. Such denunciations, like those of Tolstoi, in the second half of the nineteenth century, were destined to bear fruit. The old-established families, under whom the possession of landed property had been productive of ideal character and happiness, were to be dispossessed and their place taken by enriched grocers in revolutionary times, the title of the latter to the land being made sacred owing to the ironical fact that a wave of conservatism always follows such periods of upheaval. Oliveira Martins himself came to demand the rule of a 'tyrant' in Portugal, believing that such a strong, direct and personal government would conduce to the welfare of the people, to the exclusion of parliamentary incompetence and political intrigue. He joined the Progressista Party, but left it on the death of its leader, Braamcamp. In 1891 he was invited by King Carlos to become a member of the Ministry to be formed by the Conde de Valbom; but Oliveira Martins refused, the Conde de Valbom failed to form a Ministry, and Oliveira Martins became Minister of Finance in the government presided over by José Dias Ferreira. The post of Minister of Finance at that time, immediately after the declared bankruptcy of Portugal, offered great difficulties and great opportunities. Oliveira Martins set to work with all his strenuous activity and impetuous, not equable strength of will to carry through a well-considered plan of finance. He had the support of the King; but while his thoughts were exclusively concerned with financial measures he lived in the midst of political intrigues and fell from office in a few months. He paid a brief visit to England and wrote *A Inglaterra de Hoje* (1892), and then returned to his historical work. He happily emphasized the biographical side of his talent, and the result was *Os Filhos de D. João I* (1891), followed by what he called his swan-song: *A Vida de Nun'Alvares* (1893). At his death he was engaged upon another hero, another subject brilliantly dramatic, that of King João II, *O Principe Perfeito*, his fragment of which appeared posthumously in 1896. Oliveira Martins was worn out and discouraged. Life, as he wrote to Jayme de Magalhães Lima in November 1893, had not been for him a path of roses: 'A vida não tem sido para mim uma cousa facil nem alegre'. In the following year he died, just before attaining the fiftieth year of his age.

Oliveira Martins' business, professional, political and administrative life was sufficient to exhaust the energies of the strongest man. To this was added his literary work, in which he embraced the history of ancient and modern Portugal, the history of Spain, the history of Rome, ethnology, mythology, finance, socialism, literary criticism, and the drama (none of his dramatic works were published). In the treatment of all these subjects he claimed to be rigidly scientific and impersonal. He was of course just the reverse, always personal and subjective. One may sometimes think that he was a novelist who had mistaken his vocation, and in some respects he closely resembled his friend the contemporary Portuguese novelist, Eça de Queiroz. As a novelist he is not, of course, to be judged by his weak novel *Phebus Moniz*, written as early as 1866, but by many a brilliantly picturesque page of reconstruction of persons and events in his historical work. With his keen eye for the picturesque and dramatic he has been called ' a historical artist rather than an historian'. ' He was at once a Mommsen and a Michelet'[1] There was more of Michelet than of Mommsen in him, although there was a little of both. Oliveira Martins had not the education of a scholar nor the method of a scientific historian. Yet he persisted in being scientific, and although he had not the time or knowledge to indulge in original research, he made up for this by brilliant intuitions founded on the best authorities available in his day. It was his gift to seize the essential points of older or contemporary writers with lightning speed, to pounce eagerly on analogies, developing them according to his theories and temperament without studying the materials at first hand. Some of his reconstructions are likely to live as part of Portuguese literature; and when

[1] A. Sergio in *Dispersos*, vol. i (Lisboa, 1923), p. viii.

his patriotism and genuine interest in the people and love of democracy are concerned he can make the dullest subject interesting. But his sympathies were limited, and where they fail his method and even his literary style fail also, and his treatment of history become not scientific but pseudo-scientific. He shows from time to time a lack of clearness, a nebulous style veiling a difficulty in fitting a fact into a previous theory. His glittering and persuasive style, his apparent scientific fairness (covering subjective partiality) caused him to be widely read in the Peninsula. He in fact became one of the subversive influences in the last quarter of the nineteenth century, militating against the Braganzas, the Jesuits and England. He thus unconsciously and unwillingly contributed to the overthrow of the Portuguese Monarchy, although, in the latter part of his life at least, he had looked on the monarchy as the last stay and support of the people, to whose interests he was so genuinely and unselfishly attached. 'This [Portuguese] people,' he wrote in 1887, 'so apathetic, so melancholy, so pessimistic, injured by politics, without belief or hope in anything, clings to the monarchical tradition: an instinctive good sense tells it that its own interests are bound up with those of its king.'[1]

But we are not here concerned with Oliveira Martins' place in Portuguese politics but with his work as historian. Superficially his work may have the appearance of being coldly scientific; but if one probes into it one discovers that the materials out of which he composes his logical results are of unequal worth, varying in value according to his own knowledge and sympathies. He is thus attempting the impossible task of constructing an isosceles triangle with legs of unequal length. To those who are sceptical concerning systematic theories, brilliantly constructed with swift intuitions and neat antitheses and then forcibly imposed on the individual

[1] *Dispersos*, vol. i, p. 67.

phenomenon, it will always be at once amusing and
instructive to watch Oliveira Martins unconsciously
applying his alluring scientific net (which he believed
to be all of one material), at one time with fruitful
results, at another quite barrenly, according as his knowledge of the subject was deeper (as in the case of Portuguese literature and the character of the Portuguese
Conquistadores), or more superficial (as in the case of
English literature or sixteenth-century Spain). With
flashes of genius he could penetrate into the future
as into the past. He could often hit the nail very
accurately on the head. Forty years ago he prophesied
that King Alfonso XIII would be the link uniting the
glories of Spain's past to the Spain of a great and
prosperous future; a quarter of a century before the
Great War he was unveiling the character of Kaiser
Wilhelm II in a way which was not ordinary then and
forecasting his future; in 1893 he described the world
as having got itself into a *cul de sac*: 'O mundo acha-se
no fundo de um beco sem saida'.[1] He had intense
moments of constructive fervour; but the general effect
of his historical writings was negative and pessimistic.
He swam vigorously enough, but it was in a sea of
doubt; and there is a kernel of scepticism, even a faint
undercurrent of sneering persiflage (with some faults
of taste and some faults of grammar), which weakens
and invalidates his work. When he crystallizes history
round such figures as the Perfect Prince or Prince
Henry the Navigator, Afonso de Albuquerque, or
Dom João de Castro, he can be admirable and con-
vincing. On the other hand, in his penetrating narrowness he seemed quite unable to understand the true
greatness of sixteenth-century Spain, any more than
that of England.

Thus we find such statements as the following: that
Os Lusiadas of Camões is the greatest poem of modern

[1] *Correspondencia de J. P. Oliveira Martins* (Lisboa, 1926), p. 239.

times[1] (that is, that there is nothing to equal it in Milton or Shakespeare; although these poets are not mentioned, they are simply ignored); that there is nothing in Castilian literature to compare with *Os Lusiadas* in moral worth[2] (which is a strange confession of ignorance of Castilian literature); that the Spanish are a mixture of natural candour and violent explosions[3] (a description much better suited to the Portuguese than to the Castilians); that the Portuguese Conquistadores were tragic and just while those of Spain were external and comic[4]. That is the disadvantage of scientific history: Oliveira Martins naturally enough knew more of the Portuguese than of the Spanish Conquistadores; the real distinction between them requires different epithets. It might be said that the Spanish Conquistadores were well-balanced, whereas the Portuguese tended to run to extremes and excess, in cruelty (Almeida, Albuquerque and others), greed (Martim Afonso de Sousa and many others), or a rigid and indeed almost pedantic honesty (D. João de Castro).

There are other statements which seem to betray that the author's knowledge of sixteenth-century Spain was not profound. He speaks of it as 'a sudden, brief splendour',[5] but after all a century is a century, and it was prolonged for another brilliant half century in Spain. His reference to the 'ingenuous ignorance' of the Spanish mystics[6] might seem to indicate that St. John of the Cross grew up without study like a lily of the field, which was far from being the case. He suggests that Mariana was threatened with death, if not actually executed for openly criticizing the monarchy:[7] yet such criticism was common in the Latin writings of Spanish and Portuguese authors of that age, and Mariana, though his *De Rege* was burnt by the

---

[1] *Historia da Civilisação Iberica*, 6th ed., Lisboa, 1918, p. 289.
[2] Ibid., p. 295.   [3] Ibid., p. 247   [4] Ibid., 287, 288, 291.
[5] Ibid., p. 242.   [6] Ibid., p. 245.   [7] Ibid., p. 341.

hangman at Paris, lived comfortably in Spain to the age of nearly ninety; the view given of *Don Quixote*[4] is superficial, nor were the Catalinons and Chocolates born when *Don Quixote* was written: Sancho was rather their literary father than their heir. It is generally dangerous to treat of the Golden Age *en bloc*; thus in successive sentences[5] we find Oliveira Martins referring to the state of the population at the death of Philip II and quoting from Gil Vicente words written before Philip II was born: the difficulty confronting the historian is to discover why the same conditions apparently could spell failure and success. That age generally is described by Fray Alonso de Cabrera in 1598 as a 'golden age', and if we need not pin our faith too credulously to the praises of a funeral oration we may turn to Mariana, who so clearly saw the dangerous state of the Spanish empire at the end of the sixteenth century; and we find him corroborating Cabrera's praise, at least so far as concerns the encouragement of literature and learning. To Oliveira Martins the Counter-Reformation was merely an opponent, not an encourager of culture.

Oliveira Martins' attitude towards Philip II and sixteenth-century Spain has some excuse, for he wrote when 'History', that fascinating deceiver, had for three centuries very methodically misrepresented all that period; and just before the modern reaction, which shows it in a truer light, had set in. Philip II was still the Demon of the South and Spain was generally believed to have had a monopoly of cruelty and intolerance. More impartial research has now relegated such notions to the cupboard of History's cast-off clothes.

According to Oliveira Martins the causes of the decadence of Spain were individualism, the Jesuits, and the sixteenth-century conquests. It is, as he remarks, diffi-

[4] Ibid., p. 303.   [5] Ibid., p. 305.

cult to distinguish in this question between causes
and consequences. Probably historians will disagree as
to the real cause to the end of time. Why, it is asked,
should individualism have shortened the life of the
Spanish Empire when the more lasting British Empire
is likewise the work of a nation of individualists? One
might answer that the Spanish are as a rule more angular
than the English, less give-and-take and easy-going, and
less prone to co-operate, and that the noble qualities
of the modern Spaniard, as of the ancient Iberian, seem
to demand heroic strife and hardship, and are apt to
crumble away before success; but the fact is that no
individual enterprise can withstand constant disillusion
or persistent shackling from an incompetent political
system. Harass, overtax, or coddle the individual, and
the end of any empire is in sight; give him a free hand
and great rewards, and empires are built up.

Oliveira Martins is unfair to the Jesuits, who did
such heroic work in India and America; and as to the
Inquisition his statements were based, not on any deep
inquiry, but on books which had some reputation in his
day. Thus he can state that Torquemada burnt nine
thousand persons in eighteen years, although he might
have been perplexed if asked for any proof of his statement's truth. He could only have referred the inquirer
to Llorente or some other writer, not to contemporary
documents. The real figure was closer to ninety than
to nine thousand.

The real causes of Spain's decadence were economic.
She had wished to hold the New World and its trade
as a monopoly, and as a result her empire became
almost as artificial as Napoleon's continental system. It
is no doubt in the nature of human greatness that it
cannot endure—wealth and prosperity brought their
own dangers; but if a moral cause must be assigned for
Spain's decay it must be sought not in the Inquisition,
which by maintaining unity prolonged the Spanish

empire for a hundred years, and individual fear of whose action has been exaggerated (certainly some of the Spanish theologians and thinkers of that time were exceptionally outspoken), but in the divorce between culture and the people, which was one of the ultimate consequences of the Renaissance. Spain was exhausted, and although the nation remained individually sound and the peasantry continued to be one of the finest in Europe, the spring which impelled this people to heroic action was broken. A new people, moreover, had sprung up in the cities, a people without the moral stamina of the peasantry, a 'vulgo' who confused virtue with riches: 'introdujo por ella a las riquezas'.[1] Spain's exhaustion was the opportunity of other nations, then in the full vigour of their development, and the consequences of conflict with them, made bitter and ferocious by difference of religion, were fatal to Spain's empire and material prosperity. Later, when the Spanish saw the prosperity of other nations, in an age when prosperity counted for everything, Liberals in Spain, the men whom Oliveira Martins calls 'an élite in whom the national traditions had become effaced', came to believe that Spain had fallen behind in the race, not because the national unity of action and religious fervour of the sixteenth century had abated, but because Spain had not copied foreign methods and manners. They inferred that Spain had ceased to be great because she had clung too faithfully to the past, the real cause being that she had failed to cling faithfully enough to the great inspiring tradition of the fifteenth and sixteenth centuries. Yet Christianity and Catholicism were not as dead as Oliveira Martins seems to have imagined. The Catholic tradition, which he represents as broken in the nineteenth century, was only temporarily interrupted. Spain still possesses some of the best human

[1] Juan Perez de Moya, *Philosophia Secreta* (1585), ed. E. Gómez de Baquero, Madrid, 1928, vol. i, p. 156.

material in Europe. What it is important for her and for Europe to study is less the multifarious and often inevitable causes of the decadence of her empire than the causes which raised her for over a century to un-paralleled power and greatness. A New World is not to be discovered every day; but there can be little doubt that, with its language, literature and traditions, a great spiritual empire awaits the Spanish nation in the future.

Oliveira Martins was a thinker and an imaginative artist; and although his work sometimes lacks that vital sincerity which only sympathy and scholarship together can provide he succeeded admirably in balancing and combining thought and imagination. Frequently he plays with the names of men of action, letters, science and art as with the balls of a juggler; he appreciates, compares and contrasts them, yet many of them remain names to him and nothing more. But when his sympathy for a dramatic subject induced him to study it more closely, when he became personally interested, the effect was not mere brilliance but warmth and insight. He was as personal in his *History of Rome* and his *History of Iberian Civilization* as in his *History of Portugal* and in *Contemporary Portugal*; but this very fact gives an intimate, original interest to his work. When he was at work on a subject which appealed to his heart as well as to his head he could produce stuff which will endure.

One of his best known works, the *Historia da Civili-saçāo Iberica*, now for the first time rendered into English (it has already been done into Spanish), was first published in 1879. It is an excellent example of its author's method and will always remain interesting, even if it does not always convince. The reader will find in this book contradictions, repetitions, omissions, partly due to a lack of materials provided by subsequent re-search, partly inherent in the author's historical method; but he will also find a great deal that is sound amid the brilliance and swiftness of treatment. History, the author here tells us, deals with the dead—'it is not a discussion but a sentence'. But the historian too often has to pass sentence without having the full evidence before him, and he is necessarily affected by the thought and prejudices of his time. For Oliveira Martins, who lived when positivism was at its height, miracles were a mere popular expression: 'no one can be permitted any longer to believe in miracles'; but the miracles and mysteries of life keep breaking through the cleverly constructed systems of historians and philosophers. What will remain of Oliveira Martins' work is its suggestiveness, not its methodical deductions. He forces the reader to think and discuss and take a living interest in the great figures and social forces of the past. Oliveira Martins after all shows the profit to be won, not from scientific history but from history seen through a temperament.

A HISTORY OF
IBERIAN CIVILIZATION

INTRODUCTORY

I. THE COUNTRY

THE Spain of our time is the remains of a continent of the tertiary epoch which was united to Africa at Gibraltar and enclosed the Mediterranean in a lake, while on the north-west it may have extended as far as America. If we consider the geological map of Spain, we see that it is divided into two almost equal halves at the meridian of Madrid: to the east lake formations of the tertiary period, to the west a plateau mainly of siluric and granite formation. It was this fact that caused geology to realize the necessary existence of an Atlantis, into which great tertiary rivers, with a south-easterly course, came where now is the province of Vizcaya and formed lakes which are now the basins of the Ebro, the Douro, the Esla, and the central upland of Castille, where rise the Tagus, the Guadiana, and the Jucar. Through the present provinces of Tarragona and Murcia the lake system of tertiary Spain drained into the Mediterranean lake.

The upheavals which marked the beginning of our geological period severed Spain from Africa, opened a passage between the Mediterranean and the Atlantic, submerged Atlantis and gave Spain her Cantabrian frontier on the north, and dried up the rivers which fed the inland lakes; against the sea were raised the cretaceous barriers of Vizcaya, while the former lakes were dried up and are now a country watered by new rivers and covered with towns and vegetation. The first basin, formerly that of a lake, now that of a river, is, as one comes from France, that of the Ebro from Logroño to San Feliú. On the north it is bounded by the foothills of the Pyrenees at Huesca, Pamplona, and Barcelona, lower cretaceous and tertiary formations which reach the coast to end in the granite formation between Mataró and Gerona. It is dominated by the chain of the Pyrenees, a granitic devonian siluric mountain system, with streaks of igneous rock, which rises like a wall from the Gulf of Gascony in the Atlantic to the Gulf of Lyons in the Mediterranean. The Pyrenees are the gates of Spain which separate her from Europe and are only opened at either end, at Irún and Perpignan.

On the other side the basin of the Ebro is bound by the mesozoic country of Teruel and Calatayud, which ends in the tertiary deposits of the Mediterranean coast. From Alicante to the mouths of the Ebro and from there to Barcelona these records of geological upheavals, mingled with others jurassic, triassic, cretaceous and silurian, close the first hydrographic basin of Spain on the east. On the Cantabrian frontier the cretaceous mountains of Vizcaya prolong the Pyrenees to Santander and defend from the sea the basin of the Ebro, dominated by the famous city of Saragossa. Receiving the waters of the southern slopes of the Pyrenees, to the north the tributaries of the Cantabrian range and to the west those of the mountains of Oca, the heights of Medinaceli, and the Sierra de Molina, the Ebro flows diagonally from side to side of the Peninsula, and furnishes Aragon with the firm frontier of a separate nation, the last in modern times to be definitively incorporated in the Spanish monarchy. Bound on the north by the mountainous regions of the Basque Provinces and on the south by the broken country of Catalonia, Aragon, placed between the Pyrenees and the lofty ranges which divide it from Castille, is like another Lombardy, shut in by a circle of Nature's walls. Descending westward, the mountain range which starts from the Aragonese frontier is prolonged to the ocean at Sintra and divides this part of the Peninsula into two great basins of approximately equal size. In these ranges, which we call the backbone of Spain, are born the two principal western rivers, the Tagus and the Douro. Somosierra, Guadarrama, Alberche, Gredos, Jalama, Estrella, and Sintra are the principal names that this great range takes as it advances; it is only once interrupted for a brief space by the basin of the Alagon near Plasencia and then proceeds to Lisbon and the Atlantic, dominating the splendid basin of the Tagus.

The chain running from east to west of the Peninsula, one of the main lines of Europe's pentagonal system according to Élie de Beaumont, is at the same time the centre of Spain's orographical system and the basis of the geological structure of the Peninsula. It is a great range of granite which advances into Portugal in the Beira provinces (the Serra da Estrella), crosses the Douro, fills the whole country west of the Tamega and ends in the sea in Galicia, at Finisterre and Cape Ortegal.

In Portuguese Beira, between the Douro and the Tagus, the peninsular chain divides into two: in the north it proceeds, with its granite rock uncovered, to the sea in Galicia; on the south it follows the Tagus and, covered with mesozoic formation, finally reaches Sintra, where it for a short space reveals its fleshless bones again. From east to west this backbone of Spain is divided into two regions different in character, climate, cultivation, we would even say in race, if the successive invasions spread over the land could in historic times have determined the formation of new ethnological phenomena. To the south of this range, on the other side of the Tagus, one approaches the climate of Africa, while nature to the north is in every way European.

Madrid, situated geographically in the centre of the Peninsula, is placed at the heart of this mountain zone which separates those different climates and regions; and at the same time it is the meridian which divides the Peninsula into two countries, tertiary to the east and primary to the west. Orographically, geologically, geographically, Madrid is the centre of Spain. From this centre four lines, running north, east, west, and south, mark out four distinct regions, that of the Ebro, with its surrounding mountains; two regions to the south, of which we shall say something later; and, to the north of the Peninsula's backbone, the region of the Douro, which we will now describe.

The many confluents of the Douro, distributed like the radii of a semi-circle with Valladolid for its centre, water the vast plains of Old Castille which are Spain's granary. Bounded on the east by the dividing line of the basin of the Ebro, on the west by the mountains of León, on the north by the Cantabrian range and on the south by the backbone of the Peninsula, the basin of the Douro, containing Valladolid and Salamanca, Palencia, León, and Zamora, has for border castles Ciudad Rodrigo on the confines of Beira, Segovia at the foot of the Guadarrama range, Soria on the east, and Burgos at the foot of the Cantabrian Pyrenees. This basin of the Douro was also formerly a lake, from Burgos to Aranda, past Palencia and Valladolid to Benavente, Zamora and Salamanca; or rather the lake of Aragon, entering by the cleft channel which still joins the basins of the Ebro and Douro, past Logroño and Briviesca to Burgos, extended to the west in the opposite direction, past Osma and Almanza to Teruel. Bordered by two zones of diluvial strata, the basin of the Upper Douro, at Tierra de Campos, is the western frontier of this part of tertiary Spain. To the south of the river these diluvial strata, starting from Tordesillas, meet the granite Guadarrama at Segovia; and on the north in the basin of the confluent Esla, they reach beyond Almanza and León, joining the carboniferous formation of the Cantabrian Pyrenees between Santander and Oviedo. The range of mountains along the northern coast, the cretaceous mountains of Vizcaya, the carboniferous mountains of Asturias, form the northern boundary of the basin of the Douro,

which is shut in to the south by the central range of the
Peninsula, to the east by the dividing line of the Ebro
and to the west by the ancient mountainous country of
León, Tras-os-Montes, Entre Douro e Minho, and
Galicia. This region represents the geologically ancient
half of Spain. In the heart of Galicia on a bed of
granite there are metamorphic and igneous rocks; and
to the east of the Tamega in Portugal, to the east of
Monforte and Lugo in Spain, begin the silurian
formations of Salamanca and Tras-os-montes, Zamora
and Villa Franca, stretching to the Cantabrian sea.
It is an intricate system of mountains running in every
direction; through channels cut in them fall rivers
which are real torrents, such as the Douro from
Zamora, the Minho and the rapid streams which flow
from the Cantabrian range to the Bay of Biscay.
   The inhospitable coast from Cabo da Roca to Vigo
and from Cape Ortegal to Bayona[1] furnishes in the
north-west the fine bay of Vigo on the one hand and
that of Corunna on the other. The character of the
inhabitants, either as a result of the country or of its
history, is very different from that of their neighbours;
the climate is warm and damp, with luxuriant valleys
and mountains crowned with forests; the population is
dense, property divided into tiny holdings and emigra-
tion active. To this region belong some of the cities
most famous in the history of modern Spain: Tolosa,
Pamplona, Vitoria, Bilbao, Oviedo, Pontevedra, Orense,
Tuy, Braganza, Braga, with the primacy of the Spains,
Oporto, Coimbra, and Viseu. As the first of the regions
which the Kings of Spain gradually won back from the
Moors, this part of the Peninsula preserves the privileges
of ancient nobility. At one end it was the nucleus of
the Portuguese nation, at the other the starting-point

   [1] It would have been less confusing to keep to the same direction and
say 'from Bayona to Cape Ortegal', so as to prevent confusion with the
French Bayonne. (Trans.'s note).

of the Reconquest in the tenth century. The Reconquest began simultaneously in Asturias and in Aragon; later the Asturians and Aragonese joined forces and gradually advanced together across Castille to Andalusia like a wave, compelling the Moors to recross the Straits and return to the country whence they had come centuries earlier.

Spain is a very different country south of the parallel which starts from Coimbra in Portugal, follows the heights of the backbone of the Peninsula, and crossing the Sierra de Molina arrives at Tarragona on the Mediterranean. We have already seen how the internal valleys of eastern Spain are severed from the Mediterranean by a chain of mountains from Perpignan in the Pyrenees, past the industrial city of Barcelona, the mouths of the Ebro famous for their wines, and Tortosa to Valencia, the city of the Cid. The western part of this region may be divided into three zones: the uplands of the Castilles with the country descending to the Mediterranean at Valencia and Murcia; the valleys of the Tagus and the Guadiana falling to the Atlantic in the west, with their mountain boundaries, or in other words the Lusitania of the Romans; and, thirdly, ancient Baetica, or the basin of the Guadalquivir enclosed by the Sierra Morena, the Mariani Mountains, the Sierra Nevada, and the mountains of Ilipula. The first and last of these districts are almost exclusively tertiary and belong to the half of Spain which is geologically modern. The second region represents the remains of the primitive form of the Peninsula.

To begin with this last region, we find it bounded on the north by the Herminian mountains (this was the Roman name for our central range) and on the south by the Sierra Morena. Along the southern branches of the two ranges flow the rivers Tagus and Guadiana, limiting the Silurian region of the south of Spain. On the other side of the Tagus lies the belt of granite

formation; on the other side of the Guadiana the
tertiary country of the Mediterranean coast, clearly
marked by the course of the Guadalquivir. Parallel to
the two western rivers lies the basin of the Guadiana.
The regularity of the mountain system of this part of
Spain, shown in the parallel lines of the river-valleys
and of the direction of the ranges, finds no corresponding regularity in the geology. Great upheavals and
frequent eruptions have often here convulsed the surface of the earth. Veins of igneous rock lie among the
mountains between the Guadiana and the Guadalquivir; they are full of cracks containing veins of metals:
lead, quicksilver, silver, copper, sulphur, and manganese;
coal is found in the *cuencas* of Zafra, Belmez, and Córdoba, far up the valley of the river formerly known as the
Baetis. Granite emerges in the La Serena region south
of the Guadiana, and in the north in the ranges along
the Tagus, those of Zapata and Montanchez in Spanish
Estremadura, and those of Portalegre and Ossa in
Portugal. Our Algarve is a jurassic formation with
cretaceous strata, as is the Portuguese coast between the
rivers Tagus and Vouga and the continuation of the
Serra da Estrella to Sintra. Finally we have two considerable stretches of tertiary sea deposits: along the
Guadiana from Elvas and Olivença, past Mérida to La
Serena; the other along the valley of the Tagus, from
its mouth to Abrantes, including the basin of the
Sorraia in Alentejo and, farther to the south, that of
the Sado extending to Alcacer and Sines on the coast.

To the south of the Guadiana are steppes and
mountain-ranges with mines; to the north treeless
plains burnt by the sun and rich in corn, with hills
covered by dark evergreen oaks; this is the region of
Alentejo, Spanish Extremadura, and La Mancha, im-
mortalized in Cervantes' novel. The upland of Castille,
with Madrid situated on a small bed of diluvial soil at
the foot of the Guadarrama, this upland from which the

Jucar flows to the south and the Guadiana and Tagus to the west, was also formerly a lake, when the valleys of the Ebro and the Douro were lakes; it is now the last basin of the tertiary lakes of Spain, enclosed between Madrid, Toledo, the former capital of the Goths, Cuenca, Utiel, Albacete in Murcia, and Ciudad Real in La Mancha. Shut in by the granite peaks of Guadarrama, the mesozoic mountains to the south of the Ebro, the ranges of Lusitania and Baetica, this tertiary lake was drained into the Mediterranean along slopes where now the river Jucar flows to Cullera in the Bay of Valencia and the Segura waters the Murcian plains, forming part of the vast belt of tertiary marine formation which extends along the coast from Valencia to Alicante and Cartagena and inland as far as Albacete.

At Cartagena, at Cape Palos, rise the ranks of the metamorphic rocks which near the sea form the Sierra Nevada, beyond which flows the Guadalquivir in its tertiary bed from San Lucar to Ubeda. On the slopes and heights of the Sierra Nevada appear everywhere vestiges of the exquisite civilization of the Moors, while the whole of Andalusia bears witness to the skilful agriculture of her former masters, whose degenerate sons still tread the heights of the Alpujarras, like their brothers of the Maghreb across the Mediterranean. At Málaga and on to Gibraltar one sees the end of those chains which die out in the northern Column of Hercules. Climate, vegetation and race make of this Spanish province a region both fascinating and semi-barbarous.

The plains of Córdoba and Seville, the wines of Jérez de la Frontera, the beautiful harbour of Cadiz and the mineral wealth hidden in the chain of mountains that hem in the famous country of Tarsis and Rio Tinto to the west, Guadalcanal at the entrance of the Sierra Morena, the coal-producing basin of Belmez, the quicksilver of Almadén, the lead in the whole range from

Santa Eufemia to Linares, and following up the famous
river to its source, to Baeza, Ubeda, Jaén, Osuna, and
finally Ronda: these are the elements which characterize
the third of the almost parallel valleys of southern
Spain, that of the Tagus, that of the Guadiana, and that
of the Guadalquivir, bounded by the mountain ranges
of Toledo and Guadalupe to Evora, of the Sierra
Morena to Niebla, and of the Sierra Nevada to Ronda.
Seville is the centre of this last and fairest of the hydrographic basins of Spain. Cadiz on the sea at one end,
Córdoba, the former court of the Omayyads, at the foot of
the mountains, at the other; and the river Guadalquivir
curving through delicious plains where the olive-groves
grow as thick as the pine-woods of the wild mountains of
Asturias; vines cover the hill-sides and the whole is
shut in by sheer mountains in which precious metals
lie embedded: so that this corner of the world is a
garden, lit by the incomparable southern sun.

King Alfonso the Learned, who initiated the literary
culture of neo-Gothic Spain, gives us in his Chronicle
the following description which has an ingenuous charm
and is one of the earliest records of the Castilian
language:

> This Spain of which we speak is as the paradise of God; for
> it is watered by five principal rivers, the Duero, the Ebro, the
> Tagus, the Guadalquivir and the Guadiana, and each of them
> is divided from his neighbour by great mountain ranges, and
> the valleys and plains are great and broad, and the soil,
> rendered fertile by the rivers, produces an abundance of
> fruits. And the greater part of Spain is watered by streams
> and springs, and wherever they are needed there are wells.
> And Spain abounds in crops and delicious fruit, with plenty
> of fish and good milk and all its produce, and much game,
> large and small, and flocks and noble horses and many mules.
> It is fortified with many castles and gay with excellent wines
> and has abundance of wheat; it is rich in metals, in lead and
> tin, quicksilver, iron, copper, silver, gold and precious stones
> and all kinds of marble; in salt of the sea and land, rock salt

and many veins of lapis lazuli, red lead, chalk and alum and all the other products of the soil. It has shining silks and all the softness of honey and sugar, oil to give it light and the cheerful saffron. And especially Spain is skilful and formidably strong in battle, active in toil, loyal to its king, keen to study, courteous in word and perfect in all good; and there is no country which can equal or rival it and few in the world that are as great. Spain above all is great and famous for its loyalty. O Spain, there is none able to tell thy praises!

The geographical situation of Spain destined it to be the battle-ground between the waves of peoples migrating from Europe in search of new lands and the waves of Africans attracted by this neighbouring 'paradise of God'. Whatever may have been the clash of races here before history begins, we know that in Spain the Romans and Carthaginians met, coming from beyond the Pyrenees and from Africa to continue here the Punic wars. And in the same way here later met the Moors and the Visigoths. Twice Spain stood to Europe in the same relation as Hungary to the East, as a watch-tower and bulwark of European civilization against Moorish invasions. Thus briefly we have named four different peoples which successively occupied Spain, and before and after them came others. We shall attempt to determine what part they played in constituting the race of the Peninsula. Geography shows us that a region so diverse, divided into basins separated by broad and lofty mountain ranges, and broken up by rivers which are for the most part innavigable, tends to foster differences in national character, since, communication between the different tribes being difficult, they are slow to merge into one another. As a modern historian of Spain remarks, nothing is less like the grave and indolent Castilian than the light fantastic Andalusian. Under the same climatic conditions we see the industrious Catalan, who seeks fortune in every quarter of the globe, and the reserved and sedentary Valencian, who never leaves the fertile Huerta which his ancestors cultivated before him. Then we have the patient laborious Galician ever ready with his strong arms and shoulders to bear heavy toil and burdens. By the side of the Aragonese, noble and haughty even in his tatters, we find the fiery nervous Basque, as proud of his privileges, his *fueros*, as is the Aragonese of his famous defiance of kings. And in Portugal likewise we have great variety: the practical, laborious, and dull inhabitants of Minho, obstinate and proud, forming as it were a second Ireland, with green meadows and a granite soil; farther south dwell Portuguese as proud as the Castilians, and distant Algarve is peopled by true Andalusians. But if geographical differences preserve even to-day strong and not easily classified ethnological varieties, history nevertheless shows us the existence of a genius of the Peninsula transcending these differences, a fundamental character of the race, common to all the peoples of Spain; a genius and character marked principally on the one hand by the religious enthusiasm in our lives and on the other by the personal heroism of our actions. Hence a peculiar civilization, of a noble and original kind.

II. THE RACE

HUMBOLDT was the author of a theory which, in whole or part, is still accepted regarding the ethnology of the Peninsula. This theory was based in the study of the Basque language, the strangeness of which among romance and neo-Latin languages had excited his curiosity. The main point of the theory consisted in considering the present inhabitants of the slopes of the Pyrenees as the genuine representatives of a primitive or aboriginal Iberian race which had been driven by successive invasions of new races to take refuge in this corner of the Peninsula. The Iberians, either as autochthonous or in a simultaneous migration westward had occupied, besides Spain, the three great islands of the Mediterranean and Gallia Narbonensis; perhaps they were of the same origin as the inhabitants of northern Italy; perhaps they were only a branch separated in very early times from the great Celtic family. This last conjecture of the learned philologist was destroyed when subsequent studies proved that the Celts belonged to the Indo-European group, whereas everything tends to show that the primitive inhabitants of Spain had a different origin. As to what this origin was there are many opinions and conjectures, in the absence of scientific proof. Häckel and Müller divide the Mediterranean race, one of the twelve which they consider primitive, into four branches: Indo-European, Semite, Caucasian, and Basque. The last two, in Peschel's classification, are of origin unknown; hence the abundance and variety of hypotheses.

Broca's observations showed that the French Basques are brachycephalic, whereas the Basques on the other side of the Pyrenees are not. Moreover the dolicho-cephalic character which is common to the inhabitants of Corsica and to the races of Northern Africa was found by Morton among the peoples of America also. This gave rise to the hypothesis of a common origin for Iberians and Americans, and the hypothesis was confirmed by analogies in the language. This hypothesis, combined with the supposition that Atlantis formerly joined America to Europe, would make of the Iberians a tertiary race and of the Basques of to-day their descendants, and in the words of Peschel, the oldest inhabitants of Europe. The reader who is aware of the slight value for history of strictly anthropological investigations will not give an undue importance to these theories. Elsewhere we will examine the opinion which bases on them the existence of a Turanian race, previous to the Semite and Indo-European civilizations, and of which race the Basques would be a remnant lost in the wildnesses of the Pyrenees. To make of the Basques one of the four branches (Indo-Germanic, Semitic, Caucasian, and Basque) of the Mediterranean race opens a field for the most daring hypotheses; on the other hand such hypotheses are not needed if we consider these descendants of the ancient Iberians as forming part of the Hamite branch of the Semitic family, since this would sufficiently explain their peculiarities. The Iberian with the dark complexion and curly hair which characterize the Siculi (the 'colorati vultus et torsi plerumque crines' of Tacitus), would on this supposition have the same Hamite or Afro-Semite origin as the Tuaregs and the Berbers, the Kopts and Egyptians; the Siculi and Ligurians also belonging to the same race. The Celtic invasion destroyed these former inhabitants of Gaul, so that no vestige of their language remains; but south of the Pyrenees it was otherwise, and in this view the Basque would be the oldest representative of the Libyan languages. The suffix -tani, which in Africa and Spain marks the names of peoples, the Lusitani, Turdetani, Mauretani, is an argument in favour of the Tuareg origin of the Iberians. It is even supposed that this suffix is the same as that of -tah which characterizes Berber names, while there seems to be a similarity between the Tuareg and Turdetanian alphabets, which are both different from the Phoenician.

Leibnitz and Niebuhr had already given the Iberians an African origin; and more recently the theory of the identity of their primitive characteristics with those of the original inhabitants of North Africa, known generically as Hamites, seems to be gaining ground. The fact that there are no analogies in the roots of words between the Basque language and the group now composed of Kopt, Berber, and Tuareg, seems to militate against the African origin of the Iberians; but overmuch importance cannot be attached to the philological evidence, since it is now known that there are no written records of Basque older than the fifteenth century and that the war songs supposed to date from before the tenth century are apocryphal.[1]

The recent works in which Van Eys and Vinson have attacked Humboldt's theory show that there are no proofs of identity between the half million Basques of our time and an Iberian people speaking a kindred language; but they do not explain the strange phenomenon of the Basque, whose antiquity is proved by place-names despite the lack of written records. Yet it seems rash to affirm that in remote times a single Iberian race of Basque character was spread over the whole of the Peninsula. Strabo himself attributed to the Iberians many languages and even different alphabets; and the opinion that the name Iberia was used by the ancient geographers rather in a generical sense than to designate a particular region also deserves attention.

However this may be, it seems probable that the primitive inhabitants of Spain and those of Northern Africa had a common origin; anthropologically there is the proof of the dolichocephalic character of both peoples, while the megalolithic monuments of Spain and Africa are a further argument in favour of this supposition. Ancient writers tell us that the people or peoples called Iberian occupied not only Spain but the islands of the Mediterranean, Italy and the south coast of France. Imaginary voyages have been thought out in which Asiatic Turanians came along the coast of North Africa to Europe; but if it was this people (supposed to have preceded the Indo-European race in Europe) from which the Atlas Berbers descend, this supports the theory of a kinship between the Iberians and the North Africans. Whether they are independent

[1] This fact was mainly the discovery of the late Rev. Wentworth Webster. (Translator's note.)

or form part of the Semitic branch, we can no longer accept Humboldt's theory of a Celtic origin, since the Celts are of Indo-European stock.

The ethnologists fix the Spanish colonization of those undoubted Semites, the Phoenicians, between the twenty-second and twentieth centuries. The importance of their migration by sea is, however, as variously estimated as its date is remote. Some give a Phoenician origin to the principal names, such as Lusitania, Guadiana, and even Spain itself; others, with Mommsen, declare that the Iberians only learnt the Phoenician alphabet through the Greeks. Some place the Phoenician invasion before, others after, that of the Celts. The Celts, mingling with the Iberians, are said to have formed five great tribes, the Cantabrians, Asturians, and Vascones in the north; the Calaici and Lusitani in the west.

It is unnecessary to go farther into this inquiry to show how little value can be attached to it; we will merely say with the historian Herculano:

> He who reads impartially the frequently absurd and sometimes contradictory statements of ancient and modern writers and the contrary theories they have based on these statements concerning the distribution of the peoples of Spain can only draw one sincere conclusion: that on this subject there are extremely few facts which are certain enough to be considered historical.

Since those words were written, ethnology has furnished fresh elements to promote the craze of rash inquiry in our time. But if affirmations in matters so little susceptible of proof are always rash, cautious inferences are legitimate, and even indispensable and fruitful. From one hypothesis to another one may at last arrive at the truth. The arguments in favour of an affinity between the primitive inhabitants of Spain and those which now represent the original inhabitants of North Africa have been strengthened. After those of anthropology and pre-historic archaeology, we find in recent studies on the Kabylia proofs of undeniable importance. The Kabyles are the genuine survivors of the Numidae of Massinissa, Syphax, and Jugurtha, who proved so formidable to the Romans. The successive invasions of Romans, Vandals, Phoenicians, and Arabs expelled them and their ancient religion and language from the coast of Africa into the interior, where genuine records of their remote existence have been preserved to our own time. The Kabyle or Berber language, almost identical with the Tuareg and the languages spoken in the Sahara from Senegal to Nubia and beyond the Negroids of the Sudan, is akin to the language of Egypt, the Koptic; and if it could be proved to be akin to Basque, Basque would no longer be a unique linguistic phenomenon, and the question of the origin of the Iberian peoples would be cleared up.

The Berber race had an alphabet of its own; it had a religion which it afterwards abandoned for Islamism; of its peculiar creations, apart from the language, what survives is its system of social institutions. In accepting the religion of the Koran, the Kabyle did not accept its civil or political precepts, and along with Islamism maintained his own customary law. It is in the social institutions that we shall find singular traces of affinity between the Kabyles, the historical records in Spain and (beneath the social forms imposed by the Roman and Germanic civilizations) surviving customs and characteristics in the Peninsula.

The *jemáa* or village of the Atlas tribes so strongly resembles the Spanish *pueblo* that it is legitimate to assume in pre-Roman Spain the existence of *jemáas* which the Roman conquerors converted into *municipia* which as such have survived down to our time. Despite the centralization, first of the Roman Empire, then of the Catholic rulers, this corporation (*ayuntamiento*) has been preserved in Spain, where it still constitutes the social nucleus. The *ayuntamiento*, the *jemáa*, is the village with its elected mayor, the *amin*, the *alcalde*. In Kabylia there is no State or central power to delegate officials to the *jemáa*; in Spain European civilization has created a State, but it has no representatives in the *ayuntamiento*. Political organization in Spain proceeds upwards from below, in a federal sense; and it is only in the 'province', the group of corporations, that the State official, the *gobernador*, makes his appearance. The European State is unable to penetrate lower than these 'provinces'. Every Kabyla can become an *amin*, every Spaniard may become *alcalde*; the *jemáa* and the *ayuntamiento* are both a kind of insurance society; and if to the north of the Mediterranean there is no communal distribution of meat, the *pueblo* possesses its communal granary and a common grazing ground (every villager possesses a pig or a donkey) and also a common oven in which each villager bakes his bread. This system, common to both sides of the Mediterranean, does not foster the production of wealth but it regularizes distribution and prevents the existence of a proletariat. Poverty is an incident, not a necessity, and the beggar can retain his noble dignity; he is not a pariah, as in industrial societies, nor is he infamous, as an Englishman might call him. A sense of natural equality is imprinted on social institutions and reacts against the spontaneous forces of Nature's economy.

The *anaya* and the *sof* are further proofs of affinity: they are not to be found in the Peninsula to-day, but traces of them remain in its historical records. The *anaya* of the Kabyla is a pact of mutual protection, as in Spain was the *behetria*, while the *sof* had the name of *unión*. In the anarchy which prevailed during the reconquest of Spain from the Moors, it seems that the people remembered its old customs, forgotten under the Roman domination and under the Visigothic rule which succeeded it. On both sides of the Mediterranean *uniones* and *sofs*, formed all over the country, constituted informal independent leagues which bore no relation to the tribe in Africa nor in Spain to the feudal, municipal, and monarchical institutions of a foreign culture. It was these foreign institutions, Roman and Germanic, that in Spain replaced the tribe or group of villages which is still to be found in Kabylia and existed in Spain before the Roman conquest. The adoption of a foreign civilization gave to society in the Peninsula a character different from that which it would have had, had it been allowed to develop spontaneously in isolation, with the elements peculiar to its race.

But we need not lament as a misfortune that it was the fate of the Peninsula to become Roman and be initiated into the Indo-European civilization. The inhabitants of the Atlas country never went beyond the tribal state nor were able to attain a degree of culture comparable to that which the combination of a genius akin to their own with the Latin genius produced in ancient and modern Spain. We need not condemn the tyranny of the Romans or of the Goths before or after the Moorish invasion of Spain. Austrian Charles V, in defeating the Comuneros at Villalar and putting an end to the *uniones*, represents one of the two elements, the conflict between which constitutes the history of Spanish civilization. Of the other element there are abundant proofs throughout the Middle Ages: in the conflicts between towns, in the warfare of the *condottieri* such as the Cid and his political descendants. Nothing less resembles the heads of hereditary dynasties surrounded by their vassals in central Europe, or the sacred monarchs of the East abjectly worshipped by their subjects, than those leaders of military groups in medieval Spain, fighting against the Moors as the ancient kings of Numidia, Mauritania, and Getulia fought against the Romans. It is probable that Spain would have been divided into small independent tribes like the Berbers had she succeeded in freeing herself from her conquerors before assimilating their ideas. In the Basque Provinces and in Aragon, in the country along the Ebro, it is thought that the primitive tribes of the Peninsula survive; the life of the *jemáa* was here most intense and offered most resistance to European civilization. The almost religious love of the Basques for their language,[1] their devotion to their *fueros* are so deeply rooted that even in our days Spanish civilization has been unable to destroy them.

In the *jemáa* the only privileged person is the marabout, like the priest in Spain; but in Africa the tribe was not absorbed by a dynastic State, the priesthood did not become a power nor the clergy develop into a caste. Representing a profound religious instinct, always allied with a keen sense of personal independence, the marabout of the Peninsula, who became a clerical aristocratic class and even governed the country in the Visigothic councils, expresses the most intimate characteristic of the race. A passion for equality, which made progressive civilization impossible, prevented the constitution of a State in African tribes; in Spain there was resistance, but it was unable to withstand the Romans, and Spain was forcibly incorporated in the life of Europe. We have noted the signs of this resistance, which are still visible in a half-doctrinaire, half-historical, traditional, and anachronical theory of federalism; and in the course of our history we shall find them recur at all times of crisis. It remains to state that Iberian civilization, although formed on European models, maintains an originality due to the conflict and strong resistance of its racial characteristics. In the sixteenth century, when at last absolute monarchy is instituted in Spain and the clergy attains a political

[1] 'I love it more than my life' a farmer of Vizcaya said to me, speaking in Spanish owing to my ignorance of Basque.

power similar to that it enjoyed in the times of the Goths, the King is still the Caesar or head of a democracy; while the ex-marabout who now as a mitred Caesar and representing the faith of the nation presides over Councils of State and over the Inquisition, maintains a haughty independence towards the Khalif of Rome. It is a mistake to confuse this Catholic monarchy with the religious monarchies of the East, and it is equally different from the civil monarchies in which, as in France, there was an essential conflict between Church and State. Thus Spanish civilization has a peculiar cast which we shall attempt to emphasize as we proceed, and which, we think, is due to the combined characteristics of the primitive inhabitants and of Indo-European ideas. The series of historical invasions of Spain confirms the elements which we claimed to discover in the probable character of the pre-historic inhabitants of the Peninsula.

III. CHARACTER AND HISTORY

IF our opinion concerning the origin of the Iberian people be accepted as a scientific fact, we can see in the first and prehistoric shock between Iberians and Celts a forerunner of the successive conflicts of which history tells us. The first invasion is that of the Phoenicians[1] who, coming by sea, colonized the

[1] Gades (Cádiz) was, as is well known, the westernmost of the Phoenician factories, and the Columns of Hercules were considered the gates of the world. They survived till the year 1145. They consisted of columns of stones standing like towers on the shore or actually in the sea. Each column was fifteen cubits in circumference and ten cubits high; and the whole structure, from sixty to a hundred cubits in height, was joined together by iron bars. On this tower, without doors or inner chambers, stood a bronze statue of Melkarth, the Hercules of the Phoenicians, six cubits high, in the figure of a bearded man, with cloak and toga descending to the knees. This statue was gilt. The left hand pressed the folds of the cloak against its breast; the right arm was extended and the right hand held a key and pointed towards the

Mediterranean coast of Spain. After the Phoenicians and the Celts, the Peninsula is the scene of conflicts between Semitic and non-Semitic peoples, coming northwards across the sea from Africa, and peoples of Indo-European race which crossed the frontier of the Pyrenees. Ethnologically this constitutes the basis of Spanish history. The Greeks, however, who from the ninth to the eleventh centuries before Christ crossed the Mediterranean in every direction, came by sea and thus ran counter to the general law of Indo-European invasions in the Peninsula. Some of their colonies still exist as towns, as Rosas (Rhodas), Murviedro-Sagunto and Ampurias (Emporion); yet they seem to have left no permanent traces in Spain, not to speak of a tradition of culture such as that of Greater Greece in southern Italy.

The history of the Peninsula may be said to begin with the appearance on the scene of the Libyan-Phoenicians of Carthage on the one hand and of the Romans on the other, thus continuing the conflict of races which seems to have begun in prehistoric times. We have already noticed the influence exercised over the natives by the Indo-European invaders, or to be more exact, by the Romans, who imposed their own constitution upon the Peninsula. We have already said that to this fact we owe not only the European character of our civilization but the very fact of its existence. Otherwise we should have remained in the tribal state,

Straits. The Crusaders and Norman pirates called the Straits Karlsar, the waters of the man; and Isidore of Beja under the Moorish domination assigned a prophetic meaning to the pointing of Melkarth's right hand: its pointing finger indicated the direction which the hosts of Musa would take, while the key indicated symbolically that this was the gate of Spain. The Columns of Hercules were destroyed in 1145 by the Moorish admiral Ali Ibn Isa Ibn Maimun who had raised a revolt at Cadiz. There was a tradition that the statue was of pure gold, and that was why he pulled it down. It was only gilt, but even so produced 12,000 dinars (See Dozy, *Recherches*).

like the Kabyles; instead of the clergy we should have had marabouts, and instead of the daring soldiers of Spain Berbers mounted on thin swift steeds and engaged in tribal warfare. That is what we may infer from the customs and habits that survive in the Peninsula despite the laws and institutions of a foreign political and religious civilization. But may we not be deluding ourselves? May not the life of the Kabyla village observed in the villages of Spain, and the tribal existence developed in our indigenous state be particular instances of a general phenomenon? The tribal state and village life are common to all races at a given moment of their development, and everywhere precede the establishment of the centralizing institutions of the first empires, Assyrian, Persian, Roman. Yet in each race this development, although it may be essentially the same, produces different moral characteristics. And the main characteristic of the Berber is that which all sensible observers will find to lie at the root of the Spanish character: a manly independence. It is indeed this characteristic which condemns the Berbers to a permanent anarchy; it prevents the constitution of an aristocracy or a priesthood; it has made impossible the development of progressive institutions involving civilization. It was this characteristic which bred the spirit of the Cid and his followers, of the *behetrías*, of the *uniones*; and which, though transformed, had sufficient tenacity to impart a peculiar character to the very ideas and institutions which defeated but could not overcome it. Absolute monarchy in Spain, as we have seen, assumed the character of a democratic Caesarism, and to this victory of the independent genius of the Peninsula, which is more evident in the Castilian monarchy than in the Portuguese, was added another even more important. The religious spirit which reached its highest point in the Golden Age [1] and

[1] The Portuguese text says merely 'the sixteenth century'; but there

produced the mystic drama of Calderon, the pictures of Murillo and Ribera, the mysticism of Santa Teresa, Loyola and Jesuitism, is a phenomenon having its roots in the people. The genius of a race is like the roots of a weed which even under the plough go on living and working. Thus the submission of the Spanish as vassals is based in pride, because if to each Spaniard the monarch is a head he is also a man, an equal; they do not bow before the throne but rather feel themselves kings: 'We are as noble as the King, only less rich.' Even so the 'obedience' of the mystics reveals itself in a heroic spiritual tension, and the faithful, prostrate before the altar, feel in their heart that they are gods. In this way absolutism and theocracy, which among Eastern peoples imply political and moral abjection, are transformed when planted in a race of essential manliness. In much the same way in Germany under the iron rule of the great Frederick we find the voice of Kant hailed as the apostle of the critical liberty of reason. Nothing is more vain and illusory than to judge by external forms, for inside forms which are apparently the same the creative genius of man sets a most varied content of thought.

The fact that a formal subjection in the Peninsula existed side by side with a native freedom and dignity has given rise to the strangest opinions, the most fantastic theories and the most lamentable mistakes. Writers of great intelligence but unable to understand the co-existence of outward forms of discipline with dignity and freedom of spirit have either cut away the basis of the theocratic monarchy of Spain by declaring that it has been merely an unnatural tyranny which happens to have lasted for twenty centuries, since the time of the Romans, or have denied that independence lies at the root of the Spanish genius and have described this

is of course over a century and a half between the birth (1515) of Santa Teresa and the death (1681) of Calderón. (Translator's note.)

genius as a mixture of subservience and fear. Thus in the eyes of the modern Romantic writers Spain has always been enslaved, her natural aspirations have always been repressed, and her history should end in a federalism which will permit the genius of her various peoples to develop naturally. But surely a theory which rests on the persistent denial of a whole history must be singularly false; a theory by which everything, great deeds, splendid achievements, deep feelings, strong characters, were a mere mistake. If Roman Spain, Visigothic Spain with its kings and councils, the Catholic Monarchy ruling over Europe and the world, were mere mistakes, what is to become of the general lines of history and the very nature of things?

There is another theory which denies the existence of the spirit of Spanish independence and sees in the kings and priests the real representatives of a people debased by fear. Buckle was the author of this singular discovery. Anthropology had not then flowered in all its rashness, but the doctrine of physical causes gave rise to some curious aberrations. It is, however, not surprising that the manly independence of the Peninsular character should have been denied by an Englishman, who would naturally be incapable of understanding it. It is not surprising that Buckle should attribute the *fueros* not to popular demands but to a stroke of policy on the part of the sovereigns (he forgets the *behetrias* and *uniones*, the revolts of the towns, the battle of Villalar, the character of the Councils of Toledo and the revolution which gave the throne to Isabel) when we see that this historian, well informed as to the decadence of the Catholic Monarchy, ignores or forgets its development and has no knowledge of the works of Martínez Marina and Colmeiro, where all who run may read and perceive how submissive and timid were the Aragonese, how very timid was the Cid, that Bedouin sheik!

But the strangest part is the reason assigned for this essential baseness of the Spanish character: this reason is no other than the volcanoes and earthquakes of Spain. It is these, with plague and famine, which give birth to that reverence which lies at the heart of the Spanish character, according to Buckle. Buckle can never have heard a Castilian swearing by the bl . . . Virgin! This reverence must, however, be entirely due to the geological upheavals, not to the plagues and famines, since these devastated the whole of medieval Europe, while the earthquakes appear to be a monopoly of Spain and Italy. This philosopher forgot the island of Santorin in the Cyclades, he omitted to bestow reverence, fear, and loyalty on the Greek islanders. And that is an active volcano, whereas those of Spain have been extinct since before the beginning of history. Besides, for all the proofs and allegations of this learned and ingenious author, the region of earthquakes in the Peninsula is confined to the mouth of the Tagus and the coast of the Mediterranean from the Cabo de Gata to Cartagena. How did superstition and the consequent power of the clergy arise in the remaining nine-tenths of Spain, where indeed it originated: in the basin of the Ebro, in the basin of the Douro, in the upland of Castille, the mountains of Cantabria, Galicia, and Lusitania?

Another singular scientific discovery of Buckle was the pastoral character of life in the Peninsula and the fact that agriculture could not flourish there because it was impossible to work during a whole day. To what tremendous errors do rash theories give rise! More than half the Peninsula, the whole region of the Ebro, Asturias, part of León, Portugal, the coast of Andalusia and Catalonia, are well-watered regions with an intensive cultivation, and they were so in the days of the Moors and at the time of the Reconquest. Shepherds abound in every country which, like Spain, has vast wild mountain ranges; continual wars have deforested

Old and New Castille, La Mancha, and Estremadura;
but Latin authors describe these regions as resembling
the coasts of Berbery which now are likewise parched
and desolate.

But how are these characteristics, abject submissiveness due to the earthquakes and superstition born of
fear, according to the theory which Buckle took from
Schleiermacher, to be reconciled with the loyalty and
nobility which Buckle also finds in the Spanish character?
A timid man is always disloyal: is it possible that this
loyalty must be ascribed to the personal pride, dignity,
integrity, and manliness of the Peninsular character?
How is the essential ignorance which Buckle ascribes
to the Spanish nation to be reconciled with the intelligence [highmindedness] of the race?[1] How is this
ignorance to be reconciled with the evident existence
in Spain of great statesmen, monarchs, magistrates, and
legislators? Where did they come from? What noble
things can spring from an abject fear of earthquakes!
The evident contradiction here condemns the theory
as absurd. Those great men could not be the fruit of
an evil tree. The contradiction is as flagrant here as
is the scientific theory and the method followed by
Buckle and now by the federalist and naturalist school:
the method of judging Spanish civilization by the records
of its decadence. Great men in a weak nation ac-
complished great things, says the English historian;
then came bad or mediocre men and everything fell
to the ground. We will not inquire here how the same
atmosphere and the same race produced these two
different generations, because we are here concerned
with critics who condemn the whole and put forward
the theory that the Monarchy only existed through

[1] It is significant and characteristic that Oliveira Martins should
have translated 'highminded' by 'intelligent'. Thus his sneers at
English character and civilization are based on a palpable ignorance,
even of the English language and literature (Translator's note).

ruining the natural development of the nation. According to this theory all those great achievements were lamentable errors. The independence and dignity of the nation were crushed by the kings and clergy. The heroic sufferers of Toledo, with Padilla at their head, were martyrs and forerunners of the democratic demands of our time. Yet Padilla was a nobleman and the *unión* defeated at Villalar was principally composed of nobles. Charles V gave the people the right to wear swords to defend themselves against the nobles. The deplorable system of reading modern politics into history and seeing a tyrant wherever there is a king, a brigand in every nobleman, and a charlatan in every priest tangles and confuses everything and makes it impossible to understand history. Spirits superior to the prejudices of a school or party, thoroughly objective and scientific, such as Ranke and Gervinus, have best measured the value of the facts and character of Iberian civilization, both in its culminating sixteenth-century achievement and in its action overseas.

Buckle's rule that a civilization is only progressive when a people reacts or rebels, since a nation's strength consists in the weakness of its government, is merely a mean attempt to subordinate all kinds of genius to the British genius and the manner of development in every civilization to that of the English civilization. Radically different from it is that of Latin nations, for it consists not in dualism but unity: this is the underlying principle of the successive leaders of the continental civilization of Europe to the nineteenth century, Roman, French, and Spanish. That is why, now that England, rich and prosperous, sees in this wealth the apotheosis of her history, we are not going to bow our heads in worship of practical utilitarianism and forswear our own genius. Acting in accordance with it, we became as rich, and more noble. We fell and passed from the scene because it is the nature of all living things (and a nation is a living organism) to be born, grow, and die. But we were born, grew, and died in a natural way. Spain was a colossus, not a monster. To explain her greatness as a mere freak would require some stronger argument than that of the shepherds and earthquakes. In order to affirm that monarchy and catholicism in the Peninsula unnaturally crushed the genius of the race, it would be necessary to show whence monarchy and catholicism derived their vitality; or else to deny that vitality and ignore the history of many centuries, dwelling only on the sad days of decadence. It would be necessary, moreover, to ignore the historical records which unanimously declare the enthusiasm with which the people acclaimed the kings and priests in whom it saw itself represented and its character and genius reflected.

After the defeat of Villalar, after King John II's execution of the dukes, the political Middle Ages disappear, to make way for the universal awakening of the Renaissance. Disagreement no longer finds vent in protest. The Spanish nation lives fervently in the life of the institutions which are the symbols of its genius, the throne and altar which represent it before the world. The nation may have renounced its independence, but it did so in no spirit of abject submission, it was a free and voluntary act. Let us therefore not condemn but rather explain. If the throne and altar can no longer be the outward symbols of our thought, if the monarchy and the clergy can no longer be the instruments of our will, if new institutions and ideas have replaced the old; we are not on that account going to substitute for the calm impartiality of science and the luminous serenity of criticism the enthusiasms of our modern revolutionary spirit, the intolerance of our doctrines, and much less the illusions of our chimerical knowledge. History deals not with opponents but with the dead; criticism is not a discussion but a verdict.

BOOK I
THE CONSTITUTION OF SOCIETY

I. THE CARTHAGINIAN AND ROMAN INVASIONS

T HE first definitely historical invasion is that of the Carthaginians. Of Phoenician origin, this people so illustrious in history had conquered a considerable part of northern Africa, subduing the natives and producing to some extent a new race known as Libyo-Phoenician. Carthage fought against Rome to maintain her naval and commercial empire in the Mediterranean. After the loss of Sicily and Sardinia in the first Punic War, the Barca family, which then ruled absolutely over the African city, saw in neighbouring Spain a region which might not only indemnify their Republic for these losses but solve that difficulty which confronts every small nation in possession of a vast empire: the lack of soldiers. In the third century Carthaginian dominion in the Peninsula made good progress and in the fourth century it was definitively established. It seems to have met with a friendly reception from the Iberian peoples, since the oldest chroniclers have nothing to say of battles and sufferings such as usually follow an invasion. Recollecting what we have said above as to the origin of the two peoples, we may perhaps see an explanation of this peaceful invasion in a community of race-origin. However that may be, it is certain that an African invasion was now spread over the Peninsula. The designs of the Barcas, favoured by the ease with which the occupation was effected, proved completely successful. Spain furnished the Carthaginian army with the greater part of its strength, and the Celtiberian infantry, the Andalusian cavalry, and the Balearic slingers were the mainstay of the mercenary armies with which Hannibal overran Italy. Besides troops, Iberia gave the Carthaginian generals a base of operations, and provided them on the south of the Pyrenees and across Liguria with a rapid passage into Italy. In placing Libyan garrisons in the eastern part of Spain, which the Romans had already reached through Gaul, and sending Spanish garrisons to occupy the towns and fortresses of his Republic in Africa, the Carthaginian general was putting into practice a device always followed by the head of a military empire.

The Carthaginian troops and the Roman legions met face to face, and the war to the death which was being waged by land and sea, in the Mediterranean, in Italy, and in Africa, was continued in the Peninsula. The Romans who had come down the passes of the Pyrenees, and the Carthaginians who had landed on the coasts of the Mediterranean were to meet on the banks of the Tagus, which for a moment divided the African invaders on the south from the European invaders on the east. The Romans were unable at that time to prevent their mortal enemies from spreading over the coasts, the mountains, and valleys of Spain south of the Ebro. Their naval resources were insufficient and the war which was raging in Gaul did not permit them to send armies against the armies of Hamilcar, Hasdrubal, and Hannibal, who successively conquered Spain for Carthage. Their peaceful and undisputed possession of the greater part of the Peninsula became a fact. One can understand the anxiety of the invaders to consolidate their valuable acquisition, for, apart from its strategical value, the coast of the Mediterranean provided them with all those agricultural and mining resources which the Republic had formerly derived from Sicily. The vast remains of mines at Cartagena, or New Carthage, still attest their activity. One can also understand, given the affinity between the two races, that the relations between the Spanish and Carthaginians were so little those of conquerors and conquered that Hannibal himself did not hesitate to marry a native of Castulo, and his example was followed by many other Carthaginians.

The south of the Peninsula, then inhabited by the Turdetani or Celto-Phoenicians and by the Celts along the river Guadiana, was the first region occupied by Hamilcar; but, as one of our historians remarks, neither the occupation nor the important fact of the assimilation of the Punic races in the Peninsula, was confined to any one province of Spain: it embraced the centre, the east, the south, and the west of the Peninsula. A Spanish writer adds that it was the Carthaginians who initiated the work of national unity, by relating distant and unknown or hostile tribes and subduing their kinglets to a higher authority, by forming leagues between various cities in a common interest, by extending the ways of commerce, by intermarrying with the Celtiberians and by welding the scattered peoples in the common discipline of the army.

The condition of the towns along the shores of the Mediterranean was, however, different from that of the more or less barbarous tribes of the interior under Carthaginian rule. The Carthaginian and Greek colonies of the coast were mercantile and cosmopolitan, such as Emporias, Saguntum, Cartagena, Málaga, and Gades. The tribes of the interior were the very reverse. Emporias was a city half Greek, half Iberian: the Greek half was separated from the 'barbarian' half by a wall, where every night a detachment of soldiers of the city and one of the higher magistrates remained on guard at the only gate by which it was possible for the barbarians to invade the Greek city to which no Iberian might lawfully penetrate. This shows that the inhabitants of the Peninsula were still living, in the heroic age, a family and even a nomad existence, to which the peculiar character of the race imparted an air of chivalry. Guerrilla warfare, suited to a mountainous country, favoured their natural bent to brigandage and prevented the creation of homogeneous states. The tribes or armed bands were at the service of the highest bidder. This adventurous existence in itself maintained the traditions of 'barbarous' heroism. When the young men went out to war their mothers told them of the glorious deeds of their ancestors, and the most beautiful girl of the tribe was the reward of valour. Single combats were common, either as tournaments or to settle disputes, including those of succession to the throne; or, before battle between champions before the assembled armies, to fight for the cape and sword which were the spoils of victory.

The state of the southern tribes was nevertheless very different from that of those to the north. In the year 150 B.C. the use of gold and silver was unknown at Anticaria, although the whole of the south was then definitively Roman; while the whole of the north and west were still in a more or less barbarous state, the south and east had reached a relatively high level of civilization. Polybius speaks of the excellence of agriculture and cattle-breeding, of the splendid palaces of the kings, the magnificent plate and the wine made of barley drunk at the feasts; and the existence of a native alphabet, the traditions of legends and heroic poems are especially clear in the case of the Turdetani who apparently stood at the head of the native civilization before the time of the Carthaginians and Romans. The conquest of the Carthaginians, although of a general character, was more important racially than socially. African blood runs in the veins of the Spaniard, but the originality of the Iberian civilization consists precisely in the fact that it seeks, for a genius which is essentially non-European, forms which belong to the social and historical development of the Aryan races of Europe. That is why there is no trace of Carthaginian or Saracen institutions in Spain, although Spaniards have much Phoenician, Egyptian, and Libyan blood in their veins and the Iberian and North African races were perhaps originally identical.

The Carthaginian domination has not, therefore, strictly speaking, an historical significance; and it is with the first Roman occupation that the history of Spain may be said properly to begin. The instability of the African governments, based entirely on war and commerce, was the probable cause of the fall of their dominion in the Peninsula, despite the affinity of race; and for the same reason the fall of Carthage itself followed. It is the Romans who made Spain a European nation; they implanted their institutions, united the villages, suppressed the tribe and created the State. These changes, however, did not occur without much bloodshed. Even as early as the first quarter of the third century the Romans who came to Spain by sea had seen how heavy would be the cost of conquering the country in which their mortal foe had entrenched himself. The heroic defence of Iliturgis and of Astapa marked their first attempt at occupation. At Astapa all the able-bodied men sallied out and died to the last man, while in the town the old men killed the women and children and then set fire to the city. This first unsuccessful attempt was followed by a struggle which lasted for two centuries.

Niebuhr divides the wars in Spain into two great periods; the first period goes down to the end of the second Punic War; the second period ends with the peace made by Sempronius Gracchus, by which the Romans remained masters of Catalonia, Valencia and Andalusia, the west of Aragon and the east of Castille. These wars, in which the legions were generally victorious yet could not finally subdue the resistance of a guerrilla warfare which kept ever springing up afresh, caused the Republic to maintain permanent garrisons in the Peninsula, at Saguntum (Murviedro),[1] Gades (Cádiz), and Tarraco (Tarragona), the three bases of a

[1] The name of this ancient town has in modern times been changed back to Sagunto (Translator's note).

military occupation which proved costly and difficult. What motives induced Rome thus to break through the traditions of her external policy? Spain, which Rome had inherited from Carthage, was, in the first place, a very important commercial market; it furnished supplies of iron; and it was the country of silver: the Romans following the example of their predecessors worked these mines on a system established by Marcus Cato, as a State monopoly. And besides all this it was imperative to defend the western flank of Italy against attacks by sea and the passage across the Pyrenees and Alps, and in Spain there was no State capable of ruling the country under a Roman protectorate, as in the case of the republic of Massilia in the southern Transalpine province, of Numidia in Africa and of Pergamos in Asia Minor. It was therefore necessary to rule directly by means of a permanent occupation; and thus it came about that Spain, which had been so difficult to conquer, became Latin more quickly than any other country.

Local insurrections broke out at different places and were more or less rapidly suppressed. That of Viriathus is the most celebrated. Had fortune allowed, he would have been the Romulus of Spain, said Lucius Florus. This Lusitanian revolt appears to have failed chiefly because of the lack of co-operation among the armed tribes, a fact characteristic of semi-barbarous peoples, and especially of those which, like the Spanish, dwell in mountain valleys and, having no communications, are naturally hostile to one another.

The insurrection of Viriathus was the most widespread, that of Numancia was the most heroic. There local rivalry could be no obstacle as the struggle was confined to a single city which was offered up on the altar of patriotism. Scipio besieged Numancia with sixty thousand men entrenched behind a high palisade and a double parapet, like the Spartans at Plataea. Their engines broke down the walls, and the river Douro on either side of the town was fenced across with barriers of lances and beaks of ships, so that no provisions could get through. Numancia was reduced by famine after mothers and children had been massacred to prevent them from becoming slaves. Fifty miserable famished inhabitants adorned the victor's triumph; all the rest had been conquered but not subdued, since they preferred death. It is believed that after the fifty who graced Scipio's triumph had been beheaded not a single inhabitant of Numancia remained.

Historians generally ascribe these insurrections and stubborn resistance to the indomitable character of the Celtiberians, and it is not to be presumed that assimilation with the Carthaginians had been so complete that none of the ancient Celtiberian tribes in the mountain wilds had not retained their primitive character unaltered. But, although this may in part account for these insurrections, it would be a mistaken patriotism to imagine that it was their only or principal cause. When we see that the known pride and independence of the Celtiberians expressed itself against the Romans and not against the Carthaginians; when we see the natives frequently led against the Romans by Carthaginian leaders such as he who defeated the armies of Manilius and Piso; when we consider the story of the insurrection of Sertorius, we are persuaded that this resistance in the Peninsula represents, up to the final fall of Carthage, a prolongation of the Punic Wars, no longer expressed in pitched battles but taking the terrible form of local risings. The Celtiberians appeared in arms, but it was the Carthaginians who incited them to war and who directed their campaigns. The story of Sertorius is very significant: it shows how limited was the action of any national element and that the predominating influence was that of the Carthaginians and of the *condottieri* who, since the war between Marius and Sylla, were preparing the way for the establishment of the Empire. We shall see too that at the time of Sertorius' insurrection assimilation between Romans and natives had advanced so far that one of the main supports of the insurrection consisted in men who were half Roman by birth.

Sertorius was a Sabine; after being an advocate in Rome, he fought as a soldier in Gaul. Plutarch relates his deeds. He was as brave as he was cunning. On one occasion, when pursued by the enemy, he threw himself into the Rhine and swam the river armed with his breastplate and shield. In Gaul under Marius he feigned to be a barbarian in order to act as a spy; learnt the enemy's language, adopted their dress and manners, and remained undetected. Later he was sent to Spain and was in winter quarters at Castulo when the enemy took the city by surprise, forced an entrance and cut down the garrison. Sertorius, with a handful of followers, cut his way through the enemy, and then dressed up his soldiers in clothes of the dead, and thus was able to capture towns which supposed that he and his men were friends returning. He returned to Rome a famous man and went as quaestor to Lombardy. Sylla, by thwarting his ambition to become tribune, drove him into the party of Marius. After the frustration of many hopes Sertorius made a last attempt to achieve success by provoking the barbarian provinces of the west to rebellion, and returned to Spain. Repulsed there, he went to the Balearic Isles and passed on to Africa; it is even said that he reached the Canary Isles. When at last he had obtained a small independent command in Africa he received a message summoning him to Spain. Probably it was partisans of Marius who, taking advantage of the hatred roused by the tyrannical government of Annius, turned to the adventurer chief; for it is ridiculous to suppose that a national rising of a spontaneous character would send for a Sabine, a ruler in Africa, in order to set him at its head.

The revolt led by Sertorius was able to gain ground owing to a fact to which we have already referred: that a considerable part of the inhabitants were of hybrid birth, the sons of Roman soldiers and Spanish mothers. These men were Romans, they spoke the language of their fathers and used their name, but they had not the legal right of citizenship. Thus the revolt of Sertorius, supported by a social phenomenon which was due to the Roman occupation and representing one of the many conflicts between parties by which the great Republic was at this time torn asunder, can only by a mistaken patriotism be regarded as a monument of the spirit of national independence. The only concessions which, according to the historians, Sertorius granted to the natives of Spain were to suffer them to believe that a white fawn had been presented to him by Diana and foretold the future to him; and to take the sons of the principal inhabitants of each district and send them to the University of Osca where they learnt the Latin culture and at the same time served as hostages. From his capital at Ebora, Sertorius organized Spain as a second Latium. 'He used', says an historian, 'the arms, the money, and the cities of Spain to carry on the war, but never allowed any share in the sovereign authority to the Spanish. His captains and governors were Romans, and in fact he proposed to give liberty to his countrymen without harming their interests by increasing the power of the Spanish.' Even while waging war against Rome, she was ever in his thoughts and he lived in hope of an amnesty which would allow him to return to his country.

The insurrection of Sertorius, apart from its interest as an attempt to divide the Republic, has for us a high ethnological interest: it means the introduction of a new wave of Punic blood into Spain. Of the sixty thousand soldiers of Sertorius six thousand or more accompanied him from Africa; Perpenna brought him twenty thousand from Sardinia; and African mercenaries, men proscribed by Sylla, crossed the Straits every day to swell his ranks. If we accept the information of the Latin historians as to the composition of his army, we shall see in it the cause of the indifference of the people of the Peninsula towards a rising which was merely a personal question between generals of the Republic. And the important fact for our history is not the rising in itself but the new layer of African race brought into the country.

After the murder of Sertorius by a rival, one of his generals named Perpenna, the revolt was easily crushed by Julius Caesar; yet the wars of Rome in the Peninsula did not end until the Empire became definitively established. The duel between Caesar and Pompey had in the Peninsula one of the principal scenes of its warfare by land. Those two Roman armies, which now included men from very various and remote nations, further confused the inextricable tangle of races in the Peninsula. On the other hand Roman civilization, which in its abstract or general character was indifferent to the individuality of peoples and regions and considered itself equally suitable to Caledonia, Sarmatia and Spain, assimilated and subordinated to its principles peoples of every race. That was its greatness and enabled it with invincible strength to impose itself on the rude outlines of institutions which barbarian peoples had constructed, either instinctively, on a basis of custom, or by force, on a basis of aristocratic traditions. Against institutions of a local or personal character the Romans set the general institutions of the city state. It was under the Empire that Rome finally established civil equality, and it was naturally under the Empire that Spain became completely and organically romanized and the Spanish obtained first the *jus latinum* and then the status of Roman citizens.

II. THE ORGANIZATION OF ROMAN SPAIN

THE Roman occupation was distinguished from previous invasions by its social and administrative character. Whereas the utmost skill of the victorious barbarians
consisted in plunder, and the strange civilizations
of the Phoenicians and Carthaginians only showed
some moderation in this respect owing to their wise
commercial instinct; the Romans, without ceasing to
plunder and exploit the conquered regions, founded
everywhere new Romes and extended to all peoples
the system of rights, duties, and guarantees which
formed the basis of a real social organization.

Under the Republic Spain, still only partially subdued to Rome, was divided only into two provinces,
separated by the river Ebro (Citerior and Ulterior).
Augustus divided it into three: Tarraconensis, Lusitania, and Baetica. Otho incorporated with Spain the
northern coast of Africa, with the name of Mauretania
Tingitana, a province which belonged to the jurisdiction of Cadiz. When Diocletian divided the Empire
into four parts, the western two were Italy and the
Gauls. The latter comprised Gaul, Great Britain, and
Spain, which was divided into seven provinces, Tarraconensis, Baetica, Lusitania, Gallaecia, and Cartha-
ginensis, with Mauritania Tingitana and the Balearic
Isles. Originally the Peninsula consisted of the senatorial province of Baetica and two imperial provinces.
As their names imply one depended on the Senate and
was governed by its delegate as proconsul; the others
were governed by an imperial legate, *legatus augustalis*.
This division of authority, a sign of concessions and
agreements between the Senate and the emperors,
whose power was not yet absolute, disappeared in the
course of time. The real difference between the
senatorial and imperial provinces was that the latter

were subjected to martial law. Owing to the military character of the Empire, the provinces gradually all became imperial as the emperors succeeded in establishing their authority on an absolute basis. The governor of a province, *praeses, praesidens, legatus augustalis,* or *legatus Caesaris,* was now the representative of the Emperor. His *legati* resided in the districts, the *conventus juridici,* seats of all local administration and of the judicial and military power emanating from the central power; the quaestors were especially entrusted with taxation. Mérida, Beja, Santarem, and Braga were *conventus* of Lusitania. Under Diocletian the prefectures were divided into districts governed by a *vicarius.* Spain, in the prefecture of the Gauls, was one of these districts, governed by a *vicarius,* corresponding to the modern civil governor, and a military count (*comes militum*). The rights of the subject regions varied, not only in their government but in local administration. The provinces were governed by laws (*formulae provinciae*), by decrees sent to the governors from Rome, and finally by edicts issued by the governors. The cities were classified according to the rights conferred on them, the different rights of the cities of Italy, which had been the first to submit to Rome. These rights, however, conferred on the free men in a city did not necessarily depend on the internal organization of the city nor on its existence as part of a social and administrative system. The right of Roman citizenship formed a kind of nobility. Julius Caesar conferred it on Lisbon. Evora Mertola, Salacia (Alcacer do Sal) were *municipia* with the *jus veteris Latii*; Mérida, Beja, Medellín, Alcántara, and Santarem were colonies with the *jus italicum.* The Latin right *jus latinum, veteris Latii* or *italicum*) was extended by Vespasian to the whole of Spain; finally when Caracalla extended the privilege of Roman citizenship (originally confined to Rome) to all free subjects of the Empire, these distinctions ceased and

one of the many differences between the various cities
was at an end.

Several historians have noticed a circumstance which
distinguishes populations before and after the fall of
the Empire. The system of isolated cities in the midst
of agricultural, commercial, or mining regions and connected by military roads, was subsequently replaced by
a mixed system, and groups of houses, farms, country-
houses, convents, and churches were scattered over the
cultivated regions near the cities. We cannot now gauge
the density of population by the number of cities in
every region; but formerly, as in many parts of modern
Europe, this was not the case. In the time of Pliny
Spain, he states, contained 829 cities, of which 14 were
coloniae, 9 *municipia*; 211 had the Latin right, 6 were
free, 4 allied, 291 were tributary, and 294 contributary.
Colonies were cities inhabited either by Romans or by
natives enjoying the full Roman citizenship. They were
like so many Romes detached from the capital, to whose
existence they were closely bound. The *colonia* might
be *patricia* or *togata*, and the latter was of two kinds,
civil or military. Carteia (Tarifa) was the first colony
founded by the Romans in Spain and Córdoba was the
first Spanish city to receive Roman citizenship. Gradually, however, as the policy of the Emperors tended to
equalize all their free subjects and to abolish local
privileges and the distinctions between cities, these
various names had no longer any reason to exist, and
even under Hadrian the difference between a *colonia*
and a *municipium* was a matter for scholars. The chief
difference between them lay in the fact of Roman
citizenship, which was not inherent in the *municipia*,
although some of them might receive it. The cities
which were inhabited by Romans without right of
Roman citizenship were known as Latin, but this distinction disappeared when Vespasian granted the Latin
right to all the provinces of the Empire. The con-

federate cities were, as the name implies, allied cities
unsubdued by Rome and independent in their internal
administration; they owed their independence to the
fact that they had submitted without resistance to the
power of Rome. Some of them were *immunes*, exempt
from taxation, others were *stipendiariae* and paid taxes
to Rome. The cities called *contributae* were what we
should now call suburbs, situated within the district
of some larger city. The jurisdiction of the city was
not confined within its walls but embraced a certain
agricultural area in its neighbourhood. Having thus
sketched the system of cities which in Spain reproduced the system of Rome and the neighbouring cities
in Italy, it remains for us to examine the most intimate
and important side of the Roman administration: the
internal regime of the *municipia*, which was the essential
basis of the stability, duration, and social worth of the
institutions of Rome. To follow the Roman *municipium*
through its different kinds and slow evolution would
exceed the limits and character of this book; we will
confine ourselves to its main characteristics, its social
importance, its gradual degeneration from the unit in
an organized society to a mere cog in a huge centralized
administration.

The Roman *municipium* allows the historian to
observe one of the two essential types adopted by all
societies which emerge from a nomad state and have
a fixed existence on the indispensible basis of agriculture.
These two types are the beneficiary or aristocratic
system and the municipal system, which for want of a
better word we will call democratic. In the first case
society is constituted on the idea or fact of personal
protection; in the other on a basis of legal guarantees.
In the one case the land is the sacred property of a
protector invested with a paternal authority; in the
other the land is the common property of the inhabitants of the *municipium*, and authority centres in their

assembly. In the former case the manner of ownership of the land gives rise to an hereditary aristocracy; in the other the aristocracy consists only in the higher magistrates and powerful citizens.

At first among the Romans there were different orders and classes distinguished by peculiar rights and privileges; but these exceptions soon disappeared; whereas the very essence of the aristocratic system consists in exceptions and it tends daily to emphasize these distinctions. The system of municipal property, developing spontaneously amid the anarchy of the Middle Ages reappears, when freed from the over-rule of the Empire, as a pure democracy in the republics of Italy; while the aristocratic system under identical circumstances affirmed itself more and more definitely until it produced the feudal system. At the present time we have two nations in which actual conditions bear out these remarks. The English aristocracy, although shorn of many of its privileges, retains enough of the essential features to be characteristic of the system: it retains ownership of the land and hereditary office. On the other hand the Russian empire gives us a faithful reproduction of the social and administrative machinery of ancient Rome, without an aristocracy in the historical sense. The Russian aristocracy is, like the Roman, composed of the élite of society, civil and military magistrates (*chin*), the wealthy and men eminent in art and letters; no laws guarantee the heredity of either office or riches. This aristocracy, which we ought rather to call a social magistracy, presides over a vast democracy based juridically on civil equality, which has been universal since the abolition of slavery; administratively on a municipal system; and economically on a mixed system of individual cultivation and collective ownership. These essential characteristics of the Russian *commune* are those of the Roman *municipium*; the *mir* represents the Roman *curia*.

Thus the social problem which arises when a society becomes fixed on a limited extent of land was solved by the Romans in an entirely different way from the later solution given to it by the Germanic races, when on the ruins of the democratic Empire they set up their aristocratic or clannish institutions, characteristic of the barbaric state in which they then were. This historical fact is, we think, the most important of all when we come to estimate the significance of the Romanization of Spain. There can be no doubt that to this fact the Peninsula owed its undisputed superiority as an organized nation among the feudal people of medieval Europe. The ancient *municipium* produced citizens, and its influence was so deep and lasting that it was able to resist the Germanic aristocratic ideas which later prevailed in the whole of central Europe, so that Spain escaped the difficult position of being confronted with a complete and perfect feudal system such as those of France and England. The natural tendency of the victorious Goths was opposed on the one hand by a strong middle class sprung from the institutions of Rome, and on the other by the imperial and monarchical tradition maintained by a romanized clergy, a tradition which satisfied the personal ambition of the Gothic kings in that it curbed the greed of their warrior chiefs.

General causes which we need not here examine had brought it about at Rome that the government by magistrates and laws was gradually replaced by the government of generals induced by urgent State reasons or persuaded by caprice and ambition. This change necessarily involved a change in the character of the *municipia*. Originally by the *curia's* system of individual cultivation and collective property, due to the wish to divide the land equitably and to establish a fixed administrative and fiscal unit, the *curiales* were collectively responsible for the payment of taxes. Thus many centuries ago arose the difficulty with which the communal system in Russia is now confronted. The tax for each portion of land was fixed by law and the portions of land in each district was likewise fixed, the *municipes* being collectively responsible for the payment of the whole tax. It is evident that where the soil was fertile and agriculture remunerative the tax would not prove burdensome; but under different conditions and when the land remained uncultivated the joint responsibility to the Treasury would become a system of violent extorsion. This essential defect in the system was aggravated by unfavourable conditions of an economic order, by the arbitrary, despotic, extravagant and generally execrable administration of imperial Rome, which introduced disorder into the municipal system while at the same time unwarrantably increasing the taxation. The situation of the *curiales* was thus truly miserable, while the privileges and independence of the *municipia* gradually disappeared before the encroachments of a government which was both jealous of its power and insatiable. The *curia* was the group of all the proprietors, including both those born in the *municipium* (*municipes*) and settlers from outside (*incolae*), who owned over twenty-five *jugera* of land. To be a *curialis* was not optional, for each proprietor's name was entered in a register, called *album curiae*. We have already said that in the *municipium*, as in the Russian commune, property was collective and only the cultivation of the soil individual. It seems a contradiction now to speak of proprietors, but the contradiction disappears when we see how many checks the *municipium* placed on the right of individual property and realize that the object of the laws was to guarantee the existence of a social unit, not the independence of private property. Juridically property might not be collective, but socially and economically it was. The proprietor could not escape being a member of the *curia*, which was collectively responsible for the

administration of the *municipium* and for the total
land taxes imposed on it. Once on the register, the
proprietor could not cease to belong to the *curia* without the permission of the administrative authorities.
If the permission was refused and he refused to cultivate
the land, the tax corresponding to this neglected piece
of land was divided between the remaining properties,
unless the *curia* found somebody willing to take over the
land and pay the tax. The *curialis* might not live
outside the city nor belong to any of the higher orders
(whose members were exempt from taxation even if
they were landed proprietors) unless they had previously
filled all the posts, from mere member of the *curia* to
highest magistrate. When the Christian Church, recognized by the State, sought priests chiefly among the
middle class, the *curialis* could not take orders unless
he found someone willing to take his place in the *curia*.
This system of checks, calculated to maintain the collective character of the property, did not end with the
life of the individual. When the property of a member
of the *curia* was inherited by a person who did not
belong to the *curia*, or when girls or widows who owned
property married outside the *curia*, the *municipium*
confiscated a quarter of their entire property in favour
of the community. Three quarters of the property
of those who died childless were similarly confiscated.
Similar and in many cases identical is the lot of members
of the Russian communes, and their example shows us
that whether the communal system becomes a guarantee
of security or a source of oppression depends on the
fertility of the soil and the value of its products, on
whether the cultivation of the soil is pleasant or the
reverse, a source of gain or a cause of ruin. Apart from
the economic guarantees given by the *curia* to society
it gave certain guarantees to its members. It constituted them into a class raised above the ordinary class
of freemen; among other privileges this meant that

they were exempt from work in mines, from torture on the rack, from being burnt alive and other almost equally barbarous punishments reserved for the plebeians. They thus held a privileged position (*optimum jus*) among the mass of plebeians (*privati*) who formed the lowest layer of the class of freemen (*ingenui*); at the top of this class were the *clarissimi* who were privileged to own property without any of the drawbacks imposed on the *curiales*. This aristocracy was composed of five kinds; senators, palace officials, clergy, soldiers of the cohorts and police, and finally army officers of high rank. At the beginning of the fifth century these were the three classes into which the freemen of the Empire were divided. Placed between the plebeian *privati* and the aristocratic *clarissimi*, one can understand how great would be the ambition of the *curialis* to pass into the rank above him when one remembers how even to-day when there are no classes in the eyes of the law, the bourgeois aspires fervently to obtain the vestiges of those former privileges, the vain distinctions of noble rank. The *curialis* had the right to become a member of the aristocracy of the Roman *chin* when after passing through all the municipal offices he became one of a special class, the *honorati*.

Economically the *curia* gave its members an effective protection, since it constituted a kind of mutual assurance company and guaranteed means of subsistence to those of its member who had fallen on evil days. Politically it was a republic, and indeed it is clear from what we have said above that it could not be otherwise. Social duties of such importance could only be fulfilled on the condition of an absolutely independent political organization. And the higher kinds of *municipia* possessed this independence before the reforms which were entailed by the centralization under the Empire. Rome was unable to solve a social problem which reappears in history in the Russian Empire, the problem of the organic development of a military and agricultural nation by means of an absolute authority ruling over a vast democracy, a system of municipal institutions (or to use the modern term, of self-government) on the economic and administrative side, with an absolute centralization in the politic and supreme institutions. The future will show whether the modern Empire is able to succeed where the Roman Empire failed.

Historians divide the Spanish *municipia* at the end of the Republic into three types. In the first and perfect type, common to all cities in possession of the *jus italicum* and therefore exempt from the poll-tax, the *duumviri* are elective, like the consuls at Rome. In the second type the magistrates are not elective and the jurisdiction belongs to a *rector* or Roman administrator. In the third type there is a *curia* but there are no magistrates, unless we give this name to the decurion who was the first to be inscribed in the *album* and presided over the assembly. Municipal authority resided in the *curia*, it resembled the legislative power in modern constitutions. At the summons of the *duumvir, aedile, rector,* or *praetor* (according to the type of *municipium*) the *curia* met in assembly and its discussions went by majority of votes. The distribution of the land held in common, taxation, and the municipal finances were its principal duties. The administration belonged to the magistrates, *aedile, curator, dictator, praetor,* or *duumvir*; the first being concerned with the distribution of land, the second with the finances, and the last three exercised the same office under different names, that of mayor or president of our modern town councils. Besides these magistrates there were lower officials, the *susceptor* or notary, the aldermen (*irenarchae*), the *curatores* (inspectors) and the *scribae* or secretaries. In time, that is in the fourth century a new municipal official was created, the post of *defensor*. He was elected by all the citizens, and his duty was to defend the *curia*, maintaining its rights against higher powers and the encroachments of the provincial administrative authority, the *praesidens*, the *legatus*, and others. The post of *defensor*, which originated in *municipia* of the third type which had no magistrates to defend them, passed, as the municipal system became decadent, to those of the second and finally to those of the first type, and took the place of the post of *duumvir*. With the disorganization of the Roman administrative machine the collective character and constant interference of the *curia* became an intolerable tyranny. Collective responsibility for the taxes spelt ruin for all those who had emerged from poverty; and escape was impossible: to be born a *curialis* was to be a *curialis* all one's life. Frequently the *curiales* fled, taking refuge in the army or hiding themselves in the multitude of slaves; but the imperial administration went in search of them and forced them to retain their liberty which they found more intolerable than the life of a private soldier or even that of a slave.

It was inevitable that the centralized administration under the Empire should undermine the political privileges of the *municipia*; the internal administration of the *curia* was often oppressive, as the laws show; the *curialis* frequently longed to cease to belong to the *curia*, either to satisfy a natural ambition or to escape from intolerable oppression; but we must not, with many historians, confuse the decadence of an institution, which many causes made inevitable, with the disappearance of a class. The *curia* was destroyed by the exactions under the Empire which reduced it to a mere machinery for levying land-taxes; but it does not follow that free landed proprietors entirely died out in Spain; we shall see this middle class reappear after many an upheaval as soon as some measure of tranquillity returned. Parallel with the ruin of the municipal system by the imperial Treasury and the decay of the middle class, there arose in Spain, as is always the case where the organization of society has become corrupt although it may be economically prosperous, a strong minority of wealthy owners of *latifundia* and all movable property; dissolute men who were morally incapable of becoming the heirs of a perverted classical culture. And at the same time the number of slaves immensely increased, although in the country they had changed their name to that of permanent *coloni* when Diocletian fixed by law the new ideas which had arisen in the course of time on the subject of slavery.

From this long catalogue of facts we hope at least that the reader has arrived at the conclusion that the Roman occupation of Spain transferred that country from Africa to Europe and transformed a half barbarous, half nomad people, resembling its kin across the Straits, into a nation in the European sense; that is, a society of men united by a system of fixed and general institutions and made one not only morally but by ties of a civil, political, military, and intellectual nature. The character of the ties by which Spain was now bound was Roman and proceeded from ideas common to all the Indo-European peoples. The domination now ended had not only given an external form and constitution to the nation but had revealed to it an order of feelings and ideas which it assimilated and which separated it for ever from the peoples to which by race it belonged. Its Berber or barbarous existence was replaced by one of culture; the village became a city; the tribe was absorbed in the State. If facts of a political nature and the stability of the Roman organization of Spain were not enough to prove this, we might turn to proofs yet more decisive: to the Latin language for instance, which became national in Spain, and to the many Spaniards who figure in the annals of Roman history: Porcius Latro of Córdoba, who was an advocate at Rome; the two

Senecas; Martial of Bilbilis; Lucan, Columella, Quin-
tilian, Silius Italicus; Balbus of Cadiz, the first foreign
consul at Rome who received the honour of a triumph;
and Trajan of Seville, the first non-Italian Emperor. The
Latin of the poets of Córdoba who were taken to Rome by
Metellus after the death of Sertorius was praised by
Cicero, who only noticed in it a thick and foreign accent.

The Romanization of Spain was a central fact in the
history of the Peninsula. The construction thus raised
might fall in ruins, but it would always leave traditions
sufficient to prevent the nation from sinking back into
its former state of primitive Berber tribes. As part of
the Empire, Spain suffered from turmoils which were
foreign to her but by which she could not fail to be
affected. Social organization in the Peninsula decayed
with the decay of the Roman administration. The
Goths who advanced on Rome also crossed the Pyrenees
and invaded the fairest western province of the Empire.
The Germanic tribes were not the real cause of this
ruin, which had long been developing internally, but
they completed it. During the last centuries of the
Empire, as one more proof and symptom of its decay,
had arisen a Christian society whose Church became
a State within the State. We will quote here the words
of a celebrated historian:

> There existed a body of priests with property, a jurisdiction
> and constitution of their own; in fact a government and organ-
> ized society furnished with all the means of existence, inde-
> pendent of the society in which it lived but exercising an
> influence on it. Such was the state of the Christian Church
> at the beginning of the fifth century. The bishops and priests
> had become municipal magistrates, and almost all that was
> left of the Roman Empire was the municipal system. The
> clergy alone was morally vigorous and alive; and it thus
> became all-powerful.

The words in which Guizot thus sketches the main
lines of the history of Europe apply nowhere more

aptly than to Spain. As early as the year 313 nineteen bishops, thirty six priests and many deacons met at the Council of Iliberis; in A.D. 380 at the Council of Zaragoza and in A.D. 400 at the Council of Toledo the Spanish clergy constituted a real national parliament and their discussions were not confined to ecclesiastical matters. Amid the general decadence it took over the administration from the civil authorities which had been destroyed by a series of disorders and military seditions. In this way Spain passed from the hands of the Romans into those of Spaniards, and in the decay of the Empire these meetings of prelates and doctors presided over by the worthiest or eldest among them, was the first sketch of the future parliaments of the nation. A sketch and nothing more: for beneath the formulae of Christianity paganism survived. In the time of Constantine Spain did not yet possess a Christian Church; the change of religion had been merely an official act which did not closely affect the organization of society. Later, at the time of the Moorish conquest, despite the absolute power and intolerance of the Visigothic clergy, paganism and Christianity still appeared as rival combatants; the bishops still thundered against the worshippers of false gods and took rigorous measures against them; and as late as the sixth century Masonius Bishop of Mérida converted many pagans. The people retained a traditional polytheism or primitive fetishism; the cultured classes were sceptical; the clergy, having risen to power through a series of crises and disorder, was political. This clergy was Spanish by birth and Roman by education; the part it played was to preserve in the new invasions the tradition of ancient culture and the fragmentary remains of old institutions. Roman Spain had disappeared; modern Spain, with its original individual character, was not yet born; it was necessary that the decay should be completed in order that Nature out of the ruins might create something entirely new.

BOOK II

THE DECAY OF ANCIENT SPAIN

I. THE RISE OF THE VISIGOTHIC MONARCHY

IN the first years of the fifth century, after the Roman Empire had been divided into East and West, the treachery, or whatever it may be called, of a Roman general opened the passes of the Pyrenees to the invasion of the barbarian hordes. The gates of the Pyrenees had been entrusted by the Empire to the mercenary troops known as *honoriani*: barbarians guarded all the provincial frontiers of a nation which had ceased to be vigorous enough to bear arms. The example of Gaul's fate was lost upon the Peninsula; the rich in their egoism, the poor in their misery, the slaves as slaves, refused to take alarm. The *honoriani*, instead of guarding the frontier plundered it and then, in order to escape punishment, let in the first rush of barbarians in A.D. 411. The overwhelming character of this first invasion is noticed by the chroniclers. During the last four centuries of the Empire Spain had been so prosperous that, as Gibbon observes, she contributes but few materials to the history of the Empire during that period. In the midst of peace Mérida, Córdoba, Seville, Braga, and Tarragona had developed to such an extent that they were considered among the foremost cities of the whole Empire. The wave of barbarian tribes found here abundant material to sate their craving for enjoyment. The charms and wealth of the southern lands filled with vague desires these sons of the North, brought up in the harsh régime of fierce instincts. Their relations with the Hispano-Roman population were much the same as those of the Asturians later towards the Moors, sunk in the delights of a life of ease and exquisite culture. Such was the softness of this disorganized society that it was not necessary to besiege a single city; they all fell at the first assault, like ripe fruit when the tree is shaken. While the tempest of war raged without, in the cities men thought only of banquets and orgies, eager in their despair to enjoy the last day of their life since to-morrow they must die. And while the barbarians were engaged in plunder, the slaves, *coloni*, and ruined *curiales* broke through the harsh bonds of their servitude, formed themselves into robber bands and began to plunder on their own account.

The various tribes which poured down from the Pyrenees over-ran the Peninsula; the Vandals and Suevi remained in Galicia and Old Castille, the Alani in Lusitania and Catalonia, which was called after them (Goth-Alani: Cataulania), the Silingi in Andalusia. Idatius, the chronicler of the invasion, records with horror the massacres by which it was accompanied, as though to emphasize the transition from the old régime to the new in Spain. All the invasions of barbarians are much alike: massacres, and after the massacres plague; war followed by famine and marked by terrible examples of how low men can sink under the necessity of the harsh laws of Nature. Idatius describes the awfulness of the massacres and of the plague and shows us famished mothers devouring their children and men holding cannibal banquets. But amid all this violence and horror there is one noteworthy fact. We know why Spain, rich and densely populated, was unable to show any effective resistance to the invading hordes; but it is certainly surprising to find the chroniclers almost applauding the barbarians. Idatius, although he is revolted by their ferocity, ingenuously tells us the feelings of the clergy in this respect. Paulus Orosius in 417 says: 'magis inter barbaros pauperem libertatem quam inter romanos tributariam sollicitudinem sustinere.' The tyranny of the Roman administration must have reduced many to this state of mind; yet it is impossible to believe that the whole nation had lost the elementary notions of patriotism. With greater truth Sidonius Apollinarius writes 'You avoid those barbarians who are considered evil: I flee even from the good.' There is no doubt that the Hispano-Roman society had reached a degree of weakness which made resistance impossible; but it is inconceivable that it should actually applaud an era of massacres after several centuries of peace. But the Catholic clergy were inspired by other feelings: it had completely lost the idea of patriotism, its true country being heaven; its sectarian fervour caused it to look on the evils of the time as punishment sent by God against the contumacious pagans. The pessimism inherent in Christianity spoke by the mouth of Orosius: 'What matter how a Christian leaves this world?' Moreover the Church had everything to gain from the dissolution of society; the cultured, sceptical Hispano-Roman was by no means to be converted; but the ingenuous wave of barbarians, amazed by the glitter of civilization, more easily accepted the new fetishes with which the Catholic priests lured or threatened them. The anarchy into which Spain was thrown by the first invasion did not last many years. Wallia, elected King of the Visigoths in 415, made peace with the Emperor Honorius, accepting responsibility for the restoration of peace in the Peninsula and guaranteeing a part of it to the Romans. This agreement entailed the expulsion of the Vandals, who were driven over to Africa, but not that of the Alani and Suevi, who, amid the turmoils of war, were able to remain in Galicia and maintain their independence until Leovigild put an end to it in the year 584. But as early as 456, the date of the battle of Orvigo, the Visigoths had checked the military power of the Suevi and their expansion in the Peninsula. The second horde of invaders put Spain to fire and sword in order to eject the first; they sacked Astorga and Palencia and everywhere desecrated the churches, since they were not yet Catholics. The second half of the fifth century saw the culmination of the Visigothic monarchy. In Gaul it extended from the Pyrenees to the Atlantic and to the Alps, and in Spain, it reached Lusitania. But in the first half of the following century this empire was defeated in France, although it gained new ground in Spain. Leovigild's subjection of the Suevi in Galicia, the recognition of the Councils of Toledo as national assemblies, later the conversion of Reccared to Catholicism in 587, brought it about that the Visigothic empire, which had been destroyed in France was during the second half of the sixth century established politically and religiously in the whole of Spain. The Visigothic monarchy in Spain resembled the attempt made by Charlemagne in France to restore the Roman Empire. The institutions of the Visigoths were of great importance for the subsequent history of the Peninsula; yet it must be admitted that their domination, which degenerated in a single century, is but an episode in the history of the decay of Roman Spain which was completed by the Moors in their memorable victory of the year 711.

Much has been written concerning the influence of the Germanic races after the invasions on a population whose culture was Latin. The character of these races which so vividly impressed Tacitus has been discussed; the text of laws, the customs, literature, and monuments have been compared and commented on, in order to decide whether the chief influence in the formation of the neo-Latin peoples was that of Roman ideas or the instincts of the Germanic peoples. Often the blindness of uncritical learning and partisanship have made this problem of modern history even more difficult to unravel than it really is. Prejudice, narrowness and dogmatism, applied to a question which cannot be judged by rigorously scientific standards, and the failure to allow for the element of doubt which is often as far in the truth as it is permitted to history to penetrate, make it difficult and even dangerous to discuss this subject without the utmost caution. A statement familiar to all who have studied this subject is that the main characteristic of these Germanic races who, so it is alleged, came to free western Europe from the yoke of Rome was a natural independence, or, as it is conventionally called, individualism. It cannot be denied that the dependence which is necessarily entailed when men form themselves into a social body had been rendered excessive by the perverted and centralized character of Roman administration. It is certain also that the Germanic peoples, whose social life at the time of the invasions was in a considerably earlier state of evolution and who were for the most part nomadic and semi-barbarous, possessed that independence which is common to all primitive societies, an independence which earlier had characterized Spain, and earlier still had characterized the Romans themselves. But one must distinguish between the true feeling of independence and the anarchy which precedes the establishment of fixed institutions in a society. A stage in a people's progress is not to be confused with a racial quality inherent in a people's original character. An observer will find in modern history, which is all the history that the Germanic peoples know, exactly the opposite of what he might expect. We cannot here enter on considerations which the reader will, moreover, find in the course of this book; enough to remind him that at the crisis of Christian Europe, when religious anarchy allowed the most spontaneous feelings to find free expression, the Germany of Luther championed predestination and denied the merit of the actions of man and therefore the independence of his reason. Contradictory as it may appear, it is a fact that the Germanic genius in all its manifestations displays a moral submissiveness, on which nevertheless it builds a spiritual independence which is as it were irresponsible as forming part of a greater whole. Pantheism, reappearing in these direct descendants of the Aryan genius, lies at the base of the national religion and philosophy of Germany. These few words suffice to show that the independence of the Germanic barbarians was merely of a historic kind and not an essential characteristic of the race. Even to-day, in the nineteenth century Germany is the country of divine right; and, with the exception of Russia, she was the last country to abolish slavery. England too is a feudal or aristocratic country, in spite of the encroachments of a communal or bourgeois spirit, and still rests on a system of religious, social, and moral traditions which to-day are simply puerile.[1] Could peoples represented by such nations to-day have possibly been twelve centuries ago those bold champions of independence which many historians take pleasure in presenting to us? We think not.

True independence, which is not merely the characteristic of a certain stage of historical development but is an essential moral result expressed in institutions and character, does not in our opinion belong to the Teutonic branch of the human race but to the Greco-Italian-Celtic branch which in Greece produced a rationalist philosophy, in ancient Italy civil law and in France the type of modern monarchies. Other are the great merits of the Germanic races, but it is not part of our plan to go into that here. Whatever they be, we agree with many good authorities in thinking that their influence on the ultimate destiny of Spain was small. Spain's history is the best proof of this; if we turn once more to the religious crisis of the sixteenth century, any unprejudiced observer will see in the antagonism of temperaments and national ideas, in the difference between the characters of individuals and in the open warfare between Jesuit Spain and Protestant Germany the proof of how little Germany influenced the development of Spain. Chroniclers and historians confirm this,

[1] That is, in the eyes of a Portuguese Liberal. (Translator's note).

for they tell us that the conquerors of Roman Spain were but a small group. After the tumultuous invasion of the first barbarians, the Visigothic conquest does not present the character of military migrations. They act rather as pacifiers than as conquerors. The Romans themselves entrusted to them the task of driving out the barbarian hordes from Spain; later the natives invoked their help against the Romans, who in their despair had allied themselves with the barbarians in an attempt to drive out the heirs of the Empire. The Goths represent an aristocracy which in a sense replaced the former officials of Rome; and were it not for a partial distribution of land it would be difficult to find a trace of their occupation: apart from the change in the names of the sovereigns and their officials. Spain was conquered, but it was never Germanized. These so-called champions of independence who are supposed to have utterly transformed the Peninsula, to the extent even of constitutionally altering the character of its inhabitants, are historically a mere group of submissive men who accept everything, religion, language, laws, and institutions, from the people which they are said to have destroyed; they reserve for themselves merely the sovereign authority and the use of the riches they have won. But we must not fall into the opposite error of attributing absolutely no historical value to the Visigothic monarchy or reducing it to a mere change of authorities. It would be a paradox to assert that the conquerors who had acquired two thirds of the land and assumed sovereign authority did not introduce any of their customs, institutions and ideas into the society in which they now lived. And it is not only this circumstance that gives a place of its own to the Visigothic monarchy in the history of Spain; there were others, arising from causes with which the invasion and invaders had nothing to do.

The first of these causes is the continual degeneration

which a medley of moral and material reasons produced
in the members of the ancient society of the Peninsula,
and the change in the character of classes which was the
result. The second is the conversion of the Visigothic
monarchs to Catholicism, a fact which, in view of the
still contested pre-eminence of the Papacy, made of the
King, whose council consisted of the assembly of bishops,
both the political and religious head of the nation; the
nation became completely united under an authority,
the sanction of whose rule was undisputed. Thus the
period of the Visigothic monarchy, though short and
in a sense transitory, is very important for the study of
civilization in the Peninsula.

If on the one hand this period represents merely a
moment in the history of the decay of ancient Spain, on
the other hand it is at this time that first appear or are
first combined in a new way elements essential to the
future constitution of the nation and of its genius. In
a sense, with certain reserves, as we shall see, the later
Catholic Monarchy was merely a restoration of that of
the Visigoths. The essential characteristics are the
same in both. The person of the Gothic King unites
three characters derived from different traditions: he
is the prince of Roman law, because the Goths, as heirs
of the Emperors, maintain in modern times the institutions and ideas of antiquity; he is at the same time the
chieftain or suzerain according to the military and
aristocratic institutions and the customs of the Germans
which subsequently produced feudalism; finally he is
the priest, the anointed of the Lord, the monarchs
having, by their adoption of Christianity, added to their
legal and military character the religious sanction of the
Jewish political tradition.

We shall see how of these three characters one or the
other gains the upper hand according to the path
followed by the various nations in the development of
their history; the characters were united both in the

Kings of Spain and in the monarchs of nearly the whole of contemporary Europe, especially in the Carolingian Kings of France. In England, Germany and North Italy the type of suzerain prevailed; in France likewise under the Merovingian Kings, but afterwards the type of Roman prince gained the upper hand; finally in Spain, where the historical development of the nation was seriously interrupted by the Moorish invasion, the neo-Gothic Monarchy assumed a unique character which we will carefully study in due course.

The national character of the Catholic Monarchy was due mainly to the spontaneous way in which it arose out of the anarchy during the reconquest of the country from the Moors; and, to return to the period with which we are dealing, we find an analogous reason for the special character of the Visigothic Monarchy. In the anarchy caused by the decay of Roman Spain and increased by the havoc of the first Germanic invasions, the nation, as we have seen, found in the clergy the only element of order and authority. The Church assumed political functions. The nature of events made statesmen of the priests and turned their councils into national assemblies. When the Goths founded their monarchy in Spain, they found these institutions and authority already established. By converting themselves to Catholicism they recognized this authority; and, although they intended to use it for their own purposes, they became to a certain extent mere instruments of the authority of the Church. The Christianity of the inhabitants of the Peninsula might be pagan enough, but they accepted the hierarchy of the priesthood; and, since we are dealing here with institutions not with religious ideas, this is an important fact. The Visigothic Monarchy became theocratic to such an extent that the character of priest came to prevail in the person of its kings. Thus at this time, as later again in the sixteenth century, the genius of the nation was represented by the priesthood which consecrated the monarch and by a united religious and political government which embodied the mystical character of the people. Christianity, incoherent product of previous religious systems, was a formula which embraced various religious ideas belonging to peoples of deeply individual outlook dwelling in separate regions. In Italy Christianity was pagan; in Spain, however deep the roots of the religions of antiquity had penetrated, Christianity was what we may perhaps call African. It was the religion of Carthage in a Christian dress; it resembled the ardent mysticism and the harsh formalism of the religion of St. Augustine, combined with the imperial juridical spirit introduced into the Church of Rome and subsequently adopted by the Church in Spain. This peculiar character of the State religion of the Visigoths reappears in the Catholic Monarchy of the sixteenth century.

Although the monarch in Spain is an anointed priest, he is not an Oriental demi-god nor the Roman prince, after the fashion of the French Monarchy in modern times. Christianity in its beginnings had penetrated Europe on the one hand and on the other Egypt, Ethiopia, and Arabia, where it became a religion of mystic rites. By its schism in Europe the Greek religion preserved the pagan Alexandrine stamp, while the religion of Rome produced the Protestant idealism of the Germans, the rationalist Catholicism of Latin France and Italy, and finally the mystic Catholicism of Spain, the religious expression of the genius of the Peninsula and the political basis of the monarchy which represented it.

II. THE INSTITUTIONS OF THE VISIGOTHS

IT was not until the middle of the seventh century that the assimilation of Goths and Hispano-Romans was completed, to such an extent that all traces of invasion and conquest had vanished. Up to that time victors and vanquished were ruled by different laws: the former maintained with slight alterations their old military organization and observed their traditional customs, which wholly or in part had been written down since the time of Euricus (466–84); the latter preserved their ancient rights, and so far as possible observed Roman customs; their laws were those of Rome, the *lex Romana*, compiled in the year 506 in what was known as the Breviarium of Anianus or of Alaric. The history of legislation thus proves that during the first century of the Gothic domination, the conquerors were separated from the conquered, or rather that the aristocracy was separated from the people, since the conditions and guarantees under which the Hispano-Romans lived were rather those of a people governed by a military aristocracy than of a people subdued to the harsh laws of the conqueror. So much so, indeed, that the century and a half which separates the reigns of Euricus and Alaric (466–507) from those of Chindaswinth and Receswinth (642–72) sufficed to fuse them together, marriages being now common between the two races, so that it became necessary to promulgate a new code of laws common to both. This was the celebrated Visigothic Code of the year 649, concerning which a modern historian (Guizot) says:

> The Visigothic Code contains, not the laws of a victorious and barbarous people, but a body of general laws of the kingdom, common to victors and vanquished, Hispano-Romans and Goths. It is a system, promulgated on a fixed day and in a way becoming an established nation; whereas the laws of the Franks and Burgundians in part preceded their establishment in Roman territory. This shows that a special influence supervised the drawing up of this code, that of the clergy.

The clergy in fact, as we have said, constituted the link between Roman and Gothic Spain; and the conquerors, confronted by an organized national body, allowed themselves to be directed by it, respecting its strength, recognizing its superiority in education and above all using its power in their own interest. Although methodically drawn up, the Visigothic Code, reproduced, as could not fail to be the case, the ancient laws, but modified and subordinated to a general plan and to strictly juridical ideas; although it certainly differs from modern codes which, starting from the essential basis of natural right, are more or less subject to logic. The historical and political element predominates, and juristic historians divide the laws of the Forum Judicum into four kinds: those which emanate from the King, with or without the assistance of the *aula regia* or Council of State; those which at the suggestion of the monarch were voted at the national councils of Toledo, in which the clergy played the principal part; the laws without date or name of author, which seem to have belonged to the old Gothic collections; and finally the laws extracted from the Roman codes and adapted to the requirements of the time, *antiqua noviter emendata*.

But in spite of the necessary predominance of the historical and political element, as in all analogous systems of law, the Visigothic Code philosophically has a special character and importance which make it a document of great value. Educated under the Roman civilization, the Spanish clergy maintained the tradition of the former rulers of Spain; therefore the law is general, not personal; it is concerned not with the condition of persons or classes but with the territory; it is the rule and not a list of exceptions to the rule; it has a philosophical and not merely an historical character. The laws are 'public', not 'private', as in the rest of Europe, because preservation of the Latin tradition maintained the idea of an absolute authority, so that justice could be set above force. The king can only be king so long as he acts justly: 'Rex eris si recte facis, si autem non facis non eris'. But we must not exaggerate the historical value of such systems of law; between the written law and practical reality the difference is always great, and it was greater than ever when a wide gulf was fixed between the learned clergy who drew up the laws and the princes and barons who, more or less, applied them. Yet it is important for us to note the existence of these juridical traditions since, even when thus deformed, they exercised an influence on practical law. Thus we see that the penal legislation of the Visigoths presents an entirely different character from that of the codes of other Germanic peoples; the only thought of the latter in punishing crime is the injury inflicted by the criminal on his neighbour, whereas the Goths consider the intention: their law distinguishes in homicide between involuntary acts, carelessness, provocation, and the presence or absence of premeditation. Proof by examination of witnesses and rational inquiry into the facts exclude in principle the trial by combat, the *compurgatio*, and the different forms of the judgement of God. Punishment does not differ according to the rank of the offender (except in the distinction between freemen and slaves) but according to the degree of guilt. The law even favours the slaves to the extent that it subjects to fixed public and legal forms the right to punish them which it could not deny to their owners.

Several distinguished writers have denied the practical effectiveness of this system of laws and have pointed to real examples of the practice of the traditional juridical methods of the Germanic peoples in the heart of the neo-Gothic society formed by reaction against the Moors. Such arguments would only be valid if between that society and the Visigothic Monarchy which preceded it were not interposed the invasion of the Moors, a fact of immense importance in the history of Spain.

We have already said that the Visigothic Monarchy has the artificial and ephemeral character of an attempt to reconstruct society after the Roman plan, similar to to that of Charlemagne in France. This attempt to stay the decay of Roman Spain was unnatural and therefore doomed to failure. We agree, therefore, that the philosophical Visigothic code shares in the artificial character of the monarchy itself and represents rather a conservative ambition than the actual state of society. But it is also true that the whole spirit of the Visigothic Monarchy was conservative; it was only when the Moors invaded Spain and the decay of Roman Spain was completed that the traditions and instincts of the people gained the upper hand. It was therefore natural that traditions of Germanic origin, certainly observed previously by a part of the people, should only then come to light, such as trial by combat and other forms of the judgement of God and the systems of fines or Wergild.

We have already remarked that the Visigothic Monarchy would be of slight importance for the history of Iberian civilization if it had only this one aspect of an attempt to maintain Roman institutions in process of decay. And this would be the case if between the Romans and modern nations there were not a fact of far-reaching importance, the fact of Christianity, which through the clergy in the Councils became the political representative of the nation. The character of the Visigothic code eloquently reveals this essential fact; and this phenomenon of a general or philosophical system of legislation amid the particular or personal codes of the other Germanic peoples, although it may have its origin in ancient culture, is not based on the principles of natural law as expounded by the Roman jurists but on the dogmas of the new religion. The law, says the Forum Judicum, seeks to imitate God. For this reason and no other the law 'is the herald of justice and the sovereign lord of life; it supervises all ranks and ages; it imposes itself alike on men and women, on young and old, on the wise and ignorant, on citizens and peasants; and it does not defend any particular interest because it protects the common interest of all men'. (Forum Judicum).

This pre-eminence of religious authority undeniably gives the juridical constitution of Visigothic Spain a great superiority over the rest of Europe; it forms the basis of the unity of the nation and of the authority of the kings who are its leaders but are also subject to the Church which anoints them. This intimate relation between the religious and civil authority, between Church and State, is the cause of Spain's authority, but it is also the source of immediate facts which later, under similar circumstances, were repeated. Montesquieu remarked that the modern monks simply applied to the Jews the laws formerly enacted by the bishops; 'the modern Inquisition, he added, owes all its views and principles to the Visigothic Code'. And in fact the Catholics, who under the Aryan Gothic kings had enjoyed complete peace and freedom and were allowed to practise their religion in public and even to meet in their Councils, repaid this toleration with such a fury of persecution that St. Isidore himself condemned the violence of Sisebut (612–21) in forcing baptism on the Jews, eight or nine centuries before the Kings of Castille adopted the same methods. This religious fervour seemed to announce the future; indeed, it appears to be inseparable from the temperament of the Peninsula peoples and to form an essential element in the genius of the race.

The subordination of civil to religious authority sanctified the absolute power of the kings, and by a necessary reaction this absolute power became the protector of the Church. This gives us the key to the mutual relations of the monarchy and the councils in

Visigothic Spain. The ecclesiastical origin of authority also consecrated another fact which primarily must be traced to the traditions of the Goths and the requirements of a military society, and this fact is the election of the kings. The monarchy of the Visigoths, both before and after its definitive establishment in the Peninsula, that is to say during the fifth and nearly the whole of the sixth century, was elective. Since the conditions of a military existence were one of the causes of this system, it is not surprising to find it dying out in time of peace, although it was not denied in principle until the Gothic rule ended in the Battle of the Guadalete.

Some Spanish historians, inspired, we think, by modern Liberal ideas, have imagined the existence of great national assemblies at which the kings were elected by the people, seeking to derive from this fact an historical basis for the constitutional movement in contemporary Spain. The learned and interesting works of Martínez Marina are the best examples of this tendency. If we would form a clear opinion on this subject we must know what the Councils were. It was natural enough that before the conversion of Reccared (586–601), that is, during the period of conquest, there should be assemblies among the Goths similar to the Witenagemot of the Anglo-Saxons or the Placita generalia of the Franks, the Mallus of warrior barons presided over by the king, their elective chief. It is well known that the parliaments of aristocratic England trace their origin to those assemblies. But in Spain, in proportion as the Visigothic monarchy became nationalized after it had adopted the religion of the vanquished, these assemblies gradually disappeared before the Councils of Toledo. These Councils were in fact national assemblies because the clergy was at that time the best or only worthy representative of the Hispano-Roman peoples and because it was concerned with political and administrative matters. But it would be a complete mistake to give to the national assembly of that time a meaning similar to that which it possessed from the twelfth or thirteenth century: the more or less regular meeting of the representatives of three orders or classes constituting the nation. The Councils were an assembly of the clergy in the presence of the people, not an assembly of representatives of the nation to limit the power of the King. Therefore it is a mistake to see in those assemblies the origin of the modern parliamentary system; although we must admit that they exercised a certain influence on the authority of the king. In the meetings of warriors of the Germanic peoples the power of the barons limited the king's authority; in the councils the royal power, if it was not limited, was at least guided and enlightened by the superior culture of the clergy; hence the excellence of the laws and administration in Visigothic Spain.

From the reign of Reccared (586–601) to that of Witiza (701–10), the immediate predecessor of the unfortunate Roderick, sixteen national councils met, presided over by the Spanish metropolitan bishops of Toledo, Seville, Mérida, Braga, Tarragona, and Narbonne. The fact that it was the king who convoked the councils when he deemed it advisable proves that their function was merely to enlighten and sanction by their moral authority the acts of the king. The political strength of the clergy was due to the favour of the Crown, and the Crown through the support of the Church obtained an authority not based on force alone. These circumstances enabled the Visigothic Monarchy to attain an authority and independence unknown to the European monarchs of that day.

The councils might in the course of time have become real national assemblies if the invasion of the Moors had not put an end to the rule of the Goths. In the fifth council, convened by Swintila (621–31), the nobles appear by the side of the clergy in the assembly; and although this did not happen in all the subsequent councils, it became the rule from the beginning of the eighth century. The nobles, like the clergy, assembled at the invitation of the king, not as a right of their order. Nor was the presence of the people essential. All that one can say in this respect is that the sittings of the council were public; it is an error to imagine that the popular classes were represented or took part in the assembly: the people did not deliberate or even vote; it was not even always invited to the assembly. According to the canon law, the people attended, not in order to give their votes, but 'to defend the common faith, with arms if necessary'.

We have noticed the part played by the monarch in this kind of parliament, if we may so term the councils. Supported by the moral authority of the clergy, the kings, albeit they did not recognize the independent power of the barons, had their *aula regia*, by means of which they succeeded in grouping the chief nobles round the throne and in making use of their strength in its interest, by sharing or making a pretence of sharing a sovereignty which they refused to divide. The *officium palatinum* or *aula regia* owed its existence to Diocletian; and the Goths had inherited it from the Empire, preserving its character and its very name. The *aula regia* was composed of the chief officials of the Court, the high civil and military officials of State, and other members especially selected by the King. It thus united around the throne the bureaucratic aristocracy of the Romans and the military aristocracy of the Goths. Owing to the authority of its members it exercised an active and permanent influence on the decisions of the king, and might even supplant him, as when it deposed Wamba (672–80). But, among other causes, the inevitable lack of homogeneity in a body composed of Hispano-Romans and of Goths, and the free power of the monarch to appoint any one he chose a member, impaired its political power. And in fact this noble assembly became debased to the point of accepting from the king slaves among its members, as is evident from the fact that the twelfth council declared that only *fiscales* (we shall presently give the meaning of this word) could hold office in the palace, to the exclusion of all other slaves and freedmen. Placed between these two powers in the State, the palace officials and the councils, the natural policy of the monarchy was to play one off against the other and take advantage of the conflicts between them to strengthen its own authority. Here again it is the councils which give Spain her political originality after giving her a social superiority. It is they which moderate the influence of the nobles, who in France, after the fall of the Carlovingian dynasty, gradually usurped the royal power and finally seized absolute power. On the other hand the administration of the Visigoths in its main lines reproduces that of Rome; it is the same centralizing system and half-military régime of the ancient Empire. In the reign of Reccared we find the frontiers of Spain entrusted to the dukes, similar to the ancient *legati augustales*, governors in whom is vested both the civil and military authority. These *duces limitanei* were five in number: those of Cantabria, Carthagena, Mérida, Lusitania, and Narbonne. The civil administration of the cities was entrusted to counts (*comites civitatum*), under the higher authority of the dukes; the count appointed *vicarii* or judges and the *villici* or administrators of the villages (*pagi*); of the duties of these minor officials in the towns we shall have occasion to speak later.

Besides the councils and the *aula regia*, which in modern language we might call consultative bodies, a permanent council was attached to the monarch. Copied from the ancient Roman Empire, it was composed of officials of the king's household, of what we may rightly call ministers of State and of those who combined both these characters; and this continued down to our time, until revolutions separated the royal from the national treasury. Thus the *comes thesaurorum* was at once tax-collector and minister of finance; the *comes patrimoniorum* was a kind of minister of the empire; the *comes notariorum* resembled a modern attorney general; the *comes spathiorum* was commander-in-chief of the king's guards (different from the Army, which was then recruited from the nobility and the towns); the *comes scanciarum* was the high steward; the *comes cubiculi* was the lord high chamberlain; the *comes stabuli* was the master of the horse; and finally the *comes exercitus* was the minister of war.

Although the administration of the Visigoths is not as interesting as the constitution of the councils, the changes which the invasion of the Germans introduced into the situation of persons and classes render it of even greater importance for the understanding of the subsequent history of Spain. The people was divided into two great classes, that of the free (*ingenui*) and non-free (*servi*); and it was on the condition of the ancient slaves that the Gothic invasion had the deepest influence. The free were in turn divided into two classes, the noble and the non-noble. Beginning with the former, we have already noted that the conditions of the new conquest maintained side by side the old bureaucratic and military aristocracy of the Romans and the aristocracy of the Goths. The former, diminished by the fact that the Goths seized for themselves two thirds of the land, daily lost ground, and dismissed officials and proprietors deprived of their land sank to an inferior status without losing their liberty.

After the conversion, however, of Reccared and the promulgation of the Visigothic Code in 649, in a more united society a new kind of nobility was provided for the Hispano-Romans, who constituted the main source from which the clergy sprang. The Church was the new opportunity for the middle class to acquire a nobility which ranked with the military nobility of the Goths. This aristocracy of the Church resembled the aristocracy of ancient Rome, which was not based on birth but on the individual and the individual's high office. In spite of the different origin and the earlier traditions of the Church, the ecclesiastical nobility did not claim to be exclusive, it recognized the existence of the military nobility of the Goths and merely sought to exercise a moral influence over it.

The Gothic nobility differed from the national, bureaucratic, and ecclesiastical nobility not so much in the military character of its members, for the Roman nobles also included soldiers, as in the tenure and transmission of land, a system radically different from the Roman. There was further the great inequality in land ownership, since the Goths in taking possession of Spain had appropriated two thirds of the land by right of conquest. The military holders of land then distributed, from the king to the private *buccellarius*, provided the basis of the rights of suzerainty and vassalage in the links of a long chain. The right to transmit the land thus held, although not very sure and more or less dependent on its confirmation for the life of each successive holder, was necessarily the basis of this system. The Roman aristocracy was political, the Visigothic aristocracy was territorial; the former was held for life, the latter was hereditary in principle, whatever local or accidental exceptions might occur. The former was renewed continually from the people, the latter was bound up with the land and in course of time became a real caste. And since institutions are based on property, we may say that Roman society was essentially democratic whereas Gothic society was essentially aristocratic. If we wish to examine the matter further, passing from the essential character of these institutions to their external manifestations, we find forming part of the Gothic nobility, besides the *aula regia*, which we have already studied, and whose members were officially entitled *optimates* or *primates palatii*, the higher local authorities or *majores luci*, consisting of the dukes, counts, and gardings (a name as to which the learned have been unable to agree), and, as the lowest class, the *liti* of the king.

Large as Spain was and limited as was the number of the invaders, not all the Gothic inhabitants of Spain were fortunate enough to obtain a piece of land in the division of the confiscated territory. Thus beside the Hispano-Roman middle class there was a limited number of free but non-noble Goths, called *buccellarii*. They offered the rich and powerful baron their services in return for his protection and were to the nobles what the *liti* were to the king; they hovered on the border of nobility, and probably had no means of subsistence, being accustomed to a military life and incapable of agricultural work after the manner of the Hispano-Romans. It was these last who formed the great mass of the free population. The name of *possessores* included not only the free proprietors but the *privati*, a word which we explained in studying the Roman *municipium*. The free non-noble proprietor differed from the aristocracy in being subject to both military taxation and a territorial tax, the *jugatio*, inherited from ancient Rome; it was called a poll-tax, but was reckoned not by heads but by acreage. The land held under this system formed the *tertiae Romanorum*; it was the only land subject to taxation; and its owners, as well as all the non-proprietors, artisans, and workers, free or slaves, that is the whole mass of the non-noble population, were subject to a personal tax, the *humana capitatio*; *census* being the name which covered the two forms of taxation, personal and territorial.

Having observed the influence of the conquest on the Hispano-Roman middle class, we must see how its chief institution was affected. It is generally agreed that the Gothic invasion, instead of continuing the deleterious action of the imperial administration, restored the *municipia*. Whatever were the attributes of the Gothic count who replaced the Roman *rector*; whatever changes were introduced internally in the *municipium* (and as to this there is no agreement) it is a fact that the *curia*, the basis of the *municipium*, reacquired much of its former importance. A fact previously pointed out as one of the causes of the decay of the *curia* was no longer possible, owing to the conditions entailed by the conquest. We have seen how under Rome the ambition of the member of the *curia* was to serve all the municipal offices in order to attain the rank of *honoratus* and become member of an aristocracy which conferred every kind of privilege and exemption. The *curialis* now could no longer emerge from his own class; the doors of the aristocracy were no longer open; it was no longer a class but a caste, and unless one were born in it there was only one way to enter it, that of the Church.

Between the various kinds of freemen that we have mentioned and the various types of slavery which we shall study presently, we find the *coloni*, a class which belongs to neither of those two classes but forms as it were a transition and may be considered to be a kind of freemen among the slaves or a kind of slaves among the freemen. In the time of the Empire the *colonus* was a half-emancipated slave; but in the crisis of the invasions many freemen were reduced to become *coloni*. This class certainly now attained a new importance; and the name *plebei*, which with that of *privati* under Rome designated the mass of the people, is now applied to the *coloni*. The *colonus* is the man who cultivates another man's land, his person is free, but he is bound to the soil which he cultivates; his status is determined by the nature of the overlord's rights over the land possessed by the *litus*, not over his person. The *coloni* seem to be connected with the system of grants and protection in the Gothic ownership of land, but they already existed under the Roman administration; and accordingly we see the system applied not only to the Gothic *sortes*, exempt from taxation but to the taxed *tertiae*, that is to the land left to the Hispano-Romans. Whether it be considered as a form of mitigated slavery or as a form of rudimentary and incomplete ownership, the fact is that under feudalism the state of *colonus* was dying out in Europe whereas it was developing in the Peninsula and there became the principal means of the abolition of slavery. Thus arose a new cause of the superiority of Spain over the other nations of Europe in the Middle Ages; to such a degree that later, in the age of the Renaissance, she was able to play the principal part on the political stage, because her internal development was completed and she was thus in a position to dominate the world.

It remains for us to describe the position of the servile classes. Whatever may have been the influence of the doctrine of the ancient philosophers that slavery was unnatural, it is certainly true that the actual state of the slaves had ceased to be insupportable. Yet it is certain that in principle the Roman slave was a chattel, whereas the Gothic slave, although inferior to the *plebei* or *liti* and without any legal rights, was nevertheless a man, as it were a minor, and slavery once more received a domestic character. This was the character of slavery also among the Greeks and Romans in proportion as their development coincided with that of the Germanic civilization when it spread over the west of Europe. First wars and then industry, as new sources of slavery, had obliterated its primitive domestic character. Among the Goths it is the trade or profession which primarily characterizes slavery, a sure proof of its domestic nature. The laws always designate the slaves by the name of *ministeriales*, whence was derived the Portuguese medieval word for artisans. The good slave, the *idoneus*, is the mechanic or artisan; the rural workers are *viliores*, rustics, with a special name, that of *mancipii*. They are the lowest of the low.

In time of peace different roads led to slavery. Apart from that of birth there were various ways of falling from the status of freeman, such as insolvency, or even a fiction of sale of oneself in order to obtain a sum of money. The slaves, like the free, had their aristocracy. One of the types of this aristocracy is the freedman, the *manumissus*; but its chief representatives are the fiscal slaves whose actual situation was in fact often superior to that of the *coloni* and even to that of the *buccellarii*. These fiscal slaves were the tax-collectors and treasurers of the prince. We have already noticed their presence in the *aula regia*, and when we mention that they were permitted to own slaves of the class of *mancipii*, the existence of a slave aristocracy is sufficiently evident. We believe that we have considered the whole series of historical problems and phenomena that arose out of the constitution of the Visigothic monarchy. We hope that we have distinguished, in so far as possible in a work of this kind, between what belonged to the decay of Roman Spain in these revolutions and new institutions and what belonged to new elements for the constitution of modern Spain. These two currents continue side by side throughout the Gothic domination. The former was fatal and inevitable, the latter could only in course of time assert itself freely and independently in the direction of real progress.

The Visigothic monarchy, as being in part the artificial reproduction of the imperial monarchy of Rome, fell to pieces, a victim of internal corruption, of a corroding poison which acted with even more force on the rude and vigorous barbarians. The Gothic kings, as we have said, were the Carolingians of Spain and were obliged to yield to new invaders the sceptre that fell from their nerveless fingers. The decay of the ancient empire was thus complete. Although there was improvement in the condition of some classes, the essential ills of the Roman dominion, the concentration of land in a few hands, slavery, the general servitude, the system of ownership, the rapacity of the Treasury, continued, sometimes in an aggravated form. The miserable people may have hoped for redemption from the Church; the slaves, relying on the Gospel's doctrine of love, may have expected to become free; but the clergy, when it obtained political power, changed its mind and passed over to the enemy. St. Isidore of Seville, who for so long presided over the Councils of Toledo and was 'the glory of the Catholic Church', adhered to the ancient naturalistic theories of Aristotle and Cicero concerning slavery; and the position of the slaves, if in a sense it improved, became more burdensome, since to its former obligations were added the personal services introduced by the Visigothic lords and princes after the conquest.

The bishops who governed the kings, the priests who were their confessors, guiding the childlike yet corrupt barbarians by the fear of Hell, and who governed the nation in the councils, did nothing to improve that nation's lot. They merely introduced a new theory of government, the theocracy. Surrounded by his nobles, the king humbly knelt at the feet of the priests in the council, imploring them with groans and tears to intercede for him with God that he might be inspired to make wise laws. Faith being the supreme civic virtue, fierce intolerance became the chief duty of the government; and to all the evils of society under the Roman

Empire, which was at least sceptical, was added the evil of persecution of the Jews, formally declared in the year 616 in the reign of King Sisebut, when it was decreed that the Jews must be converted by force. The repression of the revolt of the year 694, the object of which, acting in common with the Jews of Morocco, was to set up a Mosaic State in Spain, brought to the fierceness of religious intolerance the added fierceness of political revenge. This is the reverse side of the greatness described above. Thus did all the social elements conspire for the fall of the tottering Visigothic monarchy. The Jews were ready to revolt; the slaves, apathetic in their deep misery, were indifferent towards the nation; the landed owners were the irreconcilable enemies of a system which had proved powerless to save them. And it was the slaves who formed the greater part of the infantry of King Rodrigo. That was why Tarik's twelve thousand men sufficed to conquer Spain. The new barbarian conquerors came not from the north: they were a handful of Arabs at the head of a Berber army. This new influx of African blood in the Peninsula caused Spain's history to differ from that which the second invasions brought about in central Europe.

III. THE MOORISH CONQUEST

A new conflict, like that of the Romans and Carthaginians, now become a matter of ancient history, came to put the finishing touch on the character of Spain, whose civilization seems to be a combination of the genius of two races, producing a type distinct from either. The men at the head of Spain were no longer Romans but Goths; and Carthage had sunk from among the empires, so that the generals who now led the troops of Africa across the Straits belonged to Islam. Between the two conflicts, which as far as the ethnology of Spain is concerned form one and the same movement, had occurred the historical events which we have noticed and which gave to Spain a different character from the Spain of old. At the time of the Roman invasion the Spanish, as we saw, adopted the cause of Carthage, and the Carthaginians found in the Peninsula a kindred people; but now the Spanish had become so romanized that they did not recognize in the new invaders their former comrades and perhaps their kinsmen. Such is the influence of a higher civilization on the characterless mass of half barbarous peoples that it can obliterate even the ties of kinship.

When we speak of the romanization of the Peninsula, we include in the word the important fact of the spread of a more or less pagan Christianity through the nation between the two African invasions. Similar events had occurred on the other side of the Straits. Northern Africa, subdued by the Romans, had passed into the hands of the Vandals and finally into those of the Arabs. Christianity had gained ground there, and Carthage itself was the birthplace of one of its organizers, St. Augustine; but with the Mussulman conquest the Byzantine domination, and with it the Christian religion, disappeared. It is, however, now clearly proved that neither in the thought of the Prophet nor in the system of the new religion nor in the policy of the Khalifs was there any idea or determination to wage war in order to convert the world. On the contrary conversions were a mere consequence of conquest, and often there were laments that the conquered peoples should embrace the religion of the Koran so speedily. A holy war, said Mahomet, is our duty only when the enemies of Islam attack us. It was not the worship of Allah but the empire of the Khalifs that was extended by the force of arms. The Khalifs, far from seeking proselytes, regretted the conversions, because these meant exemption from taxation and so diminished their revenues. Moreover, owing to a certain lack of originality in the religion of Islam, the conquered peoples found more or less well defined in it the dogmas of their former religion. Much the same had happened to Christianity when the romanized nations of the West introduced their pagan traditions into it. The Jews, of whose books Mahomet had made direct use, refused to accept his religion as they had refused to accept that of Christ; but it was otherwise with the Kopts of Egypt and Syria, who saw many of their own dogmas in the Koran and were not offended by the Christology of the sacred book of Mahomet. He had decreed that all who adopted the sacred book, Jews or Christians, should have liberty of worship on the payment of a tax. This permission was subsequently extended to the Persians who adopted the Bible of Zoroaster after the conquest of the province of Baharim; and later Othman (644–54) gave the same privilege to the inhabitants of the North of Africa. Thus it is clear that toleration for foreign religions increased as the conquests widened.

The glowing imagination of the Arab in the East, which is a hotbed of religious fantasies, precluded fanaticism; it was the African genius in Morocco and afterwards in Spain that gave to Islamism the character of an intolerant orthodox religion. When at Medina the descendants of the founders of Islamism were expelled from the Khalifate by the Omayyads (661–750), they took refuge in Africa, whence in their flight they passed into Spain to preach the pure truth which had been vanquished in Arabia by a pagan dynasty. The new Khalifs at Damascus represented indeed the victory of a reaction of the native polytheism of the Arab tribe and were truly impious. Walid II (743–4) ordered his concubines to represent him at public prayer and used to shoot arrows at a copy of the Koran. He lamented the conversions which impaired his revenue: Egypt brought in but half of its former taxes because the Christian Kopts had accepted the religion of Islam.

It was the same with the Berbers, whose primitive religion, if their rudimentary rites deserve this name, had disappeared before the religion of Islam. Critical investigation of our time has shown that, whatever be the moral value of a religion, the people that accepts it only takes that part of it which agrees with its genius and with its stage of development and civilization. Islamism was for the tribes of Africa in the seventh century what it is to-day for the tribes of Nigritia and will continue to be for those of central Africa. Of this religion, which unites great refinements of intelligence with a singular moral darkness and a materialism without charity, the Berber or Tuareg, the Negroid or Negro, only understand and therefore only receive the second half, which agrees with their character. At present in the region beyond the Sahara, at the sources of the Nile and in the land of the lakes, Islamism is not spread in the same way as it was by the Arabs in the seventh century among the Berbers. The tribes of North Africa have become independent, and Mecca has become a holy city like Rome, with a Khalif who is Pope but no longer Emperor. In the seventh century the religious aspect was almost always an involuntary result of conquest; and if the Berbers modelled the rites of their marabouts on the Koran, they did not submit with equal readiness to the Moorish generals. These nomad tribes, naturally independent and rebellious, fought for liberty with the fanaticism inherent in their race; and the advance made by the religion of the Koran was rather a cause of resistance than otherwise, as was proved by subsequent rebellions, of a political as well as a sectarian character. One war, in which rivers of Arab blood were shed, lasted seventy years. The Berber was infinitely superior to the degenerate inhabitants of the coast, and he gave more trouble than the corrupt empires of Persia or Byzantium.

The subjection of North Africa was the prelude to

the conquest of Spain; and in this second enterprise the Arabs found, not in the tribes of the interior but in the Byzantine colonies along the coast a repetition of what they had experienced in Africa. More or less orthodox, the Christians of Africa considered obedience to the Papacy of Constantinople an intolerable yoke; for them the victory of the Moors meant religious freedom. Later, when the heavy Byzantine taxation had been replaced by the lighter poll-tax of the Arabs, they desired exemption even from this; which was only possible by adopting the religion of the conquerors. They therefore gradually became converts to Islamism, as did many of the Christians of Spain, who exchanged a position similar to that of the Jews among Catholic nations for one of civil and religious equality.

In the last years of the seventh century Carthage, the key of Mauretania, fell into the hands of the Arabs, and with it the whole of northern Africa. But although the Greeks were expelled and the Christians conquered, the new domination was evidently not secure, since a little before the conquest of Spain there was a general insurrection of natives. Legend says that the Berbers, considering that the wealth of the cities was the incentive for foreign invasion, razed Tangier and Tripoli to the ground, cut down the trees, destroyed the small towns, and reduced a region which the Romans described as rich and luxuriant to the parched and treeless desert which is only beginning to revive under European protection. This legend, like all legends, is an echo of historic truth: the alleged voluntary act of the Berbers represents the devastation of three or four centuries of war and plunder. The insurrection, however, was a fact and not a legend. Musa, who had been appointed Emir of Africa by the Khalif of Damascus, suppressed the rising and permanently consolidated the Saracen domination in Africa.

Various causes were at work to impel the Arabs to

cross the Straits. First of all there was the allurement of a rich and delightful country so near their own; then there was the love of conquest bred in the victorious followers of Mahomet, and the inevitable expansion of civilizations until they are exhausted or meet with an insuperable obstacle. Death alone stayed the advance of Alexander; only the resistance of all Europe in arms put an end to the Napoleonic wars; only the wall of the Pyrenees checked the triumphal progress of Tarik. To these causes must be added the internal dissensions of Visigothic Spain, where political parties forgot patriotism and religion in their mutual hatred, after the fashion of their Berber neighbours.

Witiza had been dethroned and assassinated at Toledo in 709 by the usurper Roderick. The deposed king left two sons, and their followers did not hesitate to beg help from the Arabs or even to enlist in the Arab armies, hoping thus to recover the throne at the cost of a more or less serious raid. Besides this political incident there were the causes of a social nature which we have already described as eating away the vigour of the Visigothic State; prominent among these causes was the rebellious attitude of the Jews, who were numerous, rich, and influential, and were cruelly persecuted by the government and by the mob; and who hoped that their lot would be improved under the rule of a kindred race and under a religion which was tolerant in principle.

The history of the invasion of 711, which was preceded by a fruitless attempt in the previous year, is bound up with the tradition concerning a certain Count Julian, at that time Governor of Septum (Ceuta), who is said to have opened the gates of that city to the Moors and thus afforded them an easy passage across the Straits. Ceuta would thus be a Byzantine stronghold, and Julian, its governor, would be a Greek or Greek official and not a Gothic count. Ceuta, isolated from the East, is supposed to have maintained close relations

with the Court at Toledo, and Julian is said to have
sent his daughter to be brought up at the Court, where
King Roderick fell in love with her and won her by
force. Revenge for this was the cause of the invasion,
for the count invited Musa to pass into Spain. Musa
consulted the Khalif, who prudently advised him to
make sure of his ground. It is supposed that even after
the conversion of Reccared and the consequent accep-
tance of Gothic rule by Catholic Spain, certain portions
of the Southern and Western coasts remained subject
to Byzantium, which incited the natives to cast off
the yoke of the Goths. Under the rule of Theudis
(533–48) there is an account of landings on the coasts
of Africa, to attack Ceuta and to assist the Vandals.
Meanwhile Carthage fell into the hands of Justinian.
On the death of the Gothic king, his succession was
disputed, and one of the pretenders to the throne
secured the assistance of the Eastern Empire through
a treaty by which several cities of the coast were ceded
to the Roman-Byzantines, in whose power they remained until in the first quarter of the seventh century
Swintilla (621–31) definitely expelled them from Spain,
although not from their last strongholds in Africa,
where Septum and Tingis certainly remained Byzantine
until the year 711. The certain fact is that in the first
half of the year 710 Musa, Emir of the Maghreb, sent
his lieutenant Tarif to Spain with a few hundred men,
who returned to Africa after sacking Algeciras. In the
following year he sent another general, Tarik, with a
larger force which disembarked at Gibraltar (Jebel
Tarik) and captured Carteya. This force consisted of
seven thousand Berbers, with whom went Count Julian;
they were subsequently reinforced by another five thousand. These twelve thousand invaders met the army
of King Roderick in the battle of the Chryssus or
Guadalete, which seems really to have been fought
near the river Salado (Wadi-Becca) not far from the

Laguna de la Janda. The Gothic King was killed in the battle; the sons and brothers of Witiza joined the invaders in the hope that they would be given the throne; the battle was a memorable one, since it ended the Visigothic monarchy. This confirms what we said as to its artificial and ephemeral character. A single defeat does not destroy a nation when its government really represents it. This battle was followed by the conquest of the whole of Spain, if conquest be the right word for the triumphal progress of Tarik and Musa through the country virtually without meeting any resistance. The Visigothic monarchy was but an incident in the history of the decay of Roman Spain now completed by the Moors; whether it ended in the battle of the Guadalete or any other, in that or a different manner, its fall was fatally determined by the conditions of society in the Peninsula.

After winning the battle, Tarik gained another victory at Ecija and advanced on Toledo, detaching forces to occupy Córdoba, Archidona, and Elvira. While the capital, betrayed by the Jews, surrendered at discretion, Musa (in 712) disembarked in Spain with eighteen thousand Arabs and advanced to meet the victorious general whose good fortune he envied, and on his march to Toledo occupied the towns of Niebla, Carmona, Seville, Medina Sidonia, Osuna, Beja, and Mérida. At Toledo disputes occurred between the two generals as to the spoils of victory, thus preluding the future anarchy of Moorish Spain, while the last remnants of the Gothic army, which had taken refuge at Auriola, were defeated at Lorca. Tarik, deposed and imprisoned by Musa, was restored to his honours by order of the Khalif and co-operated with the Emir in subduing Spain, marching east with his Berbers while Musa with his Arabs advanced towards the north. With the capture of Zaragoza and the subjection of Galicia, the occupation was completed and the first act of the tragedy ended. It was quite a regular act in a tragedy, with the action and character of the persons clearly marked from the first; the mutual hatred and rivalry of Musa and Tarik represented the dissensions between Arabs and Berbers, the future mainspring of all the political convulsions of the new empire. There were religious dissensions in the Church founded by Mahomet, and the fanatical, orthodox temperament of the Africans was in conflict with the sceptical, poetic, imaginative temperament of the Arabs, a conflict which foreshadowed the revolutions in Moorish Spain. Tarik was of Jewish origin and belonged to the tribe of Simeon; as a Kharijite sectarian he emigrated to Africa, where he became king or chieftain of two Berber tribes. At the end of this first act the two conquerors, summoned to set forth the reasons of their dissensions before the Khalif, entrusted the government of Spain to a general whose first act was to marry King Roderick's widow. The second act of the tragedy opened according to the rules by showing the means and accessories which accompany the development of the action. The marriage of the king's widow is an epilogue which confirms our view of the state of decay of the Visigothic monarchy; and the Arabs who destroyed it certainly displayed great astuteness in dominating the rebels and making the most of their victory. They showed themselves implacable when they were resisted by force, but extended a kindly protection to all those who recognized their authority. The conquest was certainly no calamity. It was only in the south, where they met with resistance, that property was confiscated, and even there Santarem, Coimbra, and a third district were excepted. In the northern half of the Peninsula, which, practically without exception, submitted peacefully, the natives lost their movable chattels but retained their land, with the new privilege of being able to alienate it. Even in the confiscated lands of the south the slaves retained their former status; only four-fifths of this land was distributed among the soldiers, since one-fifth went to the State. On the land belonging to the soldiers the slaves gave four-fifths of the crops to their masters; on the land belonging to the State they gave only a third. All the landed proprietors were subjected to the kharaj tax of about twenty per cent.; but the Christians had to pay an additional tax, varying from 48 dirhems for the rich to 24 for the less prosperous and 12 for the peasants.[1] From this tax only conversion to Islam could free them; but women, cripples, beggars, and slaves were exempt.

Under such conditions the sceptical Arab, anxious not to deplete the Treasury, was naturally tolerant. There were, indeed, no revolts among the conquered nation, for the invasion was to some extent a blessing for the poorest inhabitants, and it protected the development of the middle class, while Islamism was more favourable to the slaves than had been the Christianity of Toledo and gave the slaves of Christians the right to become free if they ran away and became converts to Islam. Moreover, the Arabs allowed the conquered to retain their customs and laws, with their counts and national judges, and the free exercise and public profession of the Christian religion. By this means they paved the way for a hybrid population known as the Mozarabs, one of the principal phenomena of this period of Spain's history; we shall deal with them presently.

Capable as they had proved themselves to subdue and dominate Spain by that mixture of violence and astuteness which characterizes the Oriental, the invaders suffered severely from internal dissensions before more than ten years had passed since their victory. The walis or governors of provinces, corresponding to the former dukes, and the kaids, corresponding to the

[1] Roughly £12, £6, and £3.

counts, increased the disorder by opposing the central authority; and the Moorish sheiks, chieftains of Berber tribes who looked on the invasion of Spain as only a longer raid than usual, continued their nomad turbulent existence, at war among themselves and in permanent insurrection against the Arab generals. The rivalry and hatred between Arab and Berber were great. The Berbers considered themselves, not without reason, the real conquerors of Spain; Musa and the Arabs had arrived when all was over; yet they had taken the best part of the spoils, the most important posts, and the most fertile land. They divided fair Andalusia among themselves and dismissed the Berber followers of Tarik to the wastes of La Mancha and Extremadura, the wild mountains of León, Asturias, and Galicia, entrusting them with the thankless task of defending the frontier against the Christians. Such were the causes of the successive insurrections which the Arabs were only able to suppress by calling in the Syrians who had imposed their yoke on the Yemenites.

But at this time—that is, in the second half of the eighth century—two circumstances prevented the rapid decay of the Moorish domination. The Omayyad dynasty had been expelled from the Khalifate by the Abbasids in 730; and Abd-ur-Rahman I, in protest against this usurpation, founded a separate Khalifate in Spain, welding together the Moorish power in Spain and momentarily subduing the different races which had followed the standard of the prophet into the Peninsula, the Arabs of Yemen, the Modars, the Egyptians, Syrians, and Berbers. This unification effected by the Omayyads in Spain was based on orthodoxy, which was keener in the West than in the East. Nearly a century of rule, from the year 661 to 750, had consecrated the authority of the Omayyad dynasty at Damascus, and its former impiety had disappeared. Omar II (717–20) did not bewail the loss of his Egyptian revenue, but told those who lamented it that he was an apostle, not a tax-collector. For the true believers the Abbasid usurpation, carried through by one of those bloodstained tragedies common in the East, was an impiety. The Persians had defeated the Arabs; the heretics of Khorasan were now countenanced by a sacrilegious dynasty; it was a victory of the Shiites, of the Zoroastrians, even of the atheists. The Omayyads who survived the massacres took refuge in Spain or waited for a reaction to begin in Spain against these abominable impieties. Thus Córdoba became a second Damascus; and if the new Khalifate was unable to restore the old Damascus, it did maintain its independence and unite in one orthodox nation the various races of Islam in the Peninsula.

At the very time when the dynasty of the Omayyads in Spain was inaugurating the rule of the celebrated Khalifs of Córdoba, another fact compelled the Moors to unite their forces against new dangers; and this was the attacks of the exiles of Asturias, who, after fighting obscurely under the command of Pelayo (718–37 or 731–50), that Romulus of modern Spain, had become strong enough to begin the enterprise of methodical reconquest and of the restoration of the ancient Christian monarchy. There were also the attacks, more dangerous at the time although less important for subsequent history, of the Aquitanian Franks who crossed the Pyrenees and came to repay in kind the war which the Arabs had fruitlessly waged to the north of those mountains.

Despite the need of mutual assistance, the duel between Berbers and Arabs continued unabated; so great was their hatred of one another that it even made them forget their hatred against the Christians. Toledo, Zaragoza, and many cities of central Spain remained faithful to Berber rule and refused allegiance to the Emirs of Córdoba; and it was only in the first quarter of the tenth century, when the Omayyad dynasty reached its highest point of power and glory and (in 929) became an independent Khalifate, that it was able to reduce the indomitable Africans to obedience. This unification of Moorish Spain, the culminating moment of the Moorish empire, did not last beyond the end of the tenth century.

Mansur, the legendary and implacable enemy of the Christians, based on the African armies the absolute power which he enjoyed under a weakling Khalif. The Omayyad dynasty of Córdoba was dying out in the insignificant person of Hikkem II (916–1016), and the ephemeral empire of Mansur is, in itself and in the elements on which it rests, a proof of the utter decay of the unity of Arabic Spain. The Omayyads had brought to Spain from the East, together with orthodoxy, a spirit of toleration and culture which the African Islamite could not approve. His fanaticism protested against moderation and against philosophy; and the Arabs found themselves between two aggressive forms of fanaticism, that of Berber Islamism and that of Spanish Christianity. Perhaps, indeed, they were two simultaneous aspects of a common genius, a common race origin. Exploiting for his own interest the fanaticism of the Moorish priests and of the crowd of native African renegades, Mansur bade the theologians draw up an Index and consigned to the flames the scientific and philosophical books of the library formed by his predecessor, the learned Hakan II (961–76). Mansur, 'the faithful', copied the Koran with his own hand and led his armies of Africans like a prophet, blessed by the priests and acclaimed by the soldiers. It was a holy war. The old scepticism and the old toleration had vanished. What always happens happened again in Spain: a government which began by being gentle and humane degenerated into an intolerable tyranny. From the ninth century Islamism, aware of its strength, carried out to the letter the precept of the Khalif Omar: 'We must destroy the Christians and our descendants destroy their descendants until not a Christian remains.' And even from the first religion might be free, but the Church was not. The regalist rights of the Visigothic monarchy, the right to convoke the Councils, to appoint bishops, and so forth had passed into the hands of Arab Sultans who sold the bishoprics to their freedmen and gave a seat in the Councils to heretics and Jews. The Arabian scepticism of the first period of their rule had placed in the hands of the State weapons which could become means of sectarian persecution when a new spirit of religious intolerance was inspired by the zeal of the Africans.

The history of the interminable duel between the two Islamite races recommenced now with the massacre of African soldiers cut down at the gates of Córdoba in 1013, at the time of the victorious reaction of the Arab party against the soldiers of Mansur. From that moment events marched rapidly towards decay. Córdoba witnessed orgies of blood and pleasure, common in the empires of the peoples of the East, who are incapable of basing political authority on anything but force. Supreme authority passes from hand to hand, at the mercy of revolutions and civil wars, intrigues and murders, and in these ups and downs gradually loses its only support, that of force. The break up of Moorish Spain, which the mutual hatred of the various invading races had nearly brought about in the first years of the conquest, but which the foundation of the Omayyad dynasty had temporarily arrested, became natural and inevitable. The wali in his province, the kaid in his city, the sheik at the head of his tribe, declared themselves independent and made war on one another. Spain then became a bundle of nations, or rather of armies in the field, with fluctuating frontiers according as the fortune of war favoured one or other of the military chiefs. At the beginning of the eleventh century there were five principal emirates. That of Málaga, with Algeciras and, on the other side of the Straits, Ceuta and Tangier, was the property of the family of Ali, the Edrisite, to which revolutions had also given the throne of the Omayyads at Córdoba, where now at last reigned a member of the Berber race. Allies or vassals of the Emir of Málaga were the walis of Granada, Carmona, and Ecija. Seville was the seat of the second of the principal emirates; Valencia that of the third, which under the rule of the family of Amer extended its suzerainty to the Balearic Isles on one side, to Almería on the other, and in the north as far as Zaragoza and Barcelona. Badajoz and Lusitania, under the Beni-Alaftas, formed the fourth emirate, and Toledo the fifth; Algarb maintained a more or less precarious independence. This division of Spain omits the north and the east, for the Navarese and Aragonese on one side, the Asturians and Leonese on the other, men bold, warlike, and independent, had already reconquered their native country. We will describe these events later; for the present we will only say that, apart from religion, the difference between the social state of the two Spains was small. It is true that in Christian Spain there was the half-unconscious thought of future reconstruction and of its destiny finally to triumph over the enemy; but the divisions, internal strife, and general anarchy were the same as among the Moors; although among the latter this was a sign of senile decay, and among the Christians represented the vigour of youth. Among the Moors, party hatred came before patriotism; among the Christians, patriotism was so vague that history tells of alliances between Moors and Christians and of battles in which both Moors and Christians fought on either side. The celebrated Cid is a type not of romantic chivalry, loyal to God and to his lady, but of the bold adventurer who, disregarding law and loyalty, hired

himself out to the highest bidder. Half his life he spent
in the service of the Saracens as a soldier of fortune;
but, as he spent the other half in fighting against them,
Abn Bassam, the Arabic chronicler, calls him 'a Galician
dog without honour or loyalty or good faith'. The
Beni-Hud of Valencia, who had raised him to promi-
nence, paid him to defend them against the Christians;
but the cruel faithless knight turned against them and
conquered their city in 1104;[1] he burnt his prisoners
over a slow fire or threw them to his hounds; he tortured
and killed them to make them reveal hidden treasure.
But, important as is this unpatriotic indifference in
judging the spirit of those times, it could not in the
nature of things influence the final outcome of the conflict. Among the Christian chieftains and kings there was
a more or less conscious idea of a common religion, and
there was something of the same kind among the Moors
as they saw their empire fall into ruins and their frontiers
continually shrinking. The religious spirit of the people,
fostered by the clergy, unanimously condemned the
political anarchy and the impiety which pervaded the
aristocratic capitals of the various Moorish States. Sects
and heresies, schools and systems, swarmed after the
manner of the East in the small Courts which had
inherited the dominions of the Khalifate of Córdoba,
when the artificial strength momentarily given to it by
Mansur had departed. The believers foretold and invoked the wrath of heaven, and the princes, defeated
by the Christians, sought assistance from outside. On
the frontiers of Nigritia, in the Sahara, dwelt a Berber
tribe whose king, Yahya, saw visions. A foreign saint,
Abdullah, converted him to his version of Islamism,
and they joined to found a convent or fortress (*rabita*),
a hermitage in which to retire to pray. Thus arose the
sect of the Morabitun (that is, inhabitants of the

[1] The reader will not set much store on this account of the Cid when
he remembers that he died in 1099. (Trans.'s note.)

rabita), whom the Spanish Christians designated as Almoravides.

As in Arabia, once the Church was founded, conquest followed. The new apostle was both king and prophet, like Mahomet; and like Mahomet he was victorious. He conquered the whole of the Atlas country of Morocco and laid the basis of his future empire. Berber fanaticism welcomed this new creed, baptism into which was accompanied by a hundred strokes of the lash. When Abdullah died he was succeeded by Zainab, a saint or witch, and her widower, Yusuf-ibn-Tashfin, extended the empire from Senegal to Algeria. Córdoba had become a second Mecca of Islamism; Morocco was the third; and if in Spain Arabian toleration and Berber fanaticism were at strife, in Morocco the purity of the faith reigned in a sacred unchecked intolerance.

It was to Yusuf and the Almoravides that the princes of Spain turned for help. The emperor came and vanquished the Castilians at Zallaca near Badajoz in 1086. He then retired, but four years later he was again invited by the princes, the clergy, and the people. He now returned, not to defeat the Castilians, but to conquer Spain for himself. Before setting out he had sworn not to despoil the Spanish princes; but the clergy of the Peninsula, who fostered the fanaticism of the people in favour of Islam, absolved him of his oath. Yusuf then threw aside his mask. Dissimulation was no longer necessary, for, although the higher classes were against him, he had on his side a hundred thousand African soldiers blindly devoted to his cause, and in Spain itself he could count on the people and the priests; the people hoped for a reduction in taxation, the priests could not forgive the Andalusian princes for the protection they had given to freethinkers. The princes, they said, were dissolute and corrupted the people, they imposed illegal taxes on the people. Thus threatened, the Arab princes allied themselves with the

Christians of Castille against their quondam defender; but their resistance was vain. One after another they lost their thrones and died, or were banished to the deserts of Africa. Yusuf now reigned over the whole of Moorish Spain; he ruled in the name of a fanatical priesthood, and Jews and Christians alike felt the consequences; they were persecuted, expelled, and exterminated. The duel which had begun with the Moorish conquest of Spain ended at the close of the eleventh century; the Berbers, who had been merely the soldiers of the Arabs, now ruled victoriously over the victors. It was in vain that Alfonso VI, the famous King of León, to whom the reconquest owed so much, took the field; in vain the cross fought with the crescent against the Almoravide armies, as formerly the Asturians had fought with the Saracens of Toledo against the Emirs of Seville: the Berber of Morocco reigned supreme over Moorish Spain.

With supreme command, however, faith slackened, and amid the charms and seductions of lovely Spain Almoravide sternness diminished. A singular result for those who discover in the earthquakes and geological upheavals of the Peninsula the cause of the intolerance of the Catholic faith under the Goths and under the Philips! Perhaps it might be more reasonable to attribute it to the fervent temperament, the faith and personal independence of the population. When we find the Berber give Islamism in Spain the same character as the Christians gave to Spanish Catholicism, may we not believe in a community of race, strengthened by the known events of history, the successive migrations of Berbers into Spain?

Andalusian Spain, which can only seem fearful, funereal, and a source of religious terrors to one who has never seen its magnificent scenery, the sensuous charm of its women, and the careless audacity of its brigands and bull-fighters, far from paralysing with fear, corrupts with delight. That is what happened to the Almoravide of the Atlas country when he was transplanted into Spain. He gave himself up to a golden voluptuous existence, forgot his fanaticism, yielded to temptation, and accepted Arab culture. Yusuf (1090–1106) was the protector of the illustrious Ibn Tofail, and at his literary Court flourished the most celebrated writer of his time, Ibn Roch, better known as Averroes. Andalusia, where the Arabs had found a second charming and luxuriant Yemen, turned the Berber into an Arab; the harsh and arid fanatic became a lettered sceptic, fond of metaphysical speculations as a beautiful kind of poetry.

But the African genius of the populations on either side of the Straits reacted against the influence of the climate and the tradition of Arab culture. A fresh revolution in 1146 dethroned the Almoravides in Morocco, and as a result overthrew their empire in Spain. The history of the Almohades is a repetition of that of the Almoravides. Mahomet-ibn-Tumer was a Berber, one of the ferocious inhabitants of the Atlas country of Morocco. He went to Mecca and visited Baghdad, where he purified his monotheism in the orthodox theology of Al-Achari. Returning to Africa as an apostle, he built a convent, preached, collected disciples, and condemned the polytheism of those who impiously worshipped the attributes of Allah. Acclaimed by the priests and by the fanatical hordes of the people, the Almohades or unitarians won the day. From Morocco they passed into Spain, eager in their fanaticism to persecute what was left of the Jews and Christians in Andalusia. Four centuries later the parts were reversed, and it was the Moors who were persecuted, expelled, and exterminated. The Almohade said of Spain: 'In our country heresies are not tolerated, and there are nowhere any Christian churches nor any synagogues.' Later, the Christians spoke to the same effect. The religions were different, the language used was identical; and this is what makes one believe in the kindred genius of the two peoples.

It was in the middle of the twelfth century that Spain, now a province of Africa, recognized the new Almohade dynasty. Yet another dynasty, that of the Marinides, succeeded the Almohades in the middle of the thirteenth century; but the history of Saracen domination in the Peninsula may be said to end with the victory of the Almoravides, by which Spain became subject to the Emir of Fez. The emirates of Lusitania, Algarb and Andalusia had fallen one after another into the hands of the Christian kings; and in the thirteenth century the kingdom of Granada alone, which was to have an existence of another two centuries, represented the remains of the former Spain of the Moors.

The conquering sword destroyed at one blow the kingdom of the Visigoths; the nomad tribes of the Berbers prevented the establishment of a stable Arab Khalifate; but the complete victory of the Africans finally completed the decay of ancient Spain, in the same way as the second invasions of barbarians completed the destruction of Gaul and Roman Italy. But in Spain, when the decay was completed, the new edifice of modern society was rising from the ruins; birth and decay had been simultaneous.

IV. THE MOZARABS

BEFORE examining the influence of Arab civilization on Spain we must briefly describe the culture of the people which, from the ninth to the twelfth century— that is, at the time of the greatest splendour of its rule in the Peninsula—was the depository of Hellenic culture. The intellectual progress of the Arabs to the end of the twelfth century was, considered absolutely, superior to that of the Christian nations which received from this enemy the tradition of Greek science. Till the fall of the Omayyad dynasty in 750 the culture of the Arabs had been confined to the sphere which seems natural and suited to Eastern peoples: interpretation of the Koran—that is, study of religious traditions, eloquence, and indigenous poetry. Of science, properly speaking, there was no sign; and subsequent history proved that it was not congenial to the spirit of those peoples. The rise of the dynasty of the Abbasids (750–1258) and the rivalry between the Khalifs of Spain and Africa caused a craze for education to spread from Samarkand and Bokhara to Fez and Córdoba. The Khalifs of Baghdad had agents in Constantinople, Armenia, Syria, and Egypt with the mission to buy Greek books, which were immediately translated into Arabic. Ma'mun (813–33) presided in person at the assemblies of learned men, and it required many camels to transport the libraries of scholars. That of the Fatimites at Cairo is said to have numbered a hundred thousand volumes; and the Omayyads in Spain, we are told, made a collection of more than half a million. The number of libraries at Córdoba, Málaga, Almería, and Murcia exceeded seventy. The Arabs at that time were the masters, physicians and soothsayers of the barbarous Christian kings, in the same way as the Jews were their bankers and financiers. The names of Mesua and Geber, of Maimonides, Rhazes, Avicenna, and Averroes are connected with the beginnings of anatomy, botany, and chemistry in the Middle Ages. Alfonso the Learned learnt alchemy from an Arab:

> . . . the philosopher's stone he could produce
> And showed me this his skill.

The learned tell us that in these great libraries, which contained the works of Plato and Euclid, of Apollonius, Ptolemy, Hippocrates, Galen and, above all, of Aristotle, the most read and praised of all, it was nevertheless literature, rhetoric, and commentaries on the Koran which predominated. The culture of those peoples, artists rather than thinkers, more curious than scientific, literary and refined, setting store almost exclusively by imagination and scarcely employing reason, gives them a certain feminine or puerile cast; they give the preference to beautiful forms, elegant style or subtlety, and all the excesses and extravagances of imagination which supply the place of a truly rational or scientific inquiry. Their love of Greek science was a mere caprice, not a real need of their spirit. The treatises of Aristotle stood next to commentaries of the Koran on their shelves; but this Greek science did not succeed in surmounting theology or having any influence on the moral life or institutions of the people. The Arab philosopher was a mere amateur and courtier, the fashion for philosophy coming from the throne. Dilettantism is always weak, and the Arab and Persian dilettantes were incapable of transforming their intellectual exercises into a positive moral philosophy. Yet the pictures of those small Courts of Spain which succeeded the Khalifate of Córdoba are charming; at Almería under the Beni Zumadi, and in other cities kings, princes, princesses, nobles, sceptical in religion and indifferent in politics, gave themselves up to a life of almost childish literature, composing lyrics of an exquisite perfection and inditing love madrigals.

This incapacity to give serious consideration to the deepest things of the spirit was evident also in their incapacity to set up a body of social institutions. The traditions of a tribal life survived, and only war temporarily united the elements of society. Moorish society was never more than an army with a prophet as general. After the battle and the plunder, when quiet was restored, the khalif was no longer recognized as king. The union brought about by war disappeared in time of peace; and the military institutions were not transformed into civil institutions as occurs with peoples of

Indo-European race. The traditions of tribal life being still honoured, the army melted away, following the fatal tendency of the race. Seeing a ploughshare in the house of an inhabitant of Medina, Mahomet said: 'Such an object always brings shame into a household.' The tribe was the typical formation of the race, and the wandering remnants of the inhabitants of Arabia maintained their language and religion uncorrupted. Even in the days of their splendour the noble families of Spain and Africa used to send their sons to the Bedouins to complete their education.

When the absolute power of the Khalifate had diminished and the enthusiasm aroused by the conquest of Spain had subsided, anarchy and dilettantism condemned Arab society to speedy decay—the Arabs who had been so strong as invaders and so united as an army. The conquered peoples reacted against the conquerors. Islamism gave to them, as it had given to the Turks in the East and the Berbers in the West, a religious code in which their inherent fanaticism could find formal expression; and in a series of revolutions the character of society was gradually altered. We have seen how this occurred with the Berbers and with that part of the inhabitants of the Peninsula which had been converted to Islamism. In the East it was the same with the Turks. Instead of an excessive toleration bordering on scepticism there arose a blind fanaticism—the priest or marabout replaced the nobleman in the government; the chieftain or khalif was adored almost as a god; science and philosophy were condemned; and poetry changed from gay and frivolous to melancholy, sacred and almost funereal. It was the Almoravide conquest, as we have seen, which marked this revolution in Spain. In the East the thirteenth century saw the height of Arabic civilization. What happened then, says an historian, is the same as what happened in the Christian civilization of the sixteenth century. Fears arose as to the consequences of a culture which led to impiety. An attempt was made to check the movement, to react against civilization. There was as it were a Council of Trent, a Pope Pius V, a Charles Borromeo. In Europe the reaction was victorious only in Spain and Italy; but in the Moorish world it was absolutely victorious. An ephemeral civilization disappeared for ever and an irremediable decadence began which has lasted down to our time. When the sovereign, beset with scruples, set fire to the libraries and banished science, the Arabs set themselves with new fervour to comment on the Koran and to amuse themselves with the innocent pastime of well-turned phrases and elegant verse. It is only the Christians who remember there were once learned men and scholars in Islam. But if we received the precious legacy of Greek science directly from these scholars, it must be confessed that they handed it over in a sadly corrupt state. The system of practical knowledge and the structure of ancient abstract sciences of Greece had in passing through their hands undergone a transformation by which the difficulties and complications besetting studies in the Middle Ages were greatly increased. The poetical imagination and naturalistic mysticism of the Arabs gave to Greek science not only a new form but even new names; the mysterious subtleties of the kabbala wrapped the whole of ancient learning in a network of scholastic formulas and superstitions; astronomy was converted into astrology; the scholar became a magician; and chemistry, wildly seeking for the philosopher's stone, of which Alfonso the Learned claimed to have learned the secret, sank into alchemy.

A race endowed with such a character as we have described, enthusiastic for art, steeped in literary culture, must necessarily be tolerant and kindly, even if such were not the precepts of its religion. The relations between victors and vanquished show not merely disdain but an active repugnance, such as that felt by the

Christians for the Jews. The Christians and Jews were considered unclean, and true believers cautiously avoided speaking with one of the impious and being contaminated by so much as touching his garments. Generally, it may be said that the Arabs, proud of their own language and literature, disdained to learn that of the conquered. The latter were therefore obliged to learn that of the conquerors (this was an essential difference between the Arabic and the Germanic conquest of Spain), although there were not lacking men among the Arabs of the upper classes who could speak in *romance*, and although many neo-Latin words crept into the everyday speech of the Court of Abd-ur-Rahman III, in which there were certainly many natives of Spain.

The disdainful toleration of the Moors was also based, as we have seen, on their method of exploiting the conquered peoples. Their interest was to preserve the religion of the conquered and with it their own revenue derived from taxation. Since the time of Omar (717–20) they had a fixed canon of conduct towards the Christians: 'We must exploit the Christians and our descendants their descendants so long as there is a single Christian left.' The Christians were not allowed to build new churches nor to restore those fallen into ruins. The Moor had the right to enter all churches by night or day, and the churches must be always open to receive travellers and lodge them for three days. The cross was forbidden on the outside of buildings, and ceremonies were forbidden in the streets, as were singing and chants which could be heard outside the church if Moors lived in the neighbourhood. It was forbidden for Christians to proselytize or to prevent Christians from embracing the religion of Islam. In the presence of a Moor, even if he were seated, a Christian must remain standing. He was not allowed to wear Arab dress, and was obliged to wear a special girdle to show his creed; he was not suffered to speak Arabic or assume Arabic names or own Moorish slaves. One could almost believe that the Christian monarchs copied the canon of Omar in order to apply it to the Jews and Moors. But if these and other decrees were rigorously turned against them later, the Arabs themselves never scrupulously carried out the law. They were more tolerant in putting it into practice than those who had drawn it up; and the relations with Christian peoples were almost always based on a special treaty, as was the case in Spain. So tolerant were its clauses that Moors and Christians even shared the same church, the Moors using the eastern half and the Christians its western half; at Córdoba and in many other places Allah and Jehovah, Mahomet and Christ were thus worshipped under the same roof. Such a state of affairs was due not to Arab toleration alone but also to the primitive character of Christianity in the Peninsula. On this side of the Mediterranean much the same thing occurred as in the Byzantine colonies on the other side: the oppression of a corrupt government opened the doors to the invaders, as is sufficiently proved by the rapidity with which Spain was conquered; and the intolerance of the Visigothic Church caused the new régime to be considered as a kind of liberty. Christianity in the Peninsula in the eighth century was still semi-pagan; the Peninsula, which was polytheistic when Constantine made Christianity the religion of the Empire, was still more or less so when the Arab invasion came. We need not therefore be surprised at the excessive toleration shown towards the conquered people; the Arab believers in their literary pride saw in them only inferiors incapable of perceiving the sublimity of the words of the Prophet or the beauty of the language of the Koran. This feeling of superiority, based not on warlike aristocracy but on intellect, must have been the source of that somewhat disdainful toleration.

We know that the conquerors tolerated the institutions of the conquered who, under Moorish rule, were
permitted to retain their civil and ecclesiastical hierarchies. Dioceses, parishes, monasteries continued to
exist as before. In the towns the Gothic authorities
were maintained; in the palace of the Khalifs of
Córdoba noble Goths were given high positions, probably those concerned with the central administration
of the system of institutions peculiar to the natives.
We have already mentioned the fact that the Christians
did not object to serve Arab lords—we have only to
think of the alliances of the Moorish emirs with the
Leonese in the reign of Alfonso VI; the incident when
the same King Alfonso advanced against Seville but
lost the city to the Vizir in a game of chess; and the
adventures of the Cid, that legendary *condottiere*, who
alternately led Saracens against Christians and Christians
against Saracens. Many noble Goths fought in the
ranks of the Moors; and if the first Emir of Spain
married the widow of the hapless Roderick, the warlike
Alfonso VI for his part took for wife the Sevillian Zaida;
and had not their son Sancho died in the battle of
Uclés (1180) the son of a Moorish woman would
probably have sat on the throne of León. All these
circumstances demonstrate the historical fact of the
permanence of the Hispano-Roman population in the
towns and of its retention of the Christian religion.

If the persecution inherent in a conquest of extermination results in the more or less complete
destruction of the inhabitants and the formal overthrow of their institutions, it is a fact nevertheless
that it entails a certain strengthening of traditional
ideas among the scattered remnants of the population
that survive. Just the opposite happens under a foreign
but kindly government; insensibly it exercises an influence, and in time the institutions subjected to it are
modified in appearance and even in their essential char

acter. That is what occurred in Spain under the rule of the Saracens; the inhabitants became Mozarabs— that is to say, half Arabs.

The first proof of this is the Arab form taken by the names of municipal offices; the Arab *ḳā'id, ḳāẓī, wazīr,* and *muḥtasib* oust the Roman names and in modern Spain become *alcaide, alcalde, alguacil, almotacén.* In fact the Arab invasion did not entail any change in the religious or civil situation of the Hispano-Roman population, nor even any extensive expropriation of land, as was the case with the invasion of the Goths. Islamic proselytism confined itself to give renegades the privileges of the Mussulman, and the conquest was based socially merely on political and military authority and on the imposition of the same taxes as were levied by the Visigoths, the land-tax (*kharāj*), and the poll-tax (*jizyah*). If these conditions were fulfilled, Christians could only be deprived of their land if they failed to cultivate it, and were at perfect liberty to have their own civil laws and preserve both their ecclesiastical hierarchy and their classes of nobility. This manner of occupying the country could not provide that social unity which almost always results from violent conquest; but in a society undermined by an ancient and progressive decadence it had an effect which was to some extent a novelty: that of the assimilation by the conquered of the customs of the conquerors. Thus arose the Mozarab population, which is of immense importance to those who wish to understand the social history of modern Spain. It was not only in external habits that the Christians became Arabs; they even forgot their native language, to such an extent that the bishops admitted the necessity of translating the Scriptures into the language of the Koran. They neglected the Christian fathers and theologians and exchanged the reading of Latin for that of Arabic authors, so that when in 848 Eulogius brought from Navarre to Córdoba the *Aeneid* of Virgil and the *Satires* of Horace and Juvenal, these works were unknown in the country which had produced Martial. And the Christians, except for the group to which Eulogius and Albericus belonged, did not complain: they were not persecuted nor molested; on the contrary, they were free to serve in the army, to hold office at Court and in the palaces of the great and even, if they chose, to have a harem. Circumcision became general among the Christians.

But whatever the fusion between the two races resulting from this intimacy, from the use of a common language and common habits, it would, we think, be an exaggeration to infer that a new race arose. Without examining the exact meaning of the word 'race' and the possibility of natural races being formed in historical times, there is one circumstance which seems to tell decisively against any such inference. The fact that, in spite of the natural intermarriage of Moors and Christians, the Christian religion was maintained pure in its essential characteristics sufficiently shows that such intermarriages were not general enough to produce a new race. Tolerant as the religion of Islam might be on principle, it would be to deny its very existence as a religion to suppose that the emergence of a new race would not have meant the disappearance of the religion of the conquered. But the principal fact which distinguishes the Mozarab from the pure Arab is that, although they have the same customs, the same names, even the same language, their religion is different.

Although we cannot therefore consider the existence of the Mozarabs ethnologically important, we have every reason to regard it as socially one of the most significant events in the history of the Peninsula. It permitted the people to remain freely constituted in their towns; hence the peculiar character and importance of the towns in the history of modern Spain. As the reconquest advanced, the Christian kings came upon these thriving and laborious centres of population and were careful to foster and protect them. This fact, unknown in central Europe, where the invasions of barbarians fiercer than the Arabs had worked greater havoc among the population and wealth of the country, was the principal cause of the exceptional circumstance in the history of the Peninsula that feudalism was not systematically accepted there, the kings having found in the Mozarab population of the towns a strong support against the excessive demands of their warrior barons.

Dwelling on the frontier of Christian or Moorish states (for long the raids and forays on either side, penetrating far into the interior, made frontier lands of the centre and south of the Peninsula), the Mozarab hesitated between the two forces which were fighting for empire. On the one side were his friends, on the other his ancestors; on the one side were his daily habits, on the other his religion. Standing outside or indifferent to the struggle, the Mozarab for that very reason, and by reason of the ties which bound him to either side, was welcomed and protected by whatever side happened to be victorious.

We have already noticed the slight ethnological significance of the invasions. What the chronicles describe as waves of men overrunning the country are usually but a few thousand soldiers. Fear and rhetoric portray the population as being swept from off the face of the earth, and an invasion is generally represented as the substitution of one race by another. Nothing could be farther from the truth. We have shown what happened with the Goths and it remains to state what happened with the Arabs. Twelve thousand men sufficed Tarik to overthrow the Visigothic monarchy and march in triumph through Spain to the Pyrenees. And when we find the Moors in modern Spain, till their expulsion in the sixteenth century, living a life apart like the Jews, that is another excellent argument that there was not, and could not be, fusion sufficient between the two races to be of ethnological importance. The characteristics of the Mozarabs, as we have described them, point to no different conclusion.

If, however, we must insist that there is an ethnological fact here, it would not be in the Arab race in its purity that we would seek the elements composing the new type. It is undeniable that the number of Arabs in the Peninsula was extremely small, the great majority of the invaders were Africans; and in our rapid sketch of Saracen rule in Spain we saw how the Arabs and Berbers were balanced and the final decisive victory of the latter. The Mozarab race would thus spring not from Arabs but from Berbers But this fusion of the two races is but of secondary importance from our present point of view; and whatever the amount of Hamite or Arab blood that it received, it is certain that the native race of the Peninsula was sufficiently strongly constituted to assimilate it without becoming transformed. The same thing had occurred in the Germanic invasion; and if subsequently we find an aristocracy of blood with an evident foreign origin, that is due to the fact that it is in the nature of such aristocracies to remain isolated amid a conquered people. That is not to say that there were not many isolated small groups of Moors in the Peninsula, not Mozarabs but genuine Arabs, Syrians or Berbers, still easily recognizable to-day, as for instance, not to speak of the south of Spain, the dwellers along the Tagus in Portugal and, especially, the Maragatos in Spain, of whom we shall say something presently.

The toleration practised by the Arabs was certainly the chief cause of the population breaking up into groups; and the existence of the Mozarabs is the best proof that the two races were not fused into one. When Moorish rule in Spain took on a character of intolerant fanaticism, that is after the reaction of Mansur and the subsequent Almoravide invasion, the Arab empire was declining rapidly, and more than half Spain, and the most densely populated half, was once more a Christian monarchy. We must not, however, suppose that toleration from the first caused separation between the two races; we must recognize the fact, although it is historically of secondary import, that many Christians were converted to Islam and that the Hispano-Roman population was absorbed in the race which followed the banner of the Prophet. What we know of the corruption of Visigothic society and of what happened in the Byzantine population of North Africa, which resembled that of Spain, would suffice for us to presume this fact, even if it were not historically proved. Many embraced Islamism, but conversions were especially frequent among the servile class. Despite the platonic utterances of the codes and of the canon law of the Councils, the invaders were more favourable to the slaves than had been the Visigothic monarchy. Slavery among the Arabs had never been harsh nor of long duration; Mahomet in the name of Allah had allowed slaves to become free; and the freeing of a slave was considered a pious act, absolving from sins. In Spain, besides these religious ordinances, the state of society encouraged the freeing of slaves and emancipation of serfs. The Christian slave who renounced his religion ordinarily became free, and the serf became a *colonus*. All Moorish property was considered an asylum for fugitive slaves and serfs. They had but to take refuge there and confess that 'Only Allah is God and Mahomet is his prophet' in order to become emancipated, the freedmen of Allah. Working thus among the servile class, Islamism attracted, absorbed and assimilated part of the population. Without culture of any kind, Roman or Germanic, this plebeian mass of renegades lived according to its instincts, which resembled those of the African soldiers who had disembarked in the Peninsula. A fanaticism common to the people on either side of the Mediterranean caused these renegades who had become part of the Moorish people to fight on the side of the priesthood against the princes, on the side of Mansur against the Arabs, on the side of the Almoravides against the Walis, and on the side of the Almohades against the Almoravides, when the latter had become corrupted by the atmosphere of the Peninsula. With the same fervour with which in the time of the Goths they had applauded the fanaticism of the Christians against the Jews, they now applauded the fanaticism of the Moors against the Christians. Forgetting their former religion, they brought to their new belief what was unchanging in their character: an indomitable energy of moral will, the religious expression of a personal independence.

We have now reached the end of this introduction to a new period of history. We have witnessed the formation of the race and the constitution of society. We have seen how Roman civilization europeanized a people which, according to every indication, had an origin different from that of the Aryan peoples, although this had been modified by fusion with the Celts. We have seen how the basic institutions of this society were so deeply rooted that they persisted through all the upheavals and decadence. We have seen that Christianity made Spain morally one, as the Romans had made her socially one, with a common language and literary and scientific culture. We saw how in the first period of decay an aristocracy of race, with hereditary property, was grafted on the old ideas, and how the two political systems and the two systems of land ownership existed side by side; and how on the foundation of classical thought were superimposed the Germanic sentiments of the invaders. Finally we saw how the decay of ancient Spain was completed by the Saracen invasion, and that no vestiges of the Arab rule remained either in the institutions or ideas of the people of the Peninsula, owing to the toleration of the Arabs, the difference of religion, and the artificial character of Arab culture. The real influence of the Arab conquest is to be seen in the direction it gave to the national life of modern Spain. Born in the camp, in the midst of battle, the character of modern Spain springs rather from spontaneous natural sources than from the ordinances of ancient traditions, Roman or Germanic.

BOOK III
GROWTH OF NATIONALITY

I. THE SPONTANEOUS DEVELOPMENT OF THE NATIONS OF THE PENINSULA

THE kingdoms, principalities, and counties which emerge in Spain as more and more Moorish territory is reconquered, possess a completely new character. Neither by the Roman tradition alone, nor by the Germanic, can their nature be appraised or their character determined. By the side of and above those two elements appears a third condition from which they could not escape, that of spontaneous development. Everything traditional is mixed together and pounded into dust as in a mortar. As we successively discover and examine the traditional elements, we shall see how they were modified by the conditions inherent in the reconquest, and, while we recognize that tradition was an ingredient in the constitution of the new nation, we shall see that it was not an essential element. The essential elements were spontaneity and the conditions under which social facts appeared and were developed. At the same time it was natural that, since Spain before the Moorish conquest consisted of a democracy in the towns governed by an aristocracy of Germanic origin, during the subsequent disorganization and reconstruction she should revert, on the part of the people, to the municipal system of Rome and, on the part of the aristocracy, to the Germanic institutions. The conditions inherent in the reconquest were, as we have said, favourable to the former movement; on the other hand, the arrival of adventurers of Germanic origin to assist in the war and share the spoils of conquest with the descendants of the Visigoths in Spain helped to define the principles of an aristocratic or feudal rule at that time general in Europe. Thus the reconquest, in restoring the former Visigothic monarchy, did not restore the centralization of imperial Rome. This remained a vague poetical inspiration; the fact which spontaneously resulted from these wars was that of the division of Spain, not only into separate sovereign nations but into vassal principalities and counties after the feudal system, applied with more or less strictness. The loss of ancient tradition is also shown in the fact that the kingdoms are now considered the private property of the sovereigns who have conquered them and can bestow them on others. The Roman principle of national sovereignty, recognized by the Visigoths, was now extinct, as was the election of monarchs; political authority became feudal and the idea of sovereignty was merged in that of property.

We have not in this book to record the history of the various independent States of Spain, because it has little bearing on the general history of her civilization. Above individual political events is the condition of society which, with few exceptions, was common to all the States, as were the causes out of which it sprang. Moreover, the breaking up of the Peninsula into small political groups was a mere passing aspect in the development of the nation, although it lasted a long time; it merely marks the progress from disorganization to organic reconstruction.

From the reconquest, which began simultaneously in the north and east, sprang the kingdoms of León and Navarre. The latter was subsequently divided into three States—Navarre, Castille, and Aragon—of which Castille was the first to become united to León. Portugal separated from León; but in course of time Castille and León incorporated all the other States of the Peninsula, until at the end of the fifteenth and beginning of the sixteenth century, with the restoration of Navarre south of the Pyrenees, the union of Aragon, and the conquest of Granada, they became the Spanish monarchy. The first decisive act in the history of the reconquest was the expansion of the Kingdom of Asturias under Alfonso I (739–57 or 752–59) in the middle of of the eighth century. The union of the Asturian and Cantabrian States in 739 doubled the strength of the nation, while the insurrection of the Berbers in the north of Spain, who joined the Berbers recently arrived from Africa against the Arabs, presented a favourable opportunity for vaster undertakings. The whole of the Berber population, from Galicia to Estremadura, marched in arms against the Arabs, but was exterminated or took refuge in Africa (750–55). Galicia thereupon rebelled and acknowledged the Asturian king in 751; Braga, Porto, and Viseu followed suit, and of the invading Berbers only the Maragatos remained, in the mountain-ranges of Astorga and León.[1]

Alfonso I had not the means to hold so vast a region; he therefore laid waste the country to a frontier extending from north to east through Coimbra, Coria, Talavera, Toledo, Guadalajara, Tudela, and Pamplona (735–55). Cities such as Astorga and Tuy remained desolate till the ninth century; but throughout this region of the Peninsula the Arab domination had not lasted half a century.

In the conquests of King Ferdinand (1035–65), in the middle of the eleventh century, Viseu, Lamego, Coimbra, and whole region between the Douro and Mondego were lost by the Moors (1064); the Emirs of Toledo, Badajoz, Zaragoza, became vassals of the King of León; the Christians advanced in their raids as far

---

[1] The Christians of the north, in their hatred of the Berbers who remained in their country after these events of the eighth century, designated the region they inhabited as Malacoutia. Its inhabitants were mountaineers, nomad and uncivilized, although some of them had embraced Christianity. Even to-day, after ten centuries, the Maragatos, Malagoutes, or Malacoutos form a separate group in the population of León. They remain Berbers, shave their head except for a tuft of hair at the back, speak a language which is not genuinely Castilian, with a harsh, trailing pronunciation, and are for the most part muleteers, that is to say nomads.

as Seville and carried off the body of St. Isidore, and they laid siege to Valencia. King Ferdinand died during this siege. This new period of swift expansion was due to the weakness of the Moors after the Khalifate of Córdoba had split up into a number of little States in the year 1031.

There followed in the reign of Alfonso VI (1072–1109) the conquest of Toledo in 1085 and the capture of Valencia; and the Christian State became so large that the title of kingdom seemed insufficient and, following a vague tradition, the king adopted the title of emperor and called himself 'lord of the men of either religion'. The danger of the complete destruction of the Moorish States in the extreme south of Spain was so imminent that their Emirs appealed to the Almoravides, and with their help succeeded in winning back Valencia and raising the siege of Zaragoza; but they saved themselves at the price of their independence, and the Arab States that survived in the Peninsula were henceforth dependent on the African empire.

For greater clearness we will here give the principal periods of the existence of the various Christian States in the Peninsula during the Middle Ages:

NAVARRE

A.D. 755. The County of Navarre ceases to be a vassal of León.

    801. Independence of the kingdoms of Navarre and Aquitaine.

  1028. Navarre is united to Castille by dynastic marriage.

  1035. Death of Sancho II. His kingdom at the time of his death included the regions on either side of the Pyrenees which later became French and Spanish Navarre, and Castille and Aragon. By his will it was divided into four independent States: Navarre, Castille, Sobrarbe, and Aragon.

  1076. Division of Navarre between Castille and Aragon.

  1134. Restoration of independence.

1283. Union with France through dynastic marriage.
1328. Recovery of independence.
1458. Navarre is inherited by the Crown of Aragon.
1479. Restoration of its independence.
1512. Ferdinand the Catholic incorporates by conquest in the monarchy of Castille, León and Aragon, the provinces of Navarre to the south of the Pyrenees; those on the north remained independent until they were incorporated in the French monarchy when Henri IV ascended the throne.

BARCELONA

762. Creation of the County of Barcelona, recognized by Charlemagne in 801.
888. Proclamation of its independence as an hereditary State.
1077. Urgel divided from Barcelona by will.
1082. Reincorporation of the Lordship of Urgel.
1137. Accession of the Counts of Barcelona to the throne of Aragon.

URGEL

1077–82. Exists as an independent State.

ARAGON

1035. Becomes independent by the will of Sancho II.
1041. Incorporates the Lordship of Sobrarbe.
1076. Conquest and incorporation of a part of Navarre.
1109. Union with Castille by dynastic marriage.
1126. Separation from Castille.
1137. Incorporates the County of Barcelona.
1229–33. Conquers Mallorca from the Moors.
1238. Conquers Valencia.
1276. Separation of the Lordship of Mallorca by will.
1344. Conquers the Lordship of Mallorca.
1469. Union with Castille and León by dynastic marriage.
1504. On the death of Queen Isabel Aragon becomes united with Castille in the person of King Ferdinand the Catholic.

SOBRARBE

1035. Becomes independent by the will of Sancho II.
1041. Is united to Aragon.

MALLORCA

1276–1344. Is independent of Aragon.

CASTILLE

967. Becomes independent of León.
1029. Is united to Navarre by dynastic marriage.
1035. Is separated from Navarre by the will of Sancho II.
1037. Incorporates León by conquest.
1065. On the death of Fernando I the Kingdom of Castille and León is divided into five States, Castille, León, Galicia, Zamora, and Toro.
1073. The former State is reconstructed in the hands of Alfonso VI.
1076. Conquest and incorporation of part of Navarre.
1109. Union of Castille and Aragon by dynastic marriage.
1126. Separation of Aragon.
1157. Separation of León by will.
1158. Loss of independence. Conquest by León.
1170. Restoration of independence.
1230. Definitive union of León and Castille.
1250–1300. Conquest of Estremadura, New Castille, and Andalusia from the Moors.
1469. Union with Aragon through dynastic marriage.
1492. Conquest of Granada.
1512. Conquest of Navarre.

ZAMORA AND TORO

1065–73. Independence from Castille.

LEON

755. Political constitution of the Leonese State against the Moors.
783. Separation and independence of the Lordship of Biscay.

791. Loss of Biscay's independence.
863. Separation and independence of the County of Galicia.
885. Subjection of Galicia.
910. Separation and independence of the Kingdom of Oviedo and of the County of Galicia.
913. Ordoño constitutes the Asturian-Leonese kingdom and incorporates Oviedo.
924. Galicia submits to be incorporated.
967. Independent constitution of the County of Castille.
1037. Loss of independence on conquest by Castille.
1065. Separation and independence on the death of Fernando I, who bequeathed the throne of León to his third son, Alfonso VI.
1073. Alfonso VI conquers Castille.
1109. Creation of the County of Portugal in favour of Count Henry of Burgundy.
1109. Union of the monarchies of León and Castille and Aragon under the Crown of Aragon.
1126. Separation of Aragon from the monarchy of León and Castille.
1140. The Portuguese monarchy becomes independent.
1158. Separation of León and Castille. León becomes independent.
1159. Reconstruction of the Kingdom of León and Castille by the conquest of Castille.
1170. Separation of Castille.
1230. Definitive union of the Kingdoms of León and Castille through inheritance.

PORTUGAL

1097. Creation of the County.
1140. Constitution of the monarchy. Independence from León.
1139–1250. Conquest of Alentejo and Algarve from the Moors.

OVIEDO

910–13. Independence from León.

Vizcaya

783–91. Is a Lordship as vassal of León. At some date unknown Count Iñigo Lopez refuses to pay homage to León.

1379. Submission to Castille and León.

Galicia

863. Separation and independence of the County.

885. Subjection to León.

910. Restoration of Galicia's independence.

924. Definitive union with León, except for a rising quelled in 981.

1065. Constitution of the County of Galicia by will of King Fernando I of Castille.

1073. Incorporation of Galicia in the Monarchy of Castille and León under Alfonso VI.

These notes will become clearer if we add a list of the Peninsula States as they were gradually incorporated:

A.D. 755. (two States) León, Navarre.

762. (three) León, Navarre, Barcelona.

783. (four) León, Vizcaya, Navarre, Barcelona.

791. (three) León, Navarre, Barcelona.

863. (four) Galicia, León, Navarre, Barcelona.

885. (three) León, Navarre, Barcelona.

910. (five) Galicia, Oviedo, León, Navarre, Barcelona.

914. (four) Galicia, León, Navarre, Barcelona.

924. (three) León, Navarre, Barcelona.

965. (four) León, Castille, Navarre, Barcelona.

1029. (three) León, Navarre, Barcelona.

1035. (six) León, Castille, Sobrarbe, Aragon, Navarre, Barcelona.

1037. (five) Castille, Sobrarbe, Aragon, Navarre, Barcelona.

1041. (four) Castille, Aragon, Navarre, Barcelona.

1065. (eight) Galicia, León, Zamora, Toro, Castille, Aragon, Navarre, Barcelona.

1073. (four) Castille, Aragon, Navarre, Barcelona.

1076. (three) Castille, Aragon, Barcelona.
1077. (four) Castille, Aragon, Urgel, Barcelona.
1082. (three) Castille, Aragon, Barcelona.
1109. (four) Portugal, Castille, Aragon, Barcelona.
    (the same year: three) Portugal, Aragon, Barcelona.
1126. (four) Portugal, Castille, Aragon, Barcelona.
1135. (five) Portugal, Castille, Aragon, Navarre, Barcelona.
1137. (four) Portugal, Castille, Aragon, Navarre.
1157. (five) Portugal, Castille, León, Aragon, Navarre.
1158. (four) Portugal, Castille, Aragon, Navarre.
1170. (five) Portugal, Castille, León, Aragon, Navarre.
1230. (four) Portugal, Castille, Aragon, Navarre.
1276. (five) Portugal, Castille, Aragon, Mallorca, Navarre.
1344. (four) Portugal, Castille, Aragon, Navarre.
1458. (three) Portugal, Castille, Aragon.
1469. (four) Portugal, Castille, Aragon, Navarre.
1504. (three) Portugal, Castille, Navarre.
1512. (two) Portugal, Spain.
1580. (one) Spain.
1640. (two) Portugal, Spain.

We will now resume our history, and, having noted the new form which was given to the idea of political sovereignty by the influence of the reconquest, may now observe other facts deriving from the same event. The first of these facts is that of language. The spontaneous formation of the Romance or neo-Latin languages of the Peninsula proves the untraditional character of the reconstruction of the nation there; a fact common indeed to the whole of Latin Europe, where movements similar to that in Spain occurred. The neo-Latin languages of the Peninsula are different from the very first. Many were dwarfed in their development through the loss of political independence and became dialects; others, like Galician and Catalan, maintained a literary culture; two only, the Castilian and Portuguese, corresponding to the two independent nations of the Peninsula, each with its separate literature, remained completely free. All the languages, however, show in

their formation the entire spontaneity of their development. Peoples have a natural creative art of
constructing new things out of dead and scattered
materials; and this is what characterizes spontaneous
movements, whereas traditional movements are of a
learned character and propose consciously to restore
some well-defined but forgotten type. The new languages of the Peninsula are not therefore a continuation of Latin, nor a barbarous form of Latin; they
are different in kind, organically and spontaneously
formed out of the scattered remains of the ancient
Latin language of Spain. The causes already noticed
as having led to the decadence of Roman Spain were
also the causes of the decay of the Latin language, which
was formerly general throughout the Peninsula; and
the fact that Latin was forgotten is one of the many
sure signs of the total decay of the old organization of
society. However Romanized the Visigoths became,
the Germanic invasion must have been the chief cause
of the corruption of the language; and to this were
added motives of another kind due to religion. The
Christian Church, although directly descended from
the Roman society in whose image it had been formed,
found in the principles of its faith the condemnation
of the spirit which pervaded classical literature; so that
while among the clergy, as among society in general,
the traces of that ancient civilization were dying out,
scruples of conscience, and perhaps of ignorance also,
arose. St. Isidore is the last father of the Church in
the Peninsula whose writings preserve a vestige of
ancient classical purity. To these causes was added that
of the Moorish invasion. The Mozarabs totally forgot
the barbarous Latin which had been theirs under the
Visigoths, and we have seen how the bishops had to
order the translation of the sacred books into Arabic.
It was no longer a case of horror of the language of
the heathen, the horror which had induced the priests

to forbid the reading of classical authors; it was the necessity of making oneself understood by a people which had wholly forgotten Latin. Linguists tell us that the simpler grammatical construction of the Germanic languages was the chief cause of the decay and ruin of Latin; and it is in this that the Romance languages chiefly differ from it.

Such were the causes of the decay of Latin and the origin of the Romance languages of the Iberian Peninsula. Castilian and Galician from the first appear as different languages; but, besides these, other languages were formed, those in the south of Spain having a more or less important supply of Arabic elements in them. Reduced by political history to the state of dialects, most of them without a literature to fix and enrich them, these rudimentary languages failed to acquire historical importance or political independence. It was otherwise with Galician and Castilian, the national languages of the two monarchies of the Peninsula, although the former now appears as a dialect in that part of the province of Galicia which was incorporated in the Spanish monarchy, and also as the fixed and cultured language of the Portuguese monarchy, whose cradle was the part of Galicia between the rivers Minho and Douro. Galician prevailed in the Spain of the eleventh and twelfth centuries; it was the language spoken at the Court of Oviedo; and the fact that Galicia during certain periods was independent of León and Castille gave the Galician language an independence of its own. When we examine the written records of that age, we see that it was quite possible that Galician might have supplanted Castilian as the language of the monarchy of Castille and León. Had that occurred, we should have been able to see to-day what different development the same language had undergone in two nations politically independent.

The Reconquest began on the very day of the Battle

of the Guadalete. A band of soldiers commanded by Pelayo (718–37 or 731–50) revolted against the general submission of the Peninsula. Exiled in the mountains of Asturias, they preferred the life of brigands to all the comforts that might be theirs if they accepted the victor's yoke. They were joined by the sparse population of the mountains, and this first nucleus of an army descended from its eyrie like an eagle to swoop upon its prey in the valley. Courage and ability made Pelayo its leader. He was not a king of the old kind, for in this motley throng of men there were not properly speaking any institutions; these men who had been deserted by the fallen civilization, and loathed the civilization that had taken its place, were alone with Nature. The army was a horde, and Pelayo a new Heereskoenig, like those of the first invasions of Vandals and Suevi. A new kind of monarchy was outlined in a spontaneous way, by the law of Nature. It was only later, when the Asturians established their Court at Oviedo that the institutions of monarchy and the councils reappeared, and tradition was grafted on the fully developed tree. But this we will relate more fully when we study the organization of modern Spain under the influence of the spontaneous tendencies originating in the reconquest and then of the traditional elements revived after the victory.

Historical records show that Galicia was inhabited and cultivated in the last quarter of the tenth century. The provinces of Beira supplied troops to the kings of Oviedo, a proof that they were thickly populated. When the campaigns of the terrible legendary Mansur, the tyrant *condottiere* of the witless Khalif of Córdoba, carried the Moorish arms once more into the heart of Galicia, that province was covered with farms and villages, monasteries and churches. How explain this dense population if the occupation of the Moors had spelt extermination? If we recall what we have already said concerning the Mozarab population, we shall find an explanation and realize its importance. This hybrid population accepted the rule of Asturians or Saracens with equal ease, since in both camps it had relatives and friends and kindred beliefs and customs. As the re-conquest advanced, the kings of León and Navarre carefully encouraged the Mozarab population, and could thus rule over a populated and cultivated region instead of the bare soil ravaged by long and cruel wars. This population likewise furnished them with soldiers, and by taxes and military service repaid the local privileges or charters granted to them by the kings, thus crystal-lizing their ancient usages. Thus, besides Galicia, were populated Asturias, Old Castille, Zamora, Simancas, and the whole of Tierra de Campos, the geographical centre of the Kingdom of León; Avila, Salamanca, Medina, and Cuenca, the first towns of the kingdom of Castille; and finally the western slopes of the Pyrenees.

With this spontaneous movement of fixed popula-tions is connected the question of overlordship. Not only kings, but bishops and nobles, founded towns and granted charters and privileges.

'And in the land of Spain', says an ancient chronicler, 'there were but few fortresses, and he who was lord of the fields was lord of the land; and knights won places in the plain and settled there and divided the land of the new settlement among themselves; and the king's sole part in these estates was to maintain justice there.'

This text shows how the reconquest resulted in an elementary feudal or patriarchal system; the military chieftain became the protector of the town, which agreed to pay him certain taxes and render indispen-sable military service. If to this natural fact we add the existence of traditional customs in these settlements (among the warriors the tradition of Germanic feudal-ism, revived by the arrival of adventurers from Europe, and among the kings the tradition of Roman or Visi-gothic centralization) we shall have all the elements which were simultaneously at work in the reconstruction of the nation. To the interplay and balance of these elements was due the fact that a pure feudal system, such as that prevailing or tending to prevail at that time in central Europe, was impossible in Spain. The learned distinguish three kinds of vassalage in the social conditions created by the reconquest; and in all of them we shall see how natural tendencies predominate to such an extent that an aristocratic system is converted into a federal democratic system. The principal that there can be no land without a lord, which characterizes the feudal system, is likewise the rule in Spain; but it is in the kind of overlordship and the conditions of vassalage that the historian discovers a character peculiar to the Peninsula. The lordship, based on ownership of the soil, is transmitted by heredity, and the feudal system in its purity is therefore present in Spain; but the wars which gave to the king the greater part of the conquered lands bestowed on the Crown a preponderance which was supported by monarchical traditions. All were natural vassals either directly of the king or of the nobles or the Church, because all inhabited Crown land or Church land, or land belonging to the nobility.

We will not here inquire into the legal tenure or examine whether the state of vassalage possesses all the characters of the feudal system or not; it is a special rather than a general question, and one on which opinions are divided; it belongs rather to a history of law than to a history of civilization, for which the principal value of facts consists in their social significance. Whether the kings refused or consented to recognize the legally independent and hereditary sovereignty of the barons is for us a matter of secondary importance, since we know that in fact the barons were independent. After the semi-feudal overlordship came the *honra*, which the vassal received when he accepted from his lord land or arms, a horse or salary; but the transitory and voluntary character of this subjection shows that it was the first step in the transformation of the aristocratic system; a necessary transformation, since besides the aristocracy there was a numerous and wealthy middle class and a strong monarchy. As soon as the vassal renounced the *honra* he ceased to be a vassal.

But what most clearly shows the impossibility of any exact system of feudalism in practice and the subordination of traditions to the new conditions created by the reconquest is the *behetrias*. The members of a *behetria* demand and receive the military protection of an overlord, but maintain their own sovereignty. The natural and social basis of feudalism, that of protection, is here apparent; but its transformation into ownership and sovereignty does not occur. *Behetrias* were settlements or groups of settlements made during the first campaigns of the reconquest on territory won from the Moors, and which voluntarily placed themselves under the protection of a baron or warrior chief whose duty it was to defend them in case of war. It was a mutual contract in which the idea of sovereignty is not apparent. But there were *behetrias* which could only choose a new protector (the *podestá* of the Italians) in the same family, and were thus in feud, not to a person but to a family. The type of *behetrias* known as 'de mar a mar' show the form of contract in its purity, the members reserving for themselves unlimited choice of a protector. Thus natural conditions, imposing themselves on the traditional type, created the spontaneous fact of a hybrid system, a mixture of feudalism and democracy.

Facts of another kind came to increase the complexity of the elements composing the future social organization of the Peninsula; we refer to the peculiar situation of the Jews, the Moors, and foreigners, chiefly Franks, called in to colonize the dominions of the kings of Spain in the unpopulated southern half ravaged by centuries of war. It was in the beginning of the eleventh century that the Christian kings began to realize the usefulness of the Moorish population brought by conquest under their rule. Until the reign of Alfonso VI (1065–1109) prisoners of war, if they escaped massacre, were reduced to the fiercest captivity. The example of the Moorish Emirs, with the excellent results as demonstrated in the Mozarab population, had not so far been followed by the Christian sovereigns. Alfonso VI, whose admiration for the Arabic culture is well known, was better able to appreciate the fatal consequences of barren slavery and to compare them with a voluntary submission which might be a source of wealth to the country and of power for the Crown. The captives after the conquest of Toledo in 1085 are the first Moors who met with treatment from the Christians similar to that which Christians received from the Moors; they were permitted the use of their religion, they were allowed to enter into contracts with the natives, and even to intermarry. Indeed the King himself married an Islamite. Even those who remained slaves, the captives of war, were in an incomparably better situation than they were before, even when they renounced their faith in order to escape some of the worst torments of their persecutors. The precedent of Toledo was adopted at Valencia and generally; Alfonso VI's son-in-law, Don Enrique, and the latter's son, the first King of Portugal, followed the example of León when they extended their dominions to the Tagus and conquered Lisbon and Santarem, the keys of Portuguese Estremadura, in 1147. From the eleventh century the influence of the Moors in the development of the population of Spain becomes historically important.

Alfonso VI was prepared to treat the Jews in the same way as the Moors, although the hatred of the Christian peoples towards them, the envy of the poor against the rich, and the righteous indignation of popular instinct at their habits of usury and avarice tended towards their extermination. Religion, popular feeling, and history alike accused them of grave crimes. The remembrance that they had assisted the Moors to conquer Spain gave rise to thoughts of vengeance now that Spain's independence seemed near. The persecution of the Jews by the priesthood during the Visigothic period had not succeeded in expelling them from the Peninsula, and under Saracen rule they had prospered; but in the first days of the reconquest they again fell under the persecution which seemed inherent in their condition of reprobates. Alfonso VI protected them in the face of the popular hatred and gave them special privileges and charters; and in the twelfth century they had become so important and prosperous that they formed the greater part of the population of Burgos and other cities and took a weighty part in the civil wars. After their chequered lot during the Middle Ages, the Jews in the sixteenth century saw the execution of a sentence which had long been passed against them in the heart of the people. This cruel punishment was no doubt the penalty of their invincible obstinacy in carrying on their struggle against a hostile people among which they lived, and of the cold, ironical inhumanity with which they abused the position they had attained through their skill in usury.

The Frankish elements of the population of the Peninsula are less important, and the influence of central Europe was mainly felt in the institution of aristocracy and sovereignty. From France barons and adventurers, the *condottieri* of that troubled time of war, came to the Peninsula in search of land and plunder. They brought with them some troops, but such immigrations were easily absorbed in the native population. Moreover they occurred principally in the west and east, in Navarre and Portugal, Navarre on the frontier of France and Portugal the county given to a French prince; and not in León and Castille, the heart of the Peninsula, round which the other independent States united, with the exception of Portugal. Until the end of the eleventh century French influence scarcely existed in León, and it was only with the family relations of Alfonso VI to the French Court that this influence made itself felt in Spain. A friar of Cluny became Archbishop of Toledo on the restoration of that see; and for his sons-in-law the king chose two Frenchmen, one of whom was Count Enrique, founder of an independent Portugal. That is why the number of Franks was more numerous in that part of Spain. After the death of his father-in-law Count Henry went to France to levy soldiers, and we have records of towns inhabited exclusively by Franks: Atouguia, Lourinham, Villa Verde, Azambuja, Coimbra, and Ponte de Sor. Yet it is now impossible to discover any trace of this foreign element in these towns; the immigration, great as it may have been, could not escape absorption, and of the coming of the French to the Peninsula the only influence that remains is that which they exercised on the system and development of political institutions.

One last fact remains to be noticed in the development of modern Spain, and that is her isolation from the rest of the world. The old separation between the Moors of Spain and those of Africa had become, if possible, even greater after Abd-ur-Rahman III exchanged his title of Sultan for that of Khalif in 929 and became independent both in politics and religion. On the other hand, France, after the death of Charlemagne in 814 and his alliance with Alfonso II (791–842) had no further connexion with the young Asturian nation; and when the Counts of Barcelona, taking advantage of the decadence of the Carlovingian dynasty, declared themselves independent in 888, the ties between France and the Spanish marches were definitely at an end. Thus neither in the East nor in the West, neither in Asia nor in Europe, was there any one to take any interest in this corner of the world in which two religions and two races were at strife; the neo-Gothic States of Spain were therefore able to develop naturally without any external influences to complicate seriously the action of native elements.

Having now studied the ground on which the new Spain was reared, the nature of the soil and of the growth springing from it, we must proceed to consider the organization of society and finally the idea which is already obscurely at work within it.

II. THE NATURAL ELEMENTS

THE nature of the subject and the subordination of its various materials to an ordered plan entail repetitions, which are not without their use, since they serve better to fix in the memory the essential facts which we are now studying. We have already given a general sketch of the elements and conditions in the development of modern society in the Peninsula; we must now examine each of them particularly and watch the course of its development in the general reconstruction of the nation.

We have seen how the municipal system was strengthened and developed by the conditions spontaneously created by the reconquest. As the land fell beneath the sway of the Christian kings, the Mozarab *presores* and *privati* and the *coloni* (we have already studied the character of these classes) united to form new towns or remained in towns which passed without change from one régime to the other. An official delegated by the king or by some count, could easily rule a colony of serfs; but it was otherwise with settlements of free men in the possession of municipal privileges which the Emirs had not destroyed. *Presores* and *privati* were anxious for the reconstruction of the ancient 'city'; and their desire agreed with the interests of the kings who wished to repeople the devastated regions and maintain the population in the regions which had been spared by war. Hence their liberality in granting charters or privileges. These charters do not systematically represent one or more than one type, since there were no longer any fixed ideas concerning administration as in the time of the Romans. When the learned to-day, after comparing and classifying the characters, deduce certain general types, they merely prove the very natural existence of similar conditions; and we must not infer that there was any system in the drawing up of these charters. Neither the ideas of that time nor the social conditions permitted this. The charters simply fixed established customs and represented an agreement or protocol between two powers, the overlord (king, count, or Church) and the town council. It is in this double aspect that the charters must be studied. On the one hand we see how the new conditions deformed, perverted, and even destroyed that form of property as it existed among the Romans, and gave to the *municipium* a political character which effaced its former social and economic significance. On the other hand, in the increasing and almost total oblivion of ancient law the councils, which safely survived the whole period of decay, lost, with the rest of society, all idea of the general or philosophical character of the Roman laws and of the Visigothic Code which imitated them; they adopted, as must necessarily be the case, the barbarian customs and habits of the Germanic peoples or rather consecrated the native customs and habits which were likewise barbarian and which Roman civilization had not been able wholly to efface.

That is why we find in the modern town councils, as studied in their charters, the existence of the *compurgatio*, the judgement of God, the Wergild, that is to say the various forms of rudimentary trial of the barbarians without the slightest allusion to general principles of

law, which rested entirely on custom. This circumstance, added to the fact of the political character of
these towns, induced one of our modern writers to
maintain the theory, for which there is no historical
support, that the town-councils of the Peninsula in
the Middle Ages were exclusively of Germanic origin.
Learned researches have proved the existence of this
institution through all the stages of the decay of the
old organization of society, and the theory is therefore
untenable; all the more since it presumes the annihilation of the Hispano-Roman people and ascribes the existence of a middle class during the Visigothic period to
the arrival of masses of Germanic race to repeople
Spain. The mistake is easy to understand when we
consider the transformations which the ancient *municipium* underwent in the course of its history. Apart
from the perversion of ancient law, we find that the
modern town, existing by the side of feudal property
and of an aristocratic political system, is transformed
from a Roman *municipium* into a medieval commune
or republic. The Romans had transformed into *municipia* the ancient cities which were more or less independent, after the Greek pattern; during the anarchy
of the Middle Ages, when the principle of the unity of
the State disappeared, the *municipia* revert to a remote
type in such a way that in Italy and Germany reappears
a federalist system which was earlier than Rome. The
irresistible force of circumstances which had brought
about a revolution in the idea of law altered institutions
in the same way. The towns, like the property of the
nobles, became almost independent members of a
political federation. The nation is the sum of two
systems: that of aristocratic ownership and that of
democratic communes. The internal administration of
the latter is as independent as that of the former. There
were different types, but usually the municipal officials
consisted of a certain number of *alcaides* charged with

the civil and criminal jurisdiction, of a principal *alguacil* or military officer, and of a certain number of aldermen, half of whom were knights (we shall see later what villain or bourgeois knighthood meant) and half simple citizens; of certain advocates or tribunes of the people whose duty was to defend it against the excesses of judges; and of minor officials who, under the name of *alamines*, *alarifes*, and *almotacenes*, executed the municipal decrees. We have already seen that the Roman *municipium*, although like the Russian *mir*, its character was rather administrative and economic than political, enjoyed a self-government which was demanded by its very nature; now we find in the towns a real independence, since their relations to their suzerains were those of the federated cities of old to the Roman Republic. It is therefore necessary to distinguish: formerly they were independent by the very nature of the institution; now they are independent owing to the spontaneous creation of a political authority similar to that which gave independence to the property of the nobles. This parallel becomes closer with the development and decay of the municipal system. The character of the towns and of the possessions of the nobles springs from the same causes and obeys a common law. They are two currents which in the reconstruction of society represent Germanic aristocracy and Latin democracy under forms which that reconstruction renders common to both and relates them in the history of the advance towards the definitive political constitution of the nation, the monarchy.

The towns of the Middle Ages are no longer mere centres of economic importance for the life of the people in the midst of a centralized and sovereign military State; preserving its ancient character, the town is now a miniature of the State; and national unity is only expressed in the more or less slender ties confederating the democratic towns and the possessions of the nobles. The town continues to be a social unit, but is also a political and military institution; it owns troops and fortresses, and its soldiers with those of the nobles forms an army of which the monarch is the head. Each commune was a kind of republic, and in this respect the nation resembled the present federal constitution of Switzerland despite the profound alterations introduced by the influence of the institutions of her neighbours. Even sovereignty in matters of justice, always reserved for the Crown, was almost extinct; and at the end of the eleventh century the power of these town-republics was such that the kings were obliged to bow before it and to place the authority of the popular magistrates above that of officials of the Crown and allow the municipal judges to be chosen from and by the assembled householders.

Nor did their aspirations to independence end here, encouraged as they were by the independence of the towns belonging to the nobles. The ties which bound them to the Crown were sometimes entirely destroyed, as was also the case with the slender ties which bound the powerful nobles to their sovereign. The towns formed confederacies or leagues after the fashion of those of the nobles; thus arose the *union* and *hermandad* in which the cities behave like States and in their confederacies treat with the Crown as State with State. These leagues acquired a character of permanence in the midst of turbulent periods like that of the reign of Juan II of Castille, during which Murcia and Seville convoked a kind of Cortes or federal assembly. The kings could only bow before such power and acknowledge it in practice as an existing fact, a power which sent its ambassadors to the Cortes and signed treaties. 'Castille', says an historian, 'resembled a confederacy of republics acknowledging a common sovereign; but republics enjoying great liberty, where the feudal lords did not maintain the people in painful slavery.' The absence of these harsh conditions of slavery and of the heavy taxes which burdened transport and commerce in the land belonging to the nobles had contributed powerfully to the development and wealth of the free classes which grew up beside the system of aristocracy and in a sense in its image.

The coexistence of these two systems, externally alike but essentially opposed—two systems which grew up analogously under identical conditions in the new state of society but represented two irreconcilable principles, the German aristocratic and the Latin democratic, based on entirely opposite ideas of ownership of the soil—this coexistence was the chief cause of the ruin of the communal system in Spain, which in this respect follows the general tendency of the rest of Europe, especially evident in the history of the Italian republics. The wealth of the towns excited the greed of the impover- ished nobles, and the entrance of these and of their vassals into the town councils brought with it the seeds of disorder; as is shown in the bloodstained history of Seville under the Count of Arcos and under the Duke of Medina Sidonia, which reproduced in Spain the history of the *podestàs* of Italy. When the town was subjected to the tyranny of a noble, a rival noble appeared to dispute the prize, and the *forum* frequently became a battlefield. Without this interference the history of the Peninsula might have been that of Switzer- land, for, had the king and the *uniones* of the towns been left alone face to face, it is not doubtful to which side victory would have inclined. But when by the side of the towns there were nobles, the monarchy, placed between the two, could prove the truth of the Latin proverb. By subjecting now the nobles by means of the towns and now the towns by means of the nobles, the king in the nature of things became the heir of the power of both. But the victory of the Crown was not due to this alone. The towns and estates of the nobles, although based on different traditions, both sprang spontaneously out of the anarchy of the reconquest. The conditions of their development caused certain defects in their constitution which might perhaps have been corrected under a republic had not the facts of history determined that they should be subjected to a central monarchy. With the gradual development of the nation the necessity of union made itself felt and the idea of law was defined, to the condemnation in principle of the system of customs, exceptions, privileges which constituted the body of jurisprudence in the charters. The law had to re-acquire a general character and a philosophic basis, both necessities of a perfect social organism; and in view of the struggle between democracy and aristocracy, only the monarchy could make the nation take this step on the road of progress. That is why we see once more, although for different reasons, the absorption of the political authority of the towns, an absorption due under the Roman empire to economical and administrative purposes. As early as the end of the thirteenth century the monarchs arrogate to themselves the right to appoint certain officials in the towns; and the final abolition of municipal liberty dates from the fourteenth century. Alfonso XI (1312–50) decidedly claims the right to name the mayors and popular tribunes; and in 1327 Seville loses the right to elect them, the election, it was said, having been the 'occasion of much evil, scandal and uproar'. The same development occurs simultaneously in Portugal; and throughout the Peninsula from the second half of the fourteenth century the towns lose their *cabildos* and political independence; and a little later, in the reform of the charters, they lose their private forms of legislation, now condemned by the greater organic unity of the Peninsula States and by the revived learned tradition of Roman law, the historical influence of which we will examine elsewhere.

Let us now consider the other aspect of the Middle
Ages in the Peninsula, with its two faces, both obeying
simultaneously and in a parallel development the influence of causes which were at first creative and afterwards destructive but which always remained constant
and closely akin. Let us examine the main lines of the
development and ruin of the aristocratic side. The
reconquest began in the Asturias and was the work of
barbarians, a return to primitive life. The bands of
Pelayo did not constitute an army nor assemble in a
Court; they were a horde, and an Arabic chronicler
thus describes the Spanish Romulus and his comrades:
'They live like wild beasts; they never wash their bodies;
they never wash nor change their clothes but wear them
till they fall to pieces of old age.' The impression made
by these fierce and barbarous heroes on the Arabs must
have been similar to that produced on Gallo-Romans of
refined culture like Sidonius Apollinarius by the savage
companions of Attila.

The constitution of some kind of Court, the growing
extension of the Christian territory, greater skill in war
and the greater regularity of campaigns modified all
this. The bands in the tenth and eleventh centuries
become armies; instead of raids there are battles;
armies and battles resembling those of the rest of
Europe, which the Asturians and Leonese could imitate in their neighbour Navarre, their ally in the reconquest. This is the period of the Cid, the typical
knight of the Peninsula. His 'Poem', composed spontaneously or anonymously like similar poems in Europe
and Greek poems corresponding to the same stage of
development, is a picture of the warfare of the nobles
of that time crystallized in the poetic vision of the
people. These sentiments, which are those of the
knight and represent the soul of aristocracy, must be
considered to spring mainly from historical conditions;
one must give up the attempt to give them a learned

derivation in the disputed influence of the genius of the neighbouring Arabs. War is the expression of the activity of a class; and the constant danger of his existence ennobles the rough warrior:

Before their hearts the knights now clasp their shields, and as
    they ride
Their lances with their pennants they lower for the fight:
And with stout hearts ride forward, forward to attack the foe.
Smite them, ye knights, O smite them for the love of charity:
For I am Ruy Diaz the Cid, the Champion, of Bivar.

These customs and the feelings that sprang from them were the mainspring of that society when re-conquest was in the air; they were the natural and effec-tive way of carrying out a necessary achievement in spite of anarchy and disorder and internal strife, that confused web of the inner history of the Christian States; but when the collective fervour against the Moors died down, or when the Moors had been driven back and their attacks were no longer feared, or when mutual hatred exceeded the general hatred against the Moors, then all unity disappeared. Turbulence, love of fighting, primitive instincts, and rough exalted feel-ings could only be held in check when all the warriors were assembled in the field in presence of a powerful Saracen army thirsting for blood and vengeance. When the battle was won, all the personal hatreds were recalled, there were injuries to avenge, greed raised its head. The army of the previous day broke up into hostile bands and to mutual assistance in face of a common danger succeeded a mutual fury of extermination. The names of the Fuensalidas and Cienfuentes, the Sousas, Benaventes, Zuñigas, Guzmanes, Hevias,[1] Carriones, Argüelles, Bernaldos, belong to the political family of the Cid, who was the typical *condottiere* of the Peninsula in the Middle Ages. The chronicles of Seville, of

[1] Possibly misprint for Herreras. (Translator's note.)

Toledo, of Cadiz, of the north, south, centre, east, and west of Spain bear witness to the troubled life of factions which reproduced events in the Moorish part of the Peninsula and among the Christians gave rise to strange and extravagant occurrences.

The towns, more concerned with work and commerce than with war, were obliged to take precautions. The old *curia* was transformed into an armed body living in a walled and fortified town; and the municipal troops had to protect the markets and fairs by force of arms. For their part the clergy wielded the weapon of excommunication, greatly feared by the knights, who were as brave in their strength as they were timid in their great ignorance; it was thus possible periodically to create a truce of God, a sacred interval, a holiday during which fighting was forbidden.

We have already noticed that the feeling which impelled the Christian nations in a mass against the Moors was to some extent unconscious. The proof is that kings and barons did not hesitate to join the infidel, either to take part in his feuds or to fight with him against the Christians. A collective instinct nevertheless pointed to the Moors as the common enemy of the nobles, if not their only enemy.

When the kings, as traditions revived, or the people, tired of the turbulent life of the nobles, or impelled by ambition or greed, began to attack the real privileges of the nobles, it was the monarch who became the chief enemy. Need of defence created the *hermandades* and *uniones*, which one must not consider peculiar to the communes nor exclusively democratic. Before one such confederation of nobles the learned King Alfonso X (1252–84) was forced to bow his head and in Portugal King Sancho II (1223–45) lost his crown in the same way. Made prisoner in Seville, the Castilian King, attacked by his sons and brothers, by the nobles and the people and clergy, thus bewailed his lot:

How solitary now lies Castille's king!
He who was Emperor of Germany,
Whom queens implored for alms and charity,
Whose foot kissed many a royal underling.

His dominions were reduced to the loyal district of Seville; his army, which had counted a hundred thousand cavalry and three hundred thousand infantry, was now composed exclusively of the municipal troops; and the King implores the assistance of the Moorish ruler of Fez, Aben Yusuf, in whose service were a member of the Guzman family and other Spaniards:

> Since in my own country, says the King, I am deserted by those whose duty it was to serve and assist me, I must needs ask for help in a foreign land; since the Castilians have abandoned me, I must not be blamed if I turn to the men of Benamarin. Since my sons are become my enemies, I will do well to take my enemies for sons, enemies by the law of nature but not at heart, even the good king Aben Yusuf, whom I love and value.

The assistance thus sought did not come; and Sancho IV, his rebellious son (1284–95) accepted the crown from his victorious vassals, even as the Portuguese King Afonso III (1245–79) had ousted his hapless brother from the throne. When the new King of Castille made the possessions of the nobles hereditary, and their vassalage, which was in fact non-existent, became legally extinct, one might expect to see pure feudalism begin in Spain. But it was not so; for, just as the aristocracy had prevented the communes from becoming republics, the strength of the middle class, which proved a vigorous support for monarchical traditions and for the personal ambition of the kings, prevented the establishment of feudalism. This is the fitting occasion to study the third period of the aristocracy in Spain. First there were the hordes of Pelayo, then the squadrons of the Cid; it remains for us to consider how this class was composed when it tended to become a constitutional element of the monarchy. The general term *ricos hombres* included all the members of the nobility, divided into three groups; the nobility of birth, independent in principle of the monarch, who could confer usufruct of property but could not alter a man's birth; the chief government and palace officials; and, thirdly, knights ennobled by the Crown. A noble of *pendón* and *caldera* was one who could levy troops and possessed the means to support his bodyguard of retainers. He enjoyed special privileges and had a seat in the Cortes; he had civil and criminal jurisdiction in the places which he owned; he could grant charters and levy taxes; he was in fact a little king. He had his own vassals, like the king; and his lands or *honras* were exempt from intervention of the king's judges. Like the Crown, he had his *fideles*, *liti*, and *buccellarii*, and besides these military or domestic dependents, he owned rural serfs and *coloni*. He was the head of a real State, although in his person (and not directly in that of his subjects) there was the principle of vassalage by virtue of his very tenure of his domain, and he was thus linked to the nation or to the king, the idea of sovereignty being still vested in persons.

For his part the king was the first among his noble vassals, and was in a sense, paradoxical as it may seem, a vassal of the Crown. He in fact represented two persons: the sovereign, whose political authority fell into abeyance in those rough times; and the suzerain of domains larger than those of any one else, since the state of population created in Spain what central Europe lacked, a vast network of towns and a numerous and wealthy middle class. This was the strength of the kings in the Peninsula and the barrier to the spread of pure feudalism. And to this was added the revived ancient traditions of national sovereignty personified or symbolized in the monarch; the suzerain was the nation's prince. But before sufficient strength was thus

acquired to curb the power of the nobles the rights of
the sovereign for the most part had become lost and
fragmentary, and, if the kings did not renounce them,
powerful vassals were able to usurp them. The con-
vocation of the Cortes ceased to have any reality when
the nobles and the towns in their *uniones* and *hermandades* set over against the traditional Cortes of the King a
new parliament of spontaneous growth, based not on
tradition but on force. As to the supreme judicial
authority, it was an empty form, as is proved by the
violence frequently done to officers of the Crown and
the existence of the *honras* exempt from their jurisdiction. The exclusive privilege to coin money might
subsist, but not from any special respect for this attribute of majesty; rather from its slight importance,
since in a simple economic system most transactions
were made by barter or exchange and the real money
was merchandise. The most important sovereign right
at that time was precisely that which, in consequence
of the divorce between fact and principle, served to
weaken and efface the sovereign power. The vassal was
bound to answer the war summons of the king and
accompany him with his retainers in his campaigns and
forays. This duty placed military strength in the hands
of the vassal; and between answering the summons and
turning his strength against the king he might and often
did choose the latter, if it was not a question of war
against the Moors. Thus the monarchy only became
sovereign when it was able to create permanent armies,
taking for their basis the municipal troops, which,
however, often followed the rebellious example of the
nobles. Considerations similar to those concerning the
towns are here in place. Feudalism in the Peninsula
was not an institution or a system constituted in
imitation of a type or sprung from a learned tradition;
it was the spontaneous creation of circumstance,
although undeniably influenced in other ways, prin-

cipally by the example of France. If we compare, for instance, what happened in the Peninsula with what happened in Palestine when in 1099 the Crusaders founded the kingdom of Jerusalem, the truth in this matter will become clear. In Palestine the Crusaders systematically reproduced feudalism, copying its purest and most genuine manifestations in the code of Frank, German, and Lombard. This is an example of a creation springing from learned tradition; so much so that even to-day jurists consider the 'Assises de Jérusalem' as one of the principal sources in which to study and appraise the institutions of feudal Europe. Totally different was the case of Spain. The spontaneous growth of nations there created two main currents, corresponding to seeds previously sown on Spanish soil. They are the two essential forms obtaining in the whole system of social institutions: the aristocratic, beneficiary, patriarchal, feudal form, or however the theorists may care to design it, according as they give the preference to one or other of its distinguishing characteristics; and the democratic, municipal, republican, or communal form. Their coexistence proves that neither of these forms was due to a systematic restoration or an erudite tradition. Thus feudalism in the Peninsula certainly lacks juridical characteristics present in its historic type; at the same time if we give the terms a political rather than a juridical value, it is certain that a feudal system existed side by side with a communal system in medieval Spain.

Leaving to learned scholars the solution of this and other problems pertaining to Spain in the Middle Ages, we will now, after having studied the composition of the towns and of the aristocracy, examine the situation of those who were more or less subjected to slavery and the way in which they might become free. A collective movement towards freedom is at the heart of political revolutions, just as the ineluctable forces of Nature impose unknown destinies on the will of man. On this aspiration of the serf to freedom hinges the social world of the Middle Ages; and this obscure collective movement, ignored by the chroniclers, determined the whole subsequent development of the nation. It gave the victory to the Crown against communism and against feudalism; and finally, after absorbing in the people the old distinctions of classes, it absorbed the sovereignty as well and ceased to personify or symbolize it in the monarch.

A problem for the learned, much discussed by historians of the Peninsula, arises out of the question of serfdom at the time of the reconquest. Was there or was there not in the modern monarchy of Spain a personal slavery apart from the serfs attached to the soil? Different answers have been given to this question; and we need not go into the discussion nor in such a book as this record the arguments adduced on either side. The very fact that there has been all this discussion proves the slight social importance of such slavery, if it existed. It is not of great concern for us whether the *mancipia* of contemporary records meant merely the rural serfs or included real slaves, and whether these slaves were only Moorish prisoners of war or included natives. Slavery, if it existed, evidently had no social importance; it was rather linked to the past or to the daily incidents of history than to the great determining factors in the organic development of society. The discussion is, however, another decisive argument in favour of the truth of our view that society in the Peninsula grew spontaneously out of natural conditions; its institutions and its classes are not moulded systematically either on a Latin or a Germanic tradition; and the Roman or German theories of historical schools have no foundation in reality and falsify history. The necessity of reconquest and the pressing need to repeople the country gave a value to the peasant both in war and agriculture, and to this fact was due the change from slavery to serfdom, the form generally adopted by slavery in modern times. War and agriculture prevented the restoration of a vile system which was also economically unsound. Serfdom was maintained in various ways: by birth, captivity, punishment for offences, and voluntarily, when a man renounced his freedom into the hands of the Church or of a noble, from motives of piety or self-interest, in religious exaltation or in order to obtain a protection indispensable in the harsh struggle for existence.

The mass of serfs represented the Gothic *plebei* and was divided into 'fiscal', 'private' and ecclesiastical serfs. We have already examined their relative situations. Paradoxical as it may appear, the serf is the last link in an organized democracy. In considering the Roman municipal system, and subsequently, we have insisted on this point, which seems to us essential to the understanding of history. Modern serfdom did not arise out of the aristocratic system which merely altered it and gave it a domestic character; it sprang from the transformation of the old slavery of the Romans. It was an excellent feature of the democratic system, and one which helped to give it the victory over the Germanic or feudal system, that serfdom was born of a historical economic need and was therefore not permanent; whereas in the aristocratic system serfdom was based on the organic and fundamental idea of personal protection and subjection. The former leaves untouched the essential core of independence and individuality, while the latter is founded on their abasement.

Thus in the Middle Ages, as to-day in Russia, rural serfdom was a starting-point, the first step on the road to freedom, a thing utterly unknown or unforeseen in the patriarchal or feudal system. In this system serfdom, being based on essential and moral, not external and social grounds, is fixed and permanent, inherent in the system, and excludes the idea of evolution or development. In the situation of the non-free classes of the Peninsula in the Middle Ages we find every stage and gradation in the development from complete subjection to complete freedom, by which gradually subjection became extinct and freedom became a common privilege of all men. Above the serf, who changes owners with the land, we find the emphyteutic *colonus*. At first there is but slight difference between them, because the immediate overlord can compel the *colonus* to remain his serf; but as early as the fourteenth century the latter becomes personally free and is only subject to the payment of a tax. Above the *colonus* is the free man who is subject to taxation; he likewise changed owners with the land but retained his freedom and might even possess the rank of noble, since we find more than one instance of men of this class being ennobled. In this case it was not the individual who was sold, but the right of vassalage, which might consist in the payment of a tax or in military service. To this imperfect form of serfdom, this semi-freedom, the lower classes gradually attained. The hereditary serf had the certainty that his children would enjoy the fruits of his labour. In time his attachment to the soil was reduced to a mere contract or document in which his obligations were fixed; this gave not freedom but a guarantee of security. The old *libertus* likewise attained freedom, which might be modified by some passing obligations when it was so stipulated in the act of manumission. In this general aspiration of the servile classes to become free, freedom voluntarily conferred by the owners was one of the means of emancipation, but it was not the only one, nor even, as was but natural, the most important. The agreement of the overlord to receive a money payment in lieu of military service when the frontier had receded and the fear of Moorish inroads was no longer felt; the

transformation of the serf attached to the soil into the
colonus; and, last but not least, the right of immunity
given to the towns by the kings: this is the chain of
natural causes, which, arising out of natural conditions
in the organization of society, put an end to serfdom.

In the asylum of the town there were no serfs, and
any one who took refuge there was assured at least a
semi-freedom. The population of the towns, a real
middle class, consisted of Mozarabic *presores* and *privati*
and emphyteutic *coloni*, a class constantly swelled by the
serfs. The townsfolk were villains as distinguished from
the nobles and independent as distinct from the serfs;
their situation was not created by the charters, which
merely recognized the existing fact. The well-to-do
burgesses, whose situation in the modern towns corresponded to that of the Roman *curiales*, were the knights
or horsemen in the municipal army; the mass of foot-
soldiers consisted of the *coloni*. These 'villain-knights'
are in the Middle Ages the forerunners of the bourgeois
who, later, proud of their money and envious of the
brilliance and distinction of the nobility, copy it in its
habits and vices without being able to copy its traditions and birth. However much they may try to escape
from their plebeian origin, it follows them implacably
and makes them only the more ridiculous. Thus the
tares grew up with the wheat; and the aristocratic idea,
imported by the Germanic peoples into the midst of
Latin societies which were democratic in genius and
institutions, took root in the heart of the people. In
the slow evolution of the ages the genius of those
peoples, after cutting away the privileges of the nobility,
will have to destroy the results of this unfortunate
imitation of an uncongenial idea.

This then is the rapid sketch of the natural elements
working in the reconstruction of the nations of the
Peninsula. It remains for us to study the elements
brought by tradition. The division is not absolute,

since no elements are limited exclusively to a single
origin. In those we have examined we saw that tradition exercised a certain influence and in those we are
about to study we shall find that natural conditions
play their part. It could not be otherwise; but the
predominance of natural circumstances on the one hand
and of tradition on the other warrants our classification.

III. THE TRADITIONAL ELEMENTS

IN our study of the various classes of society we
omitted one, that of the clergy. The reason for this
omission is obvious. The Church in modern times is
the principal representative of tradition. The wars
and upheavals of the period of the decay of Roman
society could not introduce any essential alteration
either into the doctrines of the Church or into its
position as a social body, whatever external modifica-
tions the times imposed. On the contrary it is the
Church which gave the conquerors a new form of
religion; it acted as their guide, partly from the authority of the priestly dignity, partly as being the only
repository of learning and culture, although in a corrupt and debased form, amid a half-barbarous society.
We saw in the history of the councils during the Visigothic monarchy how real was this authority of the
priests. In the period of Moorish rule it was otherwise.
The priests could not of course impose Christianity on
the followers of Islam; nevertheless the Christian creed
was not effaced, although the people became Mozarab.
The sacred books were translated into Arabic, and the
faithful saw at the altar priests arrayed in chasubles
and dalmatics embroidered with sentences from the
Koran; but the spirit of religion remained the same,
and the ecclesiastical hierarchy was in no danger of
disappearing. Christianity is not a national but a
catholic religion; historical events in a country may
modify it locally for a time but cannot break the tradi-

tion preserved at Rome and unaffected by local influences. When the accidents of history disappear the religion is restored to its ancient purity. That is what occurred in Spain.

In the rough and violent work of reconstructing society in the Peninsula the priests took part as a class and were affected by events. The churches and monasteries became fortresses; the parish priests and bishops became warriors and lords of estates which they ruled in the same fashion as lay proprietors. Thus externally the priesthood was distinguished from the aristocracy only by certain insignia: the cross or staff beside their sword, and the stole worn over their cuirass. The bishops and abbots rode at the head of their men in the raids against the Moors; they levied taxes on their estates and owned serfs who ploughed their land or performed the more menial duties of the priestly office. The body of the priesthood was reconstructed on the model of the civil body, or rather of the military, since all the institutions shared in the military atmosphere amid which they were developed.

It was thus natural that the aristocracy's vices of greed and turbulence, and all the half barbarous practices of plunder, robbery, assassination, rape, and violence should at this time be shared by the priesthood. These vices and behaviour, however, were more noticeable in the priesthood owing to its apostolic mission. The errors of those who teach are always more serious than the errors of those who learn. Sin in a priest becomes a sacrilege. Simultaneously in Portugal and Spain at the end of the fourteenth century King Afonso IV (1325–57) and King Enrique III (1390–1406) harshly and bitterly reprimand the excesses of the priests. 'Most of the villains and criminals of my realm are tonsured' said the Spanish king; and the terms of the celebrated letter of the King of Portugal to the bishops concerning the 'crimes of the clergy' are well known.

But the corruption of the clergy was no exceptional fact in that aristocratic society; they followed the example of others; nor was the wrath of the monarchs based merely on a platonic love of justice. Although the Church with its imperial traditions was the natural ally of the throne, the ideas of Christianity concerning the origin of political power, ideas originating in the history of the Jewish people, demanded of the monarchs a submission against which they were inclined to rebel. At the same time the feudal ideas and institutions then prevailing in Europe gave to theocracy a new support, apart from that which in Spain it derived from the Visigothic monarchy. The Pope claimed for himself the suzerainty over all Christian countries; and it was not merely a spiritual suzerainty, since it was expressed in large pensions, in special privileges of the priesthood and in continual intervention in civil administration. The consecration of the Crown by the Church implied, or so the Popes claimed, a kind of feudal tenure; and the power of the Church became so great that many princes, among them the first King of Portugal, accepted its supremacy as a moral or legal support against the rebellion or independence of their own subjects. The bishops with their noble rank and estates, and the cathedrals and monasteries which by donation, inheritance, and other means had acquired privileged (*honrados*) domains, became, like the nobles, the natural enemies of the King; and they were more powerful than the nobles, since they claimed ecclesiastical as well as aristocratic privileges: their strength rested both on the force of arms and on the power of excommunication; and besides the support of their vassals they reckoned on the independent authority of the Pope, who in the name of God declared himself king of kings on earth. We have not here to chronicle the endless conflicts and civil wars provoked by the existence of these two powers face to face; we need only mark the general character of a movement which was one of the most serious with which the Middle Ages had to deal. The clergy not only demanded the same privileges as the nobility (that was never under dispute), but a universal authority over all the acts of civil life which religion sanctified. If the relations between Church and State were on this basis, it is evident that no social or political act whatever would be outside the jurisdiction of the Church, and that the power of the State would be an empty name. It is the part of religion to sanctify the acts of men; and this claim accordingly implied a government by priests, as in the East: a very different thing from a government inspired by the interests of religion, but exercised by a civil power, such as in time Spain came to possess.

As early as the thirteenth and fourteenth centuries, ever since the establishment of the monarchy at Oviedo, the restoration of the councils foretold the Catholic character of the future monarchies in the Peninsula; but even in the times of most fervent enthusiasm, in the reigns of King João III (1521–57) and Philip II (1556–98), those priest-kings, it is a mistake to imagine that Spain was ruled by the priests or by the Pope. Fervour for religion and purity of the faith were united in the heart of the sovereign with unabated zeal for the prerogatives of the Crown; and there is no better proof of this than the institution and history of the Inquisition.

Thus in the Middle Ages, while the priests claimed jurisdiction over all the acts of civil life which had the remotest ecclesiastical character (such as marriages, wills, contracts between or with priests or concerning ecclesiastical property), the kings, jealous of their own authority, always checked these claims and protected the privileges of the State, in such a way and with such compromises as at that time seemed to imply a separation between the two powers. Nor did their action stop here: just as, by revising titles and donations of property, setting up inquiries into the origin of landed estates and reincorporating in the Crown lands which seemed to rest on an insufficient title, the king attempted to prevent the vassalage of the nobles from becoming a mere form; so they attempted to oppose barriers, such as the laws of mortmain, to the enormous growth of Church property on which the power and independent influence of the clergy were based.

Although the modern monarchies in the Peninsula sprang originally directly out of war, in which the sovereign was the military chieftain of hordes or barbarian clans, they subsequently found a new source of strength in the tradition of Visigothic institutions. Thus the Crown, which in incessant warfare was merely the mark of military authority, also, in the eyes of the king, foreshadowed a civil sovereignty. Revived tradition showed him the path to follow amid change and revolt; and the monarchy sprang not so much from the forces and elements of society as from the influence of ancient traditions in the mind of the king. It was tradition, effectively supported by an agricultural non-military middle class, which prevented the spread of feudalism as the typical form of society in the Peninsula. It would be absurd nevertheless to consider tradition absolute in face of the facts which more or less decisively favoured its development: the existence of the Mozarab population and the coexistence and consequent conflict of the two opposed forces of democracy and aristocracy. In this conflict society must necessarily choose one of the rival institutions or a third with which they might combine or to which they must submit. This third institution was the monarchy; and the conflict, common to nearly the whole of Europe, had different results. In Switzerland, Italy, and Flanders democracy was victorious, although in a more or less incomplete or transitory manner;

in Germany aristocracy gained the day; England succeeded in balancing the opposing elements; while in Spain, as later in a different way in France, the outcome was submission to the monarchy. Meanwhile, although in the very beginning of the monarchy in Spain one can see the Roman-Gothic tradition defined, that tradition was only very gradually translated into fact. We have described the condition of the semi-feudal Spain of the Middle Ages, and it would be absurd to suppose the existence under such conditions of a monarchy with sovereign powers. In fact the idea of the national sovereignty being personified in the king was absolutely unknown to the early monarchs, and only arose in the twelfth century. The prince, instead of being a magistrate, exercises a merely personal authority. His collective individuality as monarch, so to speak, is not distinguished from his real individuality as chief of a clan. The wars made force the actual basis of authority and thus opposed the restoration of tradition. The king regarded the land he won as his personal estate, without remembering that, since he claimed to restore the ancient form of monarchy, it was really part of the realm. Although he was the heir of that monarchy, he bowed to present conditions and converted the realm into a personal estate, thus at one and the same time opposing and supporting the aristocratic system. This confusion between the new elements and the old marks the beginning of the incoherent and apparently unsystematic development of monarchies in the Peninsula; in their aristocratic tendency they seemed to point to a feudal solution, but in their assumption of sovereign power declared that there could be no other solution but that of monarchy. At first the monarchy wavered between election and heredity, until they finally adopted from the aristocratic system the hereditary principle, which, although it had long been the practice, only became legal in the fourteenth century. Even in the tenth century, when the Leonese monarchy was still elective, like the Visigothic monarchy before it, the electors, that is the nobles, bishops, abbots, and counts, very rarely made use of their right, which had become a mere formality. When the throne became vacant the electors merely acknowledged the new king, their sovereign by right of birth. Yet the period of transition lasted till the fourteenth century, since the right of heredity was accepted in practice but not yet recognized by law. But the monarchs considered their kingdoms their private property, and confused this with sovereignty (a confusion which is at the basis of the aristocratic system and which it was the eternal glory of the Roman legislation to have eliminated) to such an extent that, when in the Cortes of 1064 held at León, King Ferdinand the Great (1035–65) proposed that the realm should be divided among the nobles, and Sancho, his son and heir, rebelled against his decision, the King answered that he had won those realms in war and could do with them what he pleased. Thus it was that the kings openly withstood the destiny which history had in store for them and attacked the tradition which more or less definitely marked the development of the nation. The kings, unable to escape from the conditions with which they were faced, created and fostered the aristocratic system, making donations of lands, bestowing estates upon their favourites, distributing their property as they pleased and giving sovereign rights to the nobles and clergy, whose united power they were subsequently obliged to subdue. And at the same time the kings restored the Roman-Gothic administration, proving by this contradictory procedure how vague was the principle which guided them. The *aula regia* was restored, but with a different character, since posts in the palace were either hereditary privileges of the nobles or went with certain high ecclesiastical dignities, and in the Church the aristocratic principle of heredity had never been introduced. Thus the Constable, the modern equivalent of the ancient *Comes stabuli*, gives a feudal or aristocratic character to what was formerly a Court official; and in the same way the *Cancellarii* (the *Comes notariorum*) or Chancellors became in the Castilian monarchy a dignity vested in the Archbishoprics of Toledo and Santiago. As to the *Almoxarife*, that is to say the Minister of Finance or administrator of the royal treasury, he was usually a Jew; a fact which shows how the monarchy had to bow to the conditions of a society in which commerce and finance, offensive to aristocratic ideas and indeed to the Christian ideas of that time, were the privilege of a race proscribed by tradition and religion. The kings had *Adelantados* or frontier counts; but it not infrequently happened that these representatives of the royal authority, and themselves almost kings on their estates, preferred their own power and authority to that which they were supposed to represent. The tradition of royalty appears more living and vigorous in the legislation of the time. The *Fuero Viejo* of Castille says:

> Four things are inherent in the monarchy and the king may not alienate or renounce them, since they naturally belong to him; they are the administration of justice, the coining of money, summons to war, and certain taxes.

We have already seen that the royal privilege of coining money had but little value in the Middle Ages; the military system of the time shows us how illusory was the right to summon to battle; and we know how easily the payment of all taxes was evaded. It remains therefore only to see how real was the royal administration of justice. From what we have already said on this subject and what we will now mention, we may conclude that this royal privilege was in fact wholly or nearly annulled, by virtue of privileges granted by the Crown; by usurpations on the part of the nobles,

Church and lay, and of the towns; and finally by the methodical encroachment of canon law, both in theory and practice. The right to judge and condemn on their own account extended to the clergy, their land and vassals, the estates of the nobles, the military orders (an excellent example of the aristocratic character assumed by the clergy, a fact to which we have already referred), the towns, the *hermandades*, the guilds or colleges of artisans; and besides all these, several charitable establishments, such as hospitals and asylums. What then remained of the royal privilege? Apparently nothing; in fact a great deal: for among all these independent units of the social body the Crown, with its dominions, lands and vassals, was the greatest unit of all. The juridical tradition had become effaced, the monarchy had come to be considered an estate among other estates of various kinds; but since natural conditions gave the royal estate the superiority over all the rest, tradition had here a point on which to support itself and the monarchy a weapon with which it might ultimately subdue priests, nobles, and citizens. This is very evident from the fourteenth century onwards. The royal officials or *corregedores* replace the elective judges in the town councils, taking various names dating back to the days of the decay of the Roman Empire and the *municipia*, such as *majorini*, *praepositi*, *vicarii*, *villici*. The Crown officials enter private estates in pursuit of criminals; and the Councils of State (High Court, Collegiate Tribunal, Council of Castille),created anew or restored, are real supreme courts of justice which try cases of appeal from other special tribunals. In these councils, in which the monarchy shows a more definite sense of the tradition that upholds it, we find jurists replacing the priests, men educated in the schools of Italy and renovators of Roman law. This restoration of the ancient legal texts is indisputably the immediate cause of the new strength of the monarchies, for they enabled the monarchs to have a clear vision of their mission which had hitherto been vague and wavering, at the mercy of the more or less ambitious and domineering character of the prince.

An account of the Cortes will complete the picture of the traditional elements which went to form the modern nations of the Peninsula. As early as the ninth century the ancient councils of the clergy reappeared (with the same character as they had under the Visigoths) at Oviedo, León, and Astorga. The bishops, abbots, and nobles, convened by royal order (*jussu regis*), deliberated in public in the midst of a *silent* multitude, on both religious and civil affairs: *tam in ecclesia quam in palatio*, according to the expression of Alfonso the Chaste (791–842). One might think that here at least Spain was exclusively attentive to the monarchical tradition. But it was not so. The people which attended in silence now put forward new claims. The conditions which brought about the revival of the municipal system had given it a sense of its importance. The ancient *municipia* had been transformed into little States, after the fashion of the estates of the nobles, with their walls and towers, their cavalry and infantry and a more or less extensive district under their control round the walls of the town. If the estates of the nobles were represented in Cortes, why not the possessions of the towns? During the ninth and tenth centuries this question was persistently asked, and the claim gave rise to agitation and open revolts, those for instance at Sahagun and Compostela. In the renovation of the Cortes the new conditions of society, now as ever, imposed their will on the ancient traditions.

The representation of the towns was not due only to their military and economic importance; it was due to the wish of the monarch to have the usually friendly votes of the towns to oppose to the hostile votes of the clergy and nobility in the councils. The people were the support of the Crown against the nobles. Ávila sheltered, as prince, King Alfonso VIII (1158–1214), who started from that city to recover his realm from the rebellious barons. It was either at the Council of Burgos in 1169 or at the Council of León in 1188 that the delegates of the towns were first represented.

The modern parliament of the Peninsula is at length complete, with its delegates from the three estates, clergy, nobles and people. The nobles are present for two reasons, since even in the new organization of society the dual origin of the aristocracy is marked. There are no longer any personal distinctions between the aristocracy and the bureaucracy, the aristocracy of birth and that of office, the Gothic and the Roman; but they are still distinguished by the dignities they possess. The vassal princes of the Crown, the *infantes*, *ricos hombres*, *infanzones*, knights and Masters of the military orders, form the aristocracy of birth; and by their side sat the palace officials, judges, magistrates, and other high officials. The clergy likewise were represented in two ways: there were the priestly delegates of churches and monasteries, and there were lords of church lands in their own right, owing to the new aristocratic character given to the clergy in modern times. Finally the towns were represented, but only those which were vassals of the Crown; those which were vassals of the Church or of the nobles were considered sufficiently represented by those two estates. The number of the representatives varied according to the town's importance, nor was the manner of appointing them uniform. They were elected or took turns, or (and this seems to have been the most usual way) they were chosen by lot from the municipal officials; until finally the king assumed the right to appoint the proctors personally. Such were the Cortes, in which it would be a mistake to see anything similar to our modern parliaments. They had no legislative power, the proctors or representatives were not independent, nor was their meeting periodically fixed. The Cortes really only gave the king an opportunity to consult the opinion of the nation. They presented complaints to the king, gave their opinion on matters set before them by the king, and accepted and distributed the taxes which he levied. They did not legislate; and not only was it the prerogative of the Crown to convoke them, but the Crown alone had the right to select the members of the assembly from the ranks of the nobility and clergy and later from the town councils. They were a means of communication between the king and the nation and not a means for the nation to assert its rights before the monarch. Properly speaking, they were a great council of State, appointed and convened at irregular intervals, and not a political power acting in a normal and permanent fashion. They did represent the nation in an imperfect and rudimentary way, but not in such a way as to maintain its rights or carry out its will; they merely gave their opinion on the proposals or decisions submitted to them by the king.

This was their legal character, but in practice things were often very different. Conscious of representing the professional forces of the nation, its wealth and wisdom, they frequently laid claim to sovereign rights and set up their authority against that of the Crown, refusing to vote the subsidies which it demanded or presenting complaints which were rather protests and threats, if not a positive affirmation of their sovereign power or an open menace of revolt. The Cortes certainly tended to become a legislative power, instead of a merely consultative body; and this was what occurred in England, where the development of the nation took the form of a combination or balance between the opposing elements of which it was composed, as we have already pointed out. In Spain and France the same tendency existed, but it could not become a fact, because the development in both these nations was in the direction of pure monarchy. When both nations, after the strength of the monarchical principle had been exhausted in the course of four or five centuries, turned to study the historical development of England and set up monarchies of a modern parliamentary character, hoping to revive what was considered a real tradition, the disorders and revolutions of our time taught the learned renovators that history is not to be copied, that the elements composing society are not lifeless bodies for the anatomist to dissect. It is indeed evident that the monarchical solution given to the antagonism between social elements in the Peninsula in the fourteenth century could not hope to succeed in the nineteenth by a fictitious restoration of a balance between parties, when the organic conflict between them had been eliminated by five centuries of monarchy. We have already shown why the monarchical solution was unavoidable in the Peninsula, and why federalism and parliamentary control were alike impossible. We need not therefore return to the subject; but it remains to indicate the last of the traditional elements which gave a formal sanction to the centralizing tendency determined by the social elements composing modern Spain. This was the restoration of Roman law in a society beginning to revive on ancient lines, because through all the periods of decadence and foreign influences the *municipium* and its democratic form of property had succeeded in surviving and preserving the ancient form of society in its essential characteristics.

We have not here to give the history or even the chief landmarks of this gradual centralization and the consequent change from custom law to law of a systematic, general and philosophical character. In the modern codes of the Peninsula we see the coexistence of custom law, although more and more subordinate to general types, of canon law, and finally of Roman law. Of these three elements, with the addition of some special ordinances in the Castilian 'Partidas' and other codes, consisted the 'Ordenações Afonsinas' of the year 1446, revised and altered by King Manuel (1495–1521), who reformed the local privileges and from 1517 to 1521 reduced the whole body of national law to unity. If one compares this centralizing action with English law, in which neither codes nor any written constitution show a unification of authority, one sees the radical difference in the development of the Peninsula nations through centralization and the development of the English nation through the balance between irreconcilable elements, which were, however, always subordinate to the aristocracy of birth, the real sovereign. In Spain the first attempts to unify the legislation date from the middle of the twelfth century; the 'Fuero de Albedrio', promulgated by King Pedro (1196–1213), collated the municipal charters, and is the most important document in the history of the incorporation of custom into general law, which was at the same time reformed and codified. The Cortes of 1211 made a first attempt to restore civil equality and central administration of justice and to revive the tradition of the sovereignty of the Crown; and they also sought to extend the elective form of appointing municipal judges throughout the realm, to abolish the privileges of the nobles in contracts, to check the wealth of the clergy, and to encourage the conversion of Moors and Jews to Catholicism. The code of Alfonso the Learned (1252–84) in the middle of the thirteenth century marks an important epoch in the history of centralization; his 'Partidas', inspired on the one hand by Roman, on the other by canon law, are a faithful representation of the social condition of Spain, which was at once monarchical and Catholic. Tradition was at last victorious, and subdued the foreign elements originated by the events accompanying the long-drawn-out decay of the ancient world. Spain was once more Roman and Catholic; and just as her popula-

tion was able to absorb the various armies of foreign race
that invaded her, her genius now proved that it could
absorb the ideas that the foreigners had brought with
them.

The work of reconstructing the modern nation was
nearly at an end. The social tree had grown and
branched out, and the affirmation of religious faith
already indicated the nature of the fruit which this
slow evolution of the essence of the spirit of the nation
was to bring forth. But in order that the nation should
be strong enough to carry out the work which it already
unconsciously had in mind, it was necessary that the
inorganic elements still opposing unification should
disappear or be assimilated, and that a nation one in
spirit should likewise become one geographically. This
is what gives the reign of Ferdinand and Isabella (1479–
1516) its significance. The marriage of these princes
united Aragon and Castille; they proceeded to conquer
Granada in 1492, and after the queen's death King
Ferdinand in 1512 won Navarre. As two political
nations, Castille and Portugal, the Peninsula finally
took its place among the nations of Europe—two sisters
of like thought and united action. After eight centuries
of isolation, since the invasion of the Arabs placed the
frontier of Africa at the Pyrenees, Spain becomes one
of the European nations, and is soon in a position to
impose on them and on the world a hegemony founded
on the heroic force of her character and her strong arm,
on the vigorous unity of her faith and the solid strength
of her armies.

IV. THE CATHOLIC MONARCHY

THE fixed character of civilization in the Peninsula,
as shown in the various states into which it was
divided, was not effaced now that unity had been
attained. The sentiments which impelled the Castilian
or Spanish monarchy to the conquest of Oran in 1508

are the same that led the Monarchy of Avis to extend the dominions of the Portuguese Crown in Ceuta, Arzilla, and Tangier a century earlier. And not only the sentiments underlying these first rough beginnings of the expansion of their civilization were identical but many of the accidental characteristics were the same in the two sister monarchies.

We have already more than once insisted on the causes which led inevitably to the triumph of monarchy in the Peninsula. Since, in spite of all the invasions and aristocracies, Spain remained Roman and democratic, neither the aristocratic nor the federal system could suit her. To the latter the tradition of the Visigothic monarchy was an obstacle, while the coexistence of the aristocracy and the democracy and the consequent intervention of the Crown prevented the aristocracy from imposing itself. That was why the consolidation of the monarchies in the Peninsula at the end of the fifteenth century is marked by a simultaneous attack on the nobles, the towns, and the priesthood in their common share of aristocracy or feudalism: in the system of privileges, in their independence as military powers, their enormous wealth and in the fundamental characteristic of the whole system, the confusion between sovereignty and property.

In order to recover this divided sovereignty the kings had necessarily to attack those institutions and social forces and confiscate their privileges. But it is worth pointing out that they no longer act thus because they consider the realm their private property. Ideas on this point had become clearer, the restoration of Roman law, which was studied and commented at the Courts of the monarchy, having contributed to this. The kings now act as princes, conscious that the sovereignty with which they are invested is inherent in the crown, as the symbolical expression of the sovereignty of the nation; they no longer confuse their possession of power with the idea of private property belonging to the person of the suzerain. The distinction is essential; it marks the real principle of the revolution which we are studying. It is this new idea concerning sovereignty, destroying and replacing the old, which gives the monarchies strength to attack and overcome the resistance of the nobles, the citizens and the clergy, including among the latter not only the resistance of a powerful and wealthy class but the ultramontane or theocratic doctrine of the subordination of the State to the Church. Thus we find even the most enthusiastically religious and devout monarchs strenuously resisting the encroachment of the Papacy in civil administration.

The consciousness that the Crown represents and symbolizes the nation; that the sovereign is more than a mere individual since, if as a man he has his own feelings and interests, as king he represents the nation, to which even a crowned individual must subordinate himself—this consciousness gave to the monarchies their exceptional strength and to the kings a half impersonal character. Not infrequently we find the king as man humbly doing penance before a priest for acts which as prince he was constrained to perform against the Church. Even so, when the Duke of Alba victoriously entered Rome in 1557 at the head of his army, he proceeded humbly and contritely to kiss the Pope's foot and implore his pardon. This symbolical affirmation of national sovereignty gives the Spain of the fifteenth century a unique character among the nations of Europe. It was a democracy presided over by a monarchy. Charles V allowed all men to wear a sword 'that the people might be able to defend itself against the nobles'. And the people applauded the annihilation of privileges and the abasement of the nobility: the acts of the monarchs expressed the unanimous will of the nation. That is why they were so beloved; that is why there was agreement between the spirit of the nation and institutions which had grown up naturally in an organic development, and were thus the genuine expression of the national character; and this agreement gave Spain unity and strength sufficient to impose her will and thought upon the world.

The revolt of the Comuneros of Castille does not contradict this opinion; it supports it. The revolution of 1520, which carried to the scaffold the heroic Padilla and his companions, is not honoured because it was a protest against centralization. The revolution had a twofold character: it was made on behalf of special privileges; but it was more especially a revolt of the national spirit of independence against the invasion of foreigners; and hence it has become a glorious tradition. The Austrian prince who inherited the Crown of Castille in 1516 had no knowledge of Spain: from the height of his imperial throne he imagined that it was a barbarous country and that it would suffice to send a company of Flemings to take possession of the prize. This insurrection destroyed his illusions, and later Charles V, after all the chances of his dramatic life, left his empire for Spain, because experience had opened his eyes and had converted him, nationalized him a Spaniard. The revolutionary Junta of Tordesillas demanded that he should not leave Spain, that he should not give posts in his palace to foreigners, that he should not bring foreign troops into Spain, and that he should leave a Spanish regent when he was forced to absent himself—in a word, that he should be a Spaniard if he wished to reign over Spain. The prince accepted these terms and carried them out to the letter; but the revolution did not and could not stop. The Cortes of Santiago gave the answer to the last demand of the Junta of Tordesillas: that the election of proctors should be free; that is to say, that the sovereign rights of the towns should not be impaired, any more than those of the nobles and clergy; that the Middle Ages should continue and the work of Ferdinand and Isabella be disregarded. The citizens, nobles and bishops, all the little medieval princes, joined in the *hermandad* of 1520 and swore mutual alliance against the sovereign; from this point of view the revolution is the last of the revolts of a feudal as well as a communal character. The defeat of Villalar did not interrupt but confirmed the natural course of the nation's development, for Charles V realized that he must be a Spanish monarch and give up all idea of regarding Spain as a mere appendage of his empire.

Here and at other points we have broken through the chronological order of events because for us the logical order is the more important. The feudal-communal revolt of 1520 was subsequent to the consolidation of the monarchy; it belonged properly to the reign of Ferdinand and Isabella, but could only come to a head when an invasion of foreigners gave it a certain force and popularity. This proves how national was the centralizing tendency. In Castille it was only in the guise of national independence that revolution could raise its head; in Portugal it failed to break out because, as there were no foreigners, the people did not support the rebellion of the nobles. Thus in the history of the development of the institutions of the nation the revolt of the Comuneros is a last gasp of the dying aristocratic system on the part of nobles, clergy and citizens. In Portugal this dying cry of feudalism was smothered in the blood of the two dukes who raised the cry: the Duke of Braganza, who was beheaded, and the Duke of Viseu, who was stabbed to death by the king's hand.

King João II (1481–95), although he was thus an assassin, deserved in history the name of 'Perfect Prince', a proof of what we said above: that the recognition that the national sovereignty was symbolically expressed in the person of the monarch gave to the kings the ancient character of princes, who moreover were consecrated by the Catholic Church. The reason of State allowed them a different morality, and if they committed murder they were not to be confused with the assassin who kills for personal motives, since they were but carrying out the high justice of the nation. This symbolical definition of collective sovereignty as it were deprived the monarch of his individual character and gave a special meaning not only to the murders committed by kings but to their murderers. The king might be an assassin yet be considered 'perfect'; and the regicide was usually considered a hero. This was but the outcome of the principle of the reason of State—a principle underlying the political life of all peoples, whatever the form of their government, but which is especially prominent in a monarchy and loses force in proportion as the idea of national sovereignty discards its symbolical meaning and comes to be taken more and more literally. This was far from being the case in the meaning given to the idea in the fifteenth and sixteenth centuries; yet it was a necessary first step. It is objectively and historically, not by virtue of a moral, philosophical or abstract character, that the monarchies of the Peninsula in the fifteenth and sixteenth centuries mark the final step in the organic development of classes and institutions. To believe that the ideas and institutions which we now so wholeheartedly approve could exist in an abstract form at that time is to judge those times by our own—a way of writing history that has had its day, since we now realize that societies are beings which develop according to laws, not by caprice. Great as may be our knowledge and true our ideas, we can never succeed in making them enter the spirit of the nation if it is not previously ready to receive them; and for the idea of sovereignty to reach its present stage it was necessary for it to become separated from the feudal idea of property by means of the restoration of the ancient conception of the prince.

By various means the monarchs of the Peninsula succeeded in freeing their sovereignty not only from aristocratic but from ultramontane encroachments. The process was one and the same in the two countries, and the means employed were identical. King João I (1385–1433), in devising the 'mental law', and King Duarte (1433–38), in promulgating it, limited succession to property of the Crown to the eldest legitimate son, excluding women and collaterals; and, since most of the property in the Middle Ages had its origin in donations, it is easy to realize how great a blow this enforced reversion to the Crown was for the nobles. At the same time, as succession to property was thus limited, the inquiry or examination into the original titles of property continued; and in this way too many estates, held illegally under some alleged donation, reverted to the Crown. King João II restrained criminal jurisdiction and amplified the right of appeal to the royal courts; and at the same time he reinforced the oath or recognition of vassalage in the case of the mayors of the towns and all persons who received donations from the clergy or the nobles. King Manuel obtained from the Papacy not only a tithe for the crusades but a tenth part of all ecclesiastical property to do with them as he pleased. King João III, finally, incorporated the grand mastership of the military orders in the Crown. The creation of a *hermandad* in the pay and under the command of the king brought into existence a permanent army, with which it was easy to defeat the retainers of the nobles and the troops of the towns. This army was reinforced by the military orders, since the king, on becoming the grand master of Calatrava, Alcántara, and Santiago, became also the head of their troops, which had hitherto been dependent on the Papacy. The king, moreover, obtained from the Papacy the sale of bulls and right to appoint bishops; and while on the one hand the kings thus emancipate themselves from Rome, on the other hand they gradually emancipate themselves from the nobles and clergy by revising, annulling, and revoking grants of land, destroying fraudulent titles and recovering what their ancestors and even what they themselves had been constrained to part with in more difficult times.

The kings Ferdinand and Isabella, João II, and Manuel I were real sovereigns. Round the throne was grouped a galaxy of great men, the fruit of their past work: Ximenes and Columbus, the Great Captain Gonzalo de Córdoba, and Cortés, the conqueror of Mexico; Loyola, the founder of the Jesuits, Gama who discovered India, Diaz who rounded the terrible Cape of Good Hope, and the heroes of Africa, soldiers of a military school in which they learnt their subsequent task of conquering the East. The Moors were at last driven from the Peninsula; the victory at Granada was received with general rejoicing; and the wars in Africa added fuel to the religious and warlike fervour of the nation. The monarchy is the burning centre in which throbs the life of the whole body of the nation. If it annulled the privileges of the towns, it was not in favour of the aristocracy, but rather because the citizens copied the aristocracy. The monarchy now presides over a democracy; and privileges and birthrights are at an end. As in ancient Rome, aristocracy is now based on merit not on birth; the priesthood, war, and administration can ennoble, and these posts are open to the people, to every son of a serf who has the necessary talent. Pizarro had tended swine, and Ximenes from a humble friar became a second King of Castille. The aristocracy was thus renovated, and the younger sons went to the wars in search of honours, titles, and riches.

The ancient Cortes no longer had any reason to exist; the voice of the nation is heard by the king in his councils of nobles and lawyers. That was the true function of the Cortes; but when they claimed to represent the sovereignty of the nation, the monarchy, which felt that it was the real representative of this sovereignty, could by no means accept this claim. When all the privileges and classes had disappeared, how was the institution whose mission it was to balance the strife between them to be maintained ? The new situation was not a balance but unity; it was not an aristocracy nor federalism, it was a national united democracy in the old form, not of the Roman Republic, but of the Roman Empire, restored on the ruins of aristocracy and the towns, on the dead bodies of Padilla and the Duke of Braganza. The new government, so jealous of its authority, could not bow to the authority of the Pope. It is not that the kings had Protestant leanings, far otherwise: the Catholic faith was their very soul, and religious enthusiasm was the mainspring of the life of the nation. As kings and priests they were real sovereigns, since in their priestly character they faithfully represented the wishes of the people. They were indeed more Catholic than the semi-pagan Papacy itself; they charged it with indifference, and when it would not listen they claimed as kings to possess a spiritual authority, and with the goodwill of the people, and against the wishes of Rome, set up the Inquisition. The overseas discoveries and conquest brought new elements to the history of the Peninsula which were influential in the nation's decadence and not in its constitutional development or in the building up of its character. On the contrary it is the forces whose development we have described which characterized the Spanish empire overseas and in a sense made it the destiny of the Peninsula to discover and conquer new worlds. The history of those discoveries is reserved for another part of this book. We have reached the end of our voyage, like the nation itself, which has at last reached the haven to which it was sailing through the Middle Ages; and we could not better characterize this historical moment than by sketching the portrait of a man who was the real king of political Spain and the true representative of Spain's character: Cardinal Ximenes. The beginnings of the friar's life are obscure. He became a Franciscan and retired to the monastery of Castañar, where began his celebrity as a preacher and ascetic. His fame reached the ears of the throne and he became confessor of Queen Isabella and Provinical of his order. But in his new grandeur he did not abandon his ascetic life. Dressed in the coarse frock of a Fransciscan friar, the confessor of the queen visited the convents on foot, begging his way. In passing by Gibraltar he was tempted to cross into Africa to convert the heathen. He consulted a girl prophetess, a local saintly worker of miracles, but she dissuaded him. A vast work, she said, was awaiting him in Spain. We will not dwell further on this first period in the life of the all-powerful minister, for it resembles that of other mystics, and we shall have occasion later to study this side of the Peninsular character. The Ximenes we are here concerned with is the friar and *grand seigneur*, Archbishop of Toledo, and Minister of the Catholic Sovereigns. Humble in birth and character, he was in fact a king. He figured largely in the conquest of Granada and took the lead in converting and baptizing the Moors of Andalusia. He was a scholar as well as an all-powerful minister; and in publishing his Polyglot Bible(1514)[1] he showed how urgent he thought it to spread the sacred texts through the regions which Spain was daily adding to the civilization of Europe. Ximenes and the Great Captain are, with the Portuguese knights in Africa, the last figures of the Middle Ages in the Peninsula. In the government and in the field they united to consolidate the work of the monarchy. Incidents common in the life of Courts threw

[1] The Greek text of the New Testament was printed in this year. (Translator's note).

both these great men out of favour, and in their fall
they united to conquer the region of Tunis. Ximenes
was seventy years old, but he went with the army he
had raised to conquer Oran (in 1509), like a medieval
baron at the head of his vassals. This success did not
greatly please King Ferdinand, who wrote secretly to
the friar's general, Pedro Navarro: 'Prevent the man
from returning too soon to Spain. Wear him out
in purse and person. Keep him in Oran and fill his
head with new enterprises'.[1] Thus had things changed,
and the minister who had destroyed the Middle Ages
in the Peninsula now as a medieval battling prelate,
an armed apostle, suffered the consequences of the
work which he had laboured so ardently to accomplish.

[1] As a matter of fact Ximenes, aware of these intrigues, was back in
the Peninsula within eight days of setting sail from it on his victorious
enterprise, a marvellous feat in those slow times. (Translator's note.)

BOOK IV

THE SPANISH EMPIRE

I. THE GENIUS OF THE PENINSULA

HITHERTO we have studied institutions and classes; we must now change our method and seek in characters and individual lives the thread to guide us through the periods under our survey. The change is not a matter of caprice: it is imposed by the very nature of things. So far Spain has appeared to us like a great workshop in which the workmen prepare isolated pieces of the whole, and the materials lie in separate heaps in a scene of apparent confusion and disorder. The studies and learning of patient investigators make it possible for us now to classify and co-ordinate the materials of the national edifice and foresee to what purpose they are to be applied. The building now stands there finished and complete; each of its component parts occupies its proper place, in subordination to the general system; and the historian thus sees before him an harmonious effect, in which the independence and individuality of each of the parts yield to the unity of the whole. It is a superior organism, developed from the first rudimentary nucleus into a definite type. Nations are in fact collective beings, and their development is analogous to that of individual beings. Biology, the science of life, includes the history of peoples. The organs of social life appear at first as a rudimentary nucleus, and the cells gradually unite into a whole. In proportion as the action and reaction of the diverse elements force each of them to become a definite species, the principle of a common co-ordination—a kind of vital principle of the social body—makes itself felt; just as the organism develops from the primitive building up of cells. But as it develops and begins to attain the perfection of a type, the social body gives birth to thought, and this is at once the guiding principle and the internal spring which impels the organic being to develop and assert itself; just as the body, once formed, is in one sense the origin and in another the result of thought. It is the nature of thought to be expansive, and if organic life can be self-sufficient it is the peculiarity of moral life that it must imprint its own character on all its surroundings.

The history of a civilization consists therefore in three great periods, and the historian must change his point of observation accordingly. In the first period the various elements cling together and reduce history to a narrative of facts and a description of the conditions in which they occur; in the second the organism obliges the historian to study the systematic enchainment of institutions, customs, and class movements; finally, in the third period the inner thread of history is only to be found in deductions of ideas and in the expression of collective thought. It is evident therefore that the methods of observation must vary with the nature of the phenomena observed.

When a nation, after a slow and long evolution, attains that culminating moment in which all the forces of the collective organism are balanced, and all men penetrated by a common thought, which may and must be called the national soul, since it has the same character as what in individuals we call the soul, a phenomenon is seen which we shall call the synthesis of collective energy. The nation appears not as a merely mechanical being, as in its first stages; not as a merely biological being, as in the periods of more complex and advanced organization; but as human—that is, not only alive but animated by an idea. In these sublime moments in which the national tree produces its fruits the collective genius, grown definite in the thoughts of men, effects that mystery which in the symbol of religions is represented by the incarnation of a god. It becomes incarnate in the spirit of certain privileged individuals, and, clothed with that strength which only exists in the human heart, acts with heroic decision. All the great epochs of nations are marked by a galaxy of great men, in whose actions and thoughts the historian finds expressed individually those national ideas which previously had been developed collectively. The hero is great by virtue of the sum of national or collective spirit incarnate in him; and at a given moment the heroes embody the whole of that spirit. Thus it was in the Greece of the fourth century[1]; thus, after the slow development of modern nations, it was in the Italy of Leo the Tenth, the France of Louis the Fourteenth, and in the Peninsula in the sixteenth century which represented the full expression of its genius. Whereas accordingly at first we considered that the history of the nation could best be understood by following the slow anonymous evolution of institutions and classes, without dwelling on the occasional expressions of individual energy, we are now of opinion that it is only in such individual expression that we can find the thread of our history. The anonymous has become personal, and the choir of the historical tragedy ceases its chant and is replaced by the voices of the individual actors.

If these remarks apply as a philosophical law to the history of all nations, it is nevertheless certain that it is nowhere more evident than in the Peninsula, where the primary ingredients of the national character are distinguished by a spirit of heroic individualism superior to that of the inhabitants of any other nation of modern Europe. These preliminary remarks will have made the trend of our thoughts clear to the reader. 'Poetry and eloquence,' says Bouterwek in concluding his study of the literature of the Peninsula in the Middle Ages, 'during the first centuries of their existence developed spontaneously in their natural forms, without any man of superior genius to raise them or extend their frontiers.

[1] i.e. the Greece of the *fifth* century B.C. ? (Translator's note.)

Like the art of the troubadours, they were common property, under the protection of a literary democracy.' The spirit of this democracy and the basis of this property consisted in two sentiments which we shall find forming the nucleus of the souls of great men after being slowly evolved in anonymous or popular fashion in the great soul of the nation. That spontaneous literature of the Middle Ages in fact expresses on the one hand Christian mysticism and on the other the adventurous spirit which is crystallized in the romances of the Cid, the type of Spanish knight.

If the reader recalls our remarks concerning the primitive characteristics of the population of Spain, he will easily understand to what extent these fundamental marks of the national genius are the result of the natural temperament of the races which peopled the Peninsula. Everything points to the supposition that between the peoples which gave birth to the Essenians, the Therapeutae, St. Augustine, and the Christian Mystics, between those independent peoples which are still nomad in the North of Africa, and the mystical, adventurous inhabitants of the Peninsula there is a community of origin which history has not been able wholly to extinguish, although it has brought the latter into the heart of civilization and left the former in the depths of barbarism. Nothing, moreover, more resembles the monarchy of the Pharaohs than the theocratic monarchy of the Visigoths, leaving out of account the elements of European origin imported by ancient and modern conquerors and the facts which arose spontaneously out of invasion, and dwelling only on the type of clergy invented by the nation, the college of priests which in the Councils of Toledo inspire or sanction the government of the monarch. And after eight or ten centuries of slow evolution and assimilation of the new elements brought by successive invasions, Spain emerges in new strength, adventurous and mystic;

and the monarchy, permanently seeking its inspiration in those ancient traditions, raises to the throne two Pharaohs—Philip II of Spain, John III of Portugal. Let us not, however, allow ourselves to be carried away by our imagination or do violence to the facts and force them to fit into a too-general theory. The truth of considerations of this kind is not capable of proof: the mind must examine and decipher by means of the imagination those puzzles for which science provides no satisfactory solution. The exceptional and strange character of the history of the Peninsula in its greatness and its errors; the main characteristics which give this nation a place apart among the nations of Europe form one of these historical puzzles.

But history is not made up wholly of puzzles, and in considering the facts which constitute it we must always recognize how complex are its origins and how intricate the phenomena. Nothing is more false than systems of a too great simplicity in their tendency to provide an unvarying formula for diverse problems and to assign one cause alone for what is often the result of many causes acting conjointly. If organic life is so complex as, often in its phenomena and always in its origin, to elude any strict scientific definition, how should we expect to enclose within abstract rules social phenomena which are so far removed from logical or mathematical precision or from strict physical laws?

We have now studied the origins of society in the Peninsula; we have seen how various and numerous they were, in races, traditions, institutions, and in influences of every kind. This complexity of facts and of elements is the real foundation of the genius of the Peninsula, the splendid expression of which we shall now be privileged to witness. When we see the austere and squalid figure of a monk standing by the throne, at the side of a rough and daring warrior, humble only in questions of faith, it is permissible for us to inquire whether this form of monarchy has any precedents among other peoples. When, in addition to such similarity, we recall the early migrations of races, we think it allowable to put forward the theory that this adventurous and mystic spirit and priestly government represent in modern Spain the revival of an ancient growth.

We have followed the gradual development of the elements imported into the body of Spanish nations by historical events; and, by a combination and absorption of the early and later elements, those that were constitutional, and those that came by chance; we have seen the formation of a new being which has a share of all these diverse elements accumulated during centuries and assimilated in such a way as to form an organism so perfect that in the midst of the nations of Europe it has the merit of being different from all of them and therefore has the power to impose its grand originality upon them.

Up to the fifteenth century the history of the Peninsula presents the spectacle of collective and anonymous movements: the masses and the classes, confused together and impelled indefinitely by vague feelings and aspirations, collide and mingle like elements of the universe. Institutions are outlined in a shadowy, rough, incoherent fashion, like all the spontaneous manifestations of Nature. To the confusion inherent in these elements is added the greater confusion arising from perverted traditions of ancient civilizations and the broken, ruined remnants of ancient institutions. The moulding hand of society has to group harmoniously and render organic not only the incoherent spontaneous natural elements but the scattered fragments of organisms from which life has fled. This evolution is slow, painful, and obscure. From this darkness, in which the worlds travail, from the depths of this morass in which life ferments, the creative forces of Nature break forth and produce true types of a beauty which is but ephemeral: the picturesque figure of the Cid, the gentle image of the Virgin in sacred poetry; and again the 'hermandades' and the 'behetrías'. The soul of the people gets types for which it has an essential adoration, and society in its first rudimentary phase seeks the fixed organism which is its goal.

All this is now at an end; the aspirations have been attained; a unity has been constituted, both in ideas and institutions. Catholicism and monarchy, both perfected, put an end to the development which tended to define and build up those types; and this new stability coincides with the final expulsion of the Moors from Granada. The eight formative centuries are centuries of war, for while there was a Moor left on Spanish soil national unity might exist in men's minds but could not be a geographical fact. However free may be the spirit of man, it has always found it indispensable to bind down its faith with real facts, which it transforms into symbols. Catholic and monarchical, the constitution of Spain, composed exclusively of Spaniards, is now complete. Bounded by the ocean and the Pyrenees, the Peninsula is as a giant in whose breast life throbs; his arms are vigorous, his head afire with the thought of God, his heart glowing with ambition. Eight centuries of brooding have made manifest to this country a faith which for her is the eternal truth. Eight centuries of warfare have strengthened her muscles and taught her skill in arms. Eight centuries of internal and painful disquiet have filled her with ambition and with a burning thirst for conquest, pleasure, and empire. She feels herself strong; she believes that the truth is hers alone. Each of her members is a great man: Cardinal Ximenes, Loyola, Camões, Columbus, Cortés, Gama, Pizarro, Albuquerque, Calderón, Santa Teresa, Lope de Vega, Cervantes, Murillo, Ribera, Torquemada, the fierce inquisitor, the Duke of Alba, the devout and ruthless captain, Philip II of Spain and John III of Portugal, rash monarchs who reduced their realms to ashes, as a holocaust to a chimerical purity of the faith. Before the first explosion of Spanish strength and genius everything yields: nothing is able to resist those heroic arms nerved by a burning faith. Europe bows her head, Nature is forced to yield up her secrets. They conquer the known world and discover fresh worlds to conquer:

> And had there been more world they would have
> reached it! [1]

After expelling the Moors, they pass over to Morocco, advance to Tunis, and from Italy defend all Europe against the Turk, more fortunate than its defenders on the eastern bulwark of Hungary. France, Venice, even the Papacy yielded to the strength of the new barbarians, made treaties and alliances with them: only heroic Spain remained uncompromising, and her heroism was crowned on the terrible day of Lepanto (1571), which freed Europe definitively from the fearful menace of the Turk. These extraordinary exploits overstepped the limits which Nature imposes upon the daring of men. The legend of the Titans was repeated on earth, and the swift heroic splendour of the sixteenth century was succeeded by reaction and the dark workings of destiny. History then once more obeyed its ancient laws, and social life in the Peninsula, in organic dissolution, sank from stage to stage until in our time the observer may see in it something of the collective anonymous movements of the Middle Ages.

II. MYSTICISM

THE peculiar character of mystic Spain is another confirmation of our remarks concerning the probable origin of the peoples of the Peninsula. The innate mysticism of the Spaniard is not metaphysical; it is moral. Santa Teresa and San Ignacio do not reach the

[1] Camões, *Os Lusiadas*, VII. xiv.

state of vision by way of philosophical speculation, as in the case of the mystics of Alexandria; there is no intimate link between the disciples of Plotinus and those of San Ignacio. Mystic Spain has a dislike for philosophy, and thus neither the investigations of science nor the lucubrations of metaphysics illuminate the pages of her history. The mystics form no school; they spring from the soil individually and spontaneously, in the words of a modern critic. They are the expression of what is indigenous in the psychology of the nation, and one would seek in vain to connect them with a learned origin or the influence of a school. But this spontaneous birth does not imply that the influence of the Jewish schools, heirs of Averroism (an influence mainly evident in the writings of Fray Luis de León), had no share in the development of the mysticism of the Peninsula.

The spontaneous, unlearned origin and the moral non-metaphysical character of Spanish mysticism constitute the newness, eminently strange in Europe, of this mental phenomenon, which is certainly the most important factor in determining the general character of the nation and the undoubted mainspring of its extraordinary energy in the sixteenth century.

Psychological, that is, born of intimate observation and introspective analysis, created with the moral elements which the Spanish soul found within itself, this mysticism stood opposed to the heroism and the love of personal independence which had always been the distinctive characteristic of the nation, and tended, as is the wont with such mental states, to crush individual energy. We know how irreconcilable with absorption in God is the affirmation of man's independence. We know that all kinds of mysticism, starting from a system of absolute definitions of the universe and of God, of the real and transcendental, subordinate everything to the one and, as it were, annihilate everything in it.

How did the Spanish genius resolve this difficulty? The fact that the Spanish mystics were not philosophers provided them, as a privilege of ignorance, with a solution. The creative force of Nature produced spontaneously a strange phenomenon in Europe. The Spaniard discovered in mysticism a basis for his heroism and in divine love the best support for his strong arm. Instead of allowing himself to be absorbed by heaven, he absorbed the divine element. By so doing he gained a superhuman strength, the energy of his will-power becoming the will of God incarnate in him. Spanish mysticism is thus peculiar, unique and really new: it affirms the will of man; it is naturalistic. In the attempt to balance more or less stably freewill and predestination, reason and grace, scholastic theology had laboured and failed. The Spaniard, in ingenuous ignorance of that struggle but illuminated by an internal vision and impelled by a fierce innate feeling of independence—the Spaniard without systems or schools or learned traditions could not solve the problem by means of subtle combinations unless he were at the same time to renounce his own self and his heroic soul, committing suicide in God. He inquires, meditates, observes; and from the most intimate depths of his soul draws a paradoxical solution which amazes the doctors and provides Catholicism with a new support against the classical mysticism of the Reformation. And he sets out to conquer the world with the sword and the sacred word, just as the Almoravides had come from the borders of the Sahara to conquer Morocco and Spain. Everything leads to the belief that had it not been for the Jesuits the theological revolution carried through in the Council of Trent would not have occurred, and that victory would have remained with the advocates of conciliation: Charles V in politics and Contarini among the theologians.

Let us now rapidly analyse the psychological method

of Spanish mysticism. How does it reconcile Freewill and Grace? How can the love of God reign absolutely without sacrificing the will of man? How can it fail to annihilate and destroy this freewill? The love of God, says Santa Teresa, moves and guides the will, yet is the latter free. The worth of a soul is due to its choice of the object of its love, and it therefore cannot lose its freedom of such choice. Man is thus distinguished from things by the noble privilege granted him by God to determine freely his destiny, whereas things blindly obey the predestined law of their existence. We do not propose here to make a methodical study of Spanish mysticism and need not therefore pause to set forth and criticize its tenets; but we could not omit to describe its main characteristics without allowing history to remain an enigma to us. In mysticism, as we have said, is to be found the primary source of that extraordinary strength, that manysided and universal action of Spain in the sixteenth century. Were we to dismiss this as a miracle, we should be substituting for science which observes and describes a rhetorical eloquence in ecstasy, since no one may now believe in miracles, to use a popular expression. If on the other hand we were to slur over the truly exceptional character of the history of Spain in the sixteenth century we should be giving proof of limited vision or ignorance.

The history of that age is a miracle of human energy. Its light centres in mysticism, the fountain-head from which sprang action, strength, and a marvellous faith in invincible human will. It took centuries to forge the flame which now flashes forth, just as a fire works underground until in a moment it breaks into a blaze. The fuel on which the mystic fire fed in the Spanish Middle Ages was the war against the Moors and the literature of the romances of chivalry and of Scripture. Thus this mysticism at first discovered itself to us as a transformed, a divine romance of chivalry, in Santa Teresa, in the life of St. Ignatius, and in St. John of the Cross. Such titles of books as 'The Heavenly Knight', 'The Christian Knight', 'The Knight of the Gleaming Star', sufficiently declare this well-known fact. Santa Teresa and her brother, two children (she was but ten years old), feel themselves heroes, their heads are full of the strange events of the mystic romances of chivalry and of the adventures of 'The Thousand and One Nights'. One day they run away from home and set out on their adventures, their object to seek martyrdom at the hands of the Moors. A league from Avila came their rout of Alcacer Kebir, when their family found them and took them home. This heroic rage to defend the oppressed and champion the unfortunate now became general. And the divine oppressed is Christ, the victim of the Jews who crucified him. Hatred of the Jews was closely entwined round the tree of mysticism, like ivy on the trunk of an ancient olive. The mystics are tragic or ingenuous, just as the Spanish soul combines in a natural candour with violent explosions. This violence is represented in the pictures of Zurbarán and Herrera and Ribera—trivial, coarse, brutal, violent, and mad: haggard monks, dreadful visions, tortured Prometheuses, human monsters in agony lying on dark cloths against a black background, with patches here and there of blinding light. There is a glowing purity in the pictures of Murillo, bathed in light and blueness, in which bunches of fair-haired angels play amid flowers and palms and crown the Virgin's brow or twine about her throne. The pictures of Murillo correspond in paint to the hymns of Santa Teresa to her 'sweet lover'; just as the pictures of Ribera represent the visions and awful fears of St. Ignatius before his journey to Italy.

In painters and saints alike Spanish mysticism has a peculiar character which evidently springs from its peculiar growth: this character is realism. Critics have often noticed the difference between the Virgins of Murillo and the Madonnas of Raphael. The Spanish artist lacks that indefinite expression of a vague idealism which pervades the work of the Italian: the Virgins of Murillo belong to this world. They are beautiful Andalusian girls. In the same way the love of Santa Teresa is a real love, not an idealized ecstasy. These mystics feel and see the object of their love. Their feelings are real; they express emotions of the senses, not states of speculative reason. Hence an apparent contradiction which has been noticed in the Spanish mystics, and more especially in the Jesuits. They reduce the ecstatic vision to rules and thus render it paradoxical and repulsive. The method and rule, the positive and practical aspect, the exact symptoms of ecstasy and the means of producing them are dryly catalogued in the Instructions of Saint Ignatius. Santa Teresa had already given her love a local habitation: 'This secret union occurs in the inmost centre of the soul, where God himself must dwell'. What is there then wonderful or surprising that they should have actually prescribed the methods and fixed in minute and precise detail the means of attaining real communion with God? This phenomenon, even in its most paradoxical aberrations, discovers to us the peculiar and original character of Spanish mysticism. Instead of the soul shunning and denying the world and losing itself in the fire of a God of the imagination, as happened in Neo-Platonism, it was man who obliged God to descend into the soul. Spanish mysticism is naturalistic; the mysticism of Alexandria was idealist. The former makes the world divine; the latter denied the world in the name of the Absolute. We may then conclude that the Spanish made a religion out of individualism, raising the feeling of independence in the soul to the point of making it divine. The dangers and evils, the fatal consequences

of this divinization of man, of this perversion of the
conception of the Absolute, soon made themselves felt;
but it is none the less certain that without this mad
rapture no nation could have achieved what Spain
achieved in the sixteenth century. It may be said that
for a moment we were as gods and omnipotent.

III. ST. IGNATIUS OF LOYOLA

Over against the solution given by Spain to the
crisis in the Christian conscience of the sixteenth
century stands the solution given by the genius of
another race, the Germanic, personified in Luther.
More than once a formal contrast has been drawn
between the founder of Protestantism and the founder
of the Company of Jesus, in order to deduce con-
clusions concerning these two different solutions and
the genius of the peoples that devised them. An
investigation of this kind falls outside our plan. We do
not require it in order to delineate the character of the
Peninsula; we are not called upon to apply it to Germany, nor can we here embark on a study of Christianity
in the Middle Ages, which must necessarily end in the
conflict and reforms of the sixteenth century. Suffice
is to say that, given the difference between the genius
of the two peoples and the consequent difference in the
solution given to the crisis, the mental attitude of the
German monk and the hermit of Manresa are identical.
Both are torn by doubt and both seek to end their
agonies and attain peace of conscience by a reformation
of the faith. Both had dived into the obscure depths
of the soul and had despaired of being reconciled to
God by the means provided by their religion. One
seeks this reconciliation through Christ, through His
merits, through grace, without the necessity of works;
the óther finds peace in heroic obedience to the Church
which maintains the value of works and the inde-

pendence of the human will. The one rebels against the Pope: 'I plagued thee living, dead I'll kill thee, Pope'; the other offers to this same Pope the unconditional obedience of the Company of Jesus. Never before had the inherent difference between the genius of the peoples of Latin and of Germanic culture been so clearly marked as now when one of the cardinal tenets of that Christian religion in which both believed was at stake. A slackening of discipline and lukewarmness in the faith had rendered the religion of Rome incapable of satisfying scrupulous spirits, and the consequence was a crisis in many a conscience. The ancient authority being discredited, the faithful found in the living depths of their own conscience the elements for a religious reconstruction. On the one hand the Protestants protested against that authority which had been unable to maintain itself in unstained nobility; on the other hand the Jesuits sought to renew the decayed organism and reconstruct the ruined building, repeating in the sixteenth century the work of the Mendicant Orders in the twelfth.

These battles have now become a matter of history, and we can estimate the merits of the combatants with the calmness of mere spectators; for the modern spirit, rationalist and scientific, is not immediately connected with either of those parties; its origin is to be found in the sixteenth century, but between the two camps and outside the conflict. Our real ancestors are not the Jesuits nor the Protestants but the humanists, who, with Erasmus at their head, realized the dangers and uselessness of dragging those discussions from the intimate and individual ground of metaphysics to the collective ground of the religious conscience, in which they produced two illusions, different in outward aspect but equally perverse, equally vain: the Catholic formalism of the Jesuits and the Protestant ravings of the Anabaptists.

But if one were obliged to choose between them, the thinker would abandon the Protestants, as Erasmus abandoned them, to their dangerous fate. There is no doubt that the obedience of the Catholics to the authority of the Church constituted an attack on religious liberty; there is no doubt that the Jesuits carried this attack to paradoxical lengths; but there is likewise no doubt that this formal slavery was the price of moral liberty. At the price of obedience the Catholic, for whom virtue consisted in good works and the choice between good and evil, felt within himself a spring of freedom which ennobled him and made him capable of raising himself to God. The Protestant, in rebelling against the authority of the Church, gained an apparent liberty, but only apparent, because it was merely a matter of discipline and dogma. Predestination and the grace of Christ, in the name of which he denied the power of the Pope, fell on the rebel and, breaking the internal spring of his moral independence, reduced him to a transcendental slavery. Will it be rash or fantastic to see in these different ways of regarding man's destiny the principal cause of the different character of the dominion and influence of Protestants and Catholics in the world? We think not. Catholicism produced heroes. Protestantism produced sensible, happy societies, rich and free in respect to institutions and external economy but incapable of great actions because religion had begun to destroy in the heart of man that which makes him prone to daring and noble sacrifice.

The founder of the new Catholicism is St. Ignatius, and through him something of the genius of Spain passes into the body of the religion of Latin Europe: that is the first and noblest way in which Spain conquered the world in the sixteenth century. This champion or Cid, who sets out from the depths of Catalonia in order to reconquer for God the Church in jeopardy, undertakes a voyage as dangerous as that of Columbus when he set sail from the port of Palos. The life of St. Ignatius, up to the time when his journeyings cause it to belong not to one nation but to Europe, is a fine example of the mystic genius of the Peninsula, as is that of Columbus when, after leaving Italy, years of residence in the Peninsula gave a Spanish national cast to his genius, as we shall presently see.

Ignatius was a young soldier, spirited, almost a swash-buckler, a courtier, worldly, vain, proud of his good looks and of their effect on women. He was of noble birth and rich, and had a reputation for courage. There is nothing exceptional about these characteristics, but his biographers add a significant trait: he was subtle and astute in his way of dealing with questions of honour and other matters. One of the aspects of Jesuitism was derived from this circumstance. In the siege of Pamplona in 1512 a fragment of shell broke both his legs. They carried the wounded man to his home at Loyola in Vizcaya. The cure was long and painful, and through the surgeons' lack of skill he was left a cripple. This offended his vanity. How was a cripple to pay court to the fair countesses in the Madrid palace? He foresaw their covert smiles and the ridiculous part fate had in store for him. These thoughts were torture. Unable to accept the idea of such a fall, he consulted the surgeons and ordered them to break his legs again in order to effect a more radical cure. This they did, and the captain, although not completely cured, for he always limped a little, was now a different man.

During these months when he was tied to his bed, the fear of having to give up his former life of gallantry, tedium, the boredom of futile persons when they find themselves alone, pain, sleepless nights, long days, endless hours, inspired him with a desire to read, the only amusement possible in his present condition. Books to

him had been an unknown world, and reading was a
voyage of discovery. Is the world after all not limited
to war and courts? Are there so many things of which
I was ignorant? So many and so great? What madness
has been mine!

He read *Amadis*, and those knightly adventures
showed him how mean was the prowess of which he
had been vain. Then he read the *Flos Sanctorum*,
the Plutarch of Christian readers. Here was true
chivalry and mighty deeds! This is a new world; here
is the enterprise reserved for me by heaven. Chivalry
became a symbol, realized in the saints: St. Dominic,
St. Francis, these were his models: I will be as they, I
will do as they did!

And the lady of his thoughts underwent the same
transformation as the goal of his ambitions: no countess
now, no duchess, but greater than these, even the
Virgin. For the sake of the Mother he offers himself to
the Son, as a loyal vassal to his sovereign. The high
emprise of this new crusader is still the conquest of the
holy places. He will go to Jerusalem to wrest the holy
prize from the Turk; he will redeem with his blood
the sublime captive, the sepulchre of Christ.

Such thoughts fill his brain with a new excitement;
the horizons of his life are enlarged, and his blood boils
with impatience to be well, while a multitude of mystic
sentiments surge up in his heart. He cannot sleep; he
lives on his enthusiasm. One day his lady, the Virgin,
appears to him, and henceforth, his windows open wide
both day and night, his delight is to gaze at the sky, to
watch the stars and transport himself in spirit to the
El Dorado of his ambitions. Beyond those walls of
blue studded with stars dwells the lady of his thoughts
and the lord whom he has sworn to serve. When,
humbly but triumphant, will he be able to claim the
reward of his valour? His head, formerly so hollow,
is now full of visions, and the weariness of those first

weeks of loneliness is now changed into a rapture of feverish imaginings.

He is no sooner well than he leaves his home, his family. On the road he meets a Moor who as he went mocked at the Virgin. Loyola draws rein, while the Moor goes on his way. He unsheathes his dagger: shall he follow and kill him to revenge his lady? He hesitates. New ideas are already at war in his mind with the divine romance of chivalry. What shall he do? The casuist in worldly questions now reappears, the future weaver of subtle cases of conscience. He has recourse to the mule he was riding and loosens the reins for it to decide. He was at cross-roads, and the road which the mule chose would resolve the doubt in his mind. The mule decided in favour of the Moor, who certainly never knew to whom he was indebted for his life. Thus the divine Don Quixote arrived peacefully at Montserrat. Here he made his knightly vigil at the feet of the Virgin, in imitation of Amadis; he placed his worldly dress on the altar and donned a beggar's rags. He spent three days in confessing his sins to a monk. He was now fully equipped and ready, inside and out, in body and soul, to begin his campaign; and he set out for Manresa.

In proportion as his mind realized the importance of his work, grew the need to repress and chastise the rebellious body. The dualism became evident, the need of earthly degradation as an indispensable condition of heroism to win heaven. During the period of his sojourn at the hospital of Manresa his biographers describe him with the characteristics of an Indian fakir or an African hermit. He fasted daily on bread and water, only allowing himself the luxury of boiled vegetables on Sunday. Under his coarse cloth he wore a hairshirt and round his neck a chain of iron; he scourged himself thrice a day; he never washed. He presented himself in rags and dirty, his face covered with mud, dust of the earth he kissed mingling with the sweat of his sorrows; his hair, beard and nails unkempt, uncut. The street-urchins whistled as he passed and threw stones at him; he had become a general laughing-stock. One day, however, it became known that this marabout was of noble birth, and instead of being stoned as a madman he was worshipped as a saint. He fled at once, fled from everyone to his celebrated cave at Manresa. You might imagine he was an old-fashioned mystic of the first centuries of Christianity, a stylite or even a would-be suicide. You would be wrong: he was a Spanish saint or a Moroccan marabout. He flees from the world not in search of annihilation but of new strength; in his utmost abasement the enthusiasm for his high emprise does not desert him; it is as a means to that that he does what for others might be an end in itself. He does not consider himself yet sufficiently purified, or the old man in him completely dead. His abasement is the flame in which he purifies his ambition. He had confessed all his sins and received absolution; but now new scruples assail him: had he not forgotten something, omitted certain details; and if his conscience was not yet clear how could he consider himself worthy to go to Jerusalem?

Such was his spiritual state in the cave of Manresa. Good and evil seemed to him two knights engaged on a tournament within his soul, armed with lance, helmet, and shield and mounted, the one on a steed of light, the other on a black steed of darkness. Christ assisted the knight who came from Jerusalem, and Satan the knight who came from Babylonia. The thought maddened him; in his despair he attempted suicide. Prostrate, during sleepless nights, his mouth full of earth and his limbs drenched with water, he implored God to enlighten him. In vain. Illness then attacked him; he could no longer assimilate food, one of the certain conditions of the mystic. Who will save him? Will no one deliver him from these insufferable torments?

Will no merciful confessor bid him forget everything? Obedience alone can save him. When this idea dawned in the spirit of the tortured man the first nucleus of Jesuitism was found: obedience, peace of mind through being irresponsible, the supreme decision in questions of conscience, and consequently in all questions, being assigned to one's superior. So was pure monarchy established in the realm of the spirit at the same time as absolute monarchy was established in the government of Spain. This was the decisive crisis. The fact of having no one to obey completed his inability to take food and entirely deranged his mind. For a week he ate nothing, and at the end of it, as in Genesis, the world was finished. God appeared to him. He saw the Trinity. All the secrets of life, all the mysteries of the Scriptures were revealed to him. This finally decided him to find in himself the authority which he had wished to obey in another. Obedience was the mainspring of his doctrine, but it was his part now not to obey but to command. The old man was dead; the new felt able to carry out his enterprise.

At this period his biographers place his connexion with the devout woman of Manresa, another celebrated seer who was consulted by King Ferdinand himself, and generally with the sect of the Alumbrados, whose spiritual history is that of Santa Teresa or of St. Ignatius. Nothing is more natural than such a connexion based on identical states of conscience; but, whatever may have been its value, the fact is that the solution of obedience discovered by St. Ignatius and the subsequent character of his life prevents this connexion from having a moral or historical importance.

At length, being now enlightened, he leaves Barcelona for the Holy Land. The sea air restores his health, and observations made in Italy and France modify his ideas, giving his madness a practical cast. He returned a different man. He saw how chimerical was his enter-

prise; he realized that the sepulchre of Christ to be
redeemed was not at Jerusalem but Rome. At Rome
the living Christ was buried and awaited the hour of
His resurrection. He realized that in the sixteenth
century, in a Europe intoxicated by intellectual culture,
mendicant knights without culture or means of subsistence had little to expect. Finally he realized that
obedience must be not merely internal but a practical
rule, and that it was not by creating a new authority
but by giving new life to the old authority of the papacy
that the crisis of Christianity could be solved. He left
Spain as a seer; he returned from Jerusalem as a mis-
sionary of a new kind suited to the times in which he
lived. It is this adaptability and the moral grandeur of
his genius that make him the first of the epic figures of
sixteenth-century Spain.

Realizing his ignorance and the madness of his ways,
he began to live a more ordinary life; he considered
that he required a new initiation in order to appear on
the world's scene. He lays aside his pilgrim's scrip and
iron chain and contents himself with a hairshirt and an
ordinary, not too ragged, cassock. He goes to Barcelona
in order to prepare himself to be able to study theology
at Paris. His sphere of observation becomes general
because he has seen the world and knows that he is
going to act on it in a certain special way. He has
passed from dreams to reality. Study is now his main
business, and the doubts that now assail him are quite
different from the old. Other thoughts distract his
mind from grammar as he studies Latin verbs, thoughts
of his lady as he conjugates *Amo amas*. He takes hours
from prayer in order to give them to study. When
setting out for Paris he does not refuse the money
offered him by his friends as he had refused when he
set out for Jerusalem, because he has learnt that without money he would be able to effect nothing. Was
he growing worldly? No. The inner strength of his

will was not being bent and could not be broken. That flame did not cease to burn; it had been steadfast in his delirium of mystic abasement; it was steady now before the needs of practical method. His thoughts underwent various phases, as it grew clear and definite, but it remained essentially unchanged. Yet in proportion as he adapted himself to the conditions around him he became less national. In Paris St. Ignatius only remains a Spaniard in his vigour of spirit, in all else he is a European, French or Italian. Ever since the time of the Visigoths the Church in the Peninsula, with the King at its head, had in spite of intricate conflicts constituted a body opposed to the Italian organization at Rome; and in the sixteenth century itself the Inquisition in Spain and Portugal was a royal institution created and maintained in the teeth of the opposition of Rome. Yet we must not forget that the papacy which the Jesuits were to obey was to be an institution reformed in Spanish fashion. For obedience to be possible a revolution was first required.

In Paris and with Spaniards the Order was founded and received the name of the Company of Jesus. Fellow students and religious comrades, Francisco Xavier, Bobadilla, Laynez, Salmerón, Rodriguez, the Savoyard Lefèvre, form the nucleus of the future all-powerful society. For a moment the old rhapsodies seem to return. The new Company remembers the old dreams of the Holy Land. They felt their conscience bound by this old pledge. They assembled at Venice and referred their destiny to chance: if during the next year there were a ship to take them to the East they would go; if not, they would remain in Europe. It was a repetition of the device of St. Ignatius on the road to Montserrat. The thought of the Holy Land revives old memories, and for a moment at Venice these first Jesuits recall the fakir of Manresa. On the same day, and at the same hour, says an historian, they appeared in various streets, and, standing on milestones and waving their hats, vehemently exhorted the faithful to repentance in a garbled Spanish-Italian which nobody could understand. Finally they pass onward to Rome, whither their destiny called them, and entirely abandoned monasticism. Their company included men of exceptional ability: Laynez and Salmerón, as theologians, guide, inspire, and lead the renewal of Catholicism in the Council of Trent; Azevedo founds at Coimbra a college which is the first step in the reform of studies at the University; Xavier sets out for the New World to convert it to the faith, and fills the old world with amazement at a charity and heroism which eclipse even the courage of the soldiers and discoverers. For his part Loyola, at the centre of Christianity, at Rome, at the head of the Order, is the real Pope of the new Catholicism.

Thus the Spanish genius spread over and conquered Europe by reforming its religion. If this reform subsequently proved suicidal, the responsibility for the fact does not rest with Spain.

> The character of Jesuitism (says a modern historian) born in Spain, nurtured in France, developed at Rome, consists in the assimilation of that cosmopolitan spirit which Italy at that time brought to every aspect of life. On this account it is in agreement with the spirit of the South in the Renaissance. It is so on another account also, in that it gave over the asceticism and self-torture of the Middle Ages. Its first dream in Spain was that of the conquest of the Holy Land; in Italy it became practical: its desire was no longer to obtain possession of a tomb but to obtain possession of the living in order to reduce them to dead bodies.

After the renaissance of classical naturalism it was indispensable that the pessimistic Christianity of the Middle Ages should be reformed and brought into line with the spirit of the age in Europe. The Protestants carried out such a reform; they gave a place of honour to free examination of conscience, honest work, serious marriage and family life, honest wealth: all the sober qualities which predominate in the genius of the Northern peoples. The Jesuits conceived and carried through a reform of the religion of the peoples of the South in a different spirit, by modifying the terrible doctrine of grace, glossing over the rigid rules of the doctors of the Church, and inventing a tolerant spiritual direction, a lax morality, an easy casuistry, a facile devotion, and the doctrine of probabilism. They made a suitable and indulgent religion, and, to make it consistent, entrusted to a methodical and mechanical guidance of the imagination the part which in Protestantism belonged to the voice of conscience and an orderly existence. With the clear vision of genius the Company discovered the true principle of educating men: to build up a sensuous atmosphere of the imagination which might give birth to ideas, suitably to prepare the material in which to mould and fashion thoughts. Protestantism proceeded from the inside to the outside of man, Jesuitism reversed the process. The one was a republic, with the problems of all its doctrines treated idealistically, the other was Caesarism, with all the practical problems of a religious State.

IV. CHARLES V AND THE COUNCIL OF TRENT

THE Spanish monarchy was the first among those of modern Europe to succeed in making the power of the throne absolute. As a result of historical traditions and special events, Ferdinand and Isabella, even before their subjects had discovered America, were the richest and most powerful monarchs in Europe. Acknowledged autocrats of a nation which found its true expression in its kings, they were monarchs in the fullest sense, for they might almost be said to be popes as well as princes. They were the head of the nation in civil affairs and its patriarchs in religion. All the moral, social, and material resources of the nation were in their hands. There was no need for them to consider how they should maintain their authority, because the nation, considering them its true representatives, placed itself wholly at their disposal. They were free to command, free to act; they were, in fact, real monarchs.

An historical chance caused this monarchy to be inherited by a prince of the House of Austria in the year 1519. Elected Emperor and completely ignorant of Spain, Charles V imagined at first that he had acquired a territory populous indeed and rich, but not essentially different from the countries and peoples which formed the rest of his realm. The national spirit of Spain resented this, and in a nation resentment involves rebellion. He had sent to his Spanish 'province', as the Romans of old, a proconsul and his legions: the Spanish proved to him that they were a nation. As a nation they were willing to identify themselves with their king, but the king on his part must identify himself with them. This obliged Charles V to meditate and observe, and he came to the conclusion that the throne of the Peninsula was worth more than all the rest of his fragmentary empire of kingdoms honeycombed by individual claims and privileges. And when in 1556 he abdicated, he first renounced Germany and only later gave Spain into the hands of his son.

When Charles saw the loyalty and strength of the Spanish nation and sounded the depths of its character, his political genius made it clear to him that it was the destiny of Spain to intervene actively in the affairs of Europe. He therefore guided and directed a movement which had begun in the time of Queen Isabella, when in 1504 the Spanish throne succeeded to the crown of Naples, and which must have occurred quite apart from whether an historical chance had united on the same head the imperial crown and the crown of

Spain. Yet it is as head of Catholic heroic Spain, not as one of the Emperors of Germany, that Charles V stands out as a great figure in history. Nationalized a Spaniard, surrounded by his statesmen and soldiers, relying on the invincible infantry of the Peninsula, with the wealth of the Indies at his disposal, when he crosses Europe from one end to the other, speaking to each people in its own language, fighting against François I and the Protestants of Germany, against Suleiman and the Emperors of Barbary, Charles V is the true successor of Charlemagne, the defender of Christendom, and, with a power greater than that of the Pope, almost as great a monarch spiritually as he is temporally. He is the image of Spain dominating the world through the expansion of that genius which only now, after a slow development, imposes itself on men's minds and on the nations.

In Charles V the prince comes before the soldier, reasons of State are more to him than the strong arm. He is the head of a nation and the first modern sovereign, whereas his French rival, François I (1515–47) is the last king of the chivalric system and belongs to the Middle Ages. Germany, France, and Italy had not yet emerged from the old feudal forms when in Spain Ferdinand and Isabella were reigning as real monarchs and Cardinal Ximenes, from the steps of the throne, crushed all the medieval privileges that remained and constructed the model of a modern nation. It is Spain that speaks by the mouth of Charles V, emperor and almost pope, prince and statesman, who had learnt the maxims of the new political system in Spain. It is Spain, her genius, her civilization, that, stepping across the plans of the politician and imposing themselves on his will, seat themselves with Charles V on the imperial throne, a throne ruling the old world and the new.

We cannot accompany the Emperor on his endless campaigns. Having marked their character from our point of view, we leave the details of his wars and alliances, the intrigues and achievements that make up his dramatic life, to history proper; to history and not such a book as this must this be left. From the point of view of the development of Iberian civilization Charles V's great campaign is the Council of Trent (1545). In this assembly, in which every act of the statesman, every victory or defeat of the soldier, find an echo—this assembly which, even in a plain narrative of events, is the centre on which all the meshes of the intricate web of European politics converge—we must now see rather the activity of the genius of Spain reforming religion than the intervention of a prince anxious to defend himself from his rivals.

It was in 1530, at the Diet of Augsburg, that Charles V and the Protestant princes had agreed to call a general council to restore peace to the Church and recall the dissidents to its fold. Rome, however, proved disinclined to grant the Emperor's urgent request. The Pope had had to resign himself to accept the supremacy of Charles V, but he hoped that in return the powerful monarch would hurl against the Protestants his legions of Spanish fanatics. The papal legate at the Emperor's court urged him to violence, tempting him with the rich spoils of the Protestant princes; but the political genius of Charles V foresaw the dangers of such a war, and he was inclined to be conciliatory. A year later, threatened by the league of Skalmalden and by the Turk (secretly supported by François I), the Emperor became more urgent with Clement VII; but the Pope still delayed, prompted to do so by personal motives as well as by those of a political nature, which indeed seemed to make it necessary to defer indefinitely a resolution which he could not openly oppose. Persecuted by his troublesome protector, the Pope had recourse to his rival, who was then the ally of the enemies of the Church; and to Europe was given the extravagant spectacle of a Pope, allied with Turks and Protestants, waging war on the Catholic Emperor. What better proof could he give of the decay of the authority of the Church? What better proof of the urgent necessity of a reform, either Protestant, as Luther had demanded, or Catholic, as now conceived by the Jesuits?

The unhappy Clement VII died in 1534, after four years of heavy trials; and it was not till 1542, after twelve years of war, that the Papacy resolved to convoke the assembly which might become a court to try its crimes; an assembly which came too late to effect a reconciliation but in time to serve the reforming ambitions of the new army of Christ. Convoked in 1542, it assembled in 1545, but could no longer answer to the political designs of Charles V; and the Spanish genius, which in the form of armies was his strength, left on one side his plans as statesman in order through the Jesuits to give a new character to Catholicism. The strength of the Protestants was now too great for the ideas of Cardinal Campeggi to prevail; but the ultramontane and unitarian spirit, if it could not conquer by force of arms, was able to affirm itself in a decisive spirit of intolerance within the Church. The result of the Council from which Charles expected a political solution was that he was obliged to abdicate and all his plans miscarried.

There was still, in 1545, as earlier, a party at Rome in favour of the reform of papal abuses; there were still some who believed that this could lead to reconciliation and reunion. Cardinal del Monte saw abuses everywhere: he wished to sweep clean and uproot the tares; everything, he said, was covered with dirt and rubbish. Hence arose the first disputes in the Council: what were they going to discuss, discipline or dogma? the reform of ecclesiastical manners or the renovation of the faith? Fiery discussions ensued between those who pinned all their hopes on a confession of past sins and sincere repentance and those who expected everything from the strength of authority renewed by a fresh religious spirit. The latter, the Jesuits, won; and their victory decided the Protestants at the Diet of Ratisbon in 1546 to declare that they would not accept the decisions of the Council. The project which the Emperor had fostered during sixteen years was thus destroyed despite all the wars and intrigues which he had undertaken in order to attain it. As a politician he was the victim of the proverb of the nation which he had used as an instrument to further his own plans: he had played with fire and it had burnt him.

At the head of his Spanish soldiers and of the troops of the Pope, Charles V now invaded Protestant Germany and entered Wittenberg in triumph. There in 1547 he saw the tomb of Luther. The Spanish wished to disinter and burn the remains of that 'demon'. But the Emperor, thoughtful and perhaps dimly aware of the folly of this religious strife, perhaps inspired by the genius of Erasmus, gave his decision with true humanity: 'Let him alone, I wage war on the living, not on the dead.'

In spite of the war and these victories, the French party in favour of a reform of discipline had not yet been destroyed in the Council of Trent. There were daily conflicts, which were not confined to words; two bishops came to blows and the face of one of them was bathed in blood: a symbol of the state of Europe. Contarini at Trent represented the French party; Laynez and Salmerón were at the head of the Spanish party which was finally victorious and set aside questions of discipline in order to attend to dogma. By giving a new vigour and purity to the faith which they were preaching in the New World, by supplying a new, stronger, and surer support for the authority of the Church, the Jesuits brought to the Church the ardent faith and monarchical unity of Spain, and hoped, not through any concessions, but by authority, to recall Protestantism to the fold of the faith, which must be purified before it could become truly Catholic and one.

The problem of justification was the crux of the theological questions which were now without demur preferred in the Council to questions of discipline. Contarini proposed a conciliatory doctrine, supporting himself with the arguments of Pflug and Gropper, the opponents of Luther. The Council was to recognize the coexistence of two justifications, one inherent and immanent in man, expressed in his actions and evident in his virtues, by which justification men are the sons of God, but which is by itself alone insufficient; and, side by side or above it, the divine justification, the justification of Christ, through whose merits we are redeemed and forgiven; this alone gives real salvation and redemption and is truly complete. The Jesuits Salmerón and Laynez had no difficulty in defeating this plan of a dangerous reconciliation. It cannot be denied, they said, that divine is different from human justification, but this difference does not imply that it is remote from the world, since it is only revealed through faith and works. Man is not simultaneously impelled by both forms of justification, by freewill and predestination, existing and working side by side. God reveals himself through faith and good works, the merit of which can raise to a state of grace. The Protestants do not exclude good works, but according to them it is not through their merit that redemption is attained, but solely through the merit of Christ independently of man's action. To reconcile this independent grace with the merit inherent in good works is absurd and dangerous: it is almost Protestantism and leads straight to the errors of Luther.

Thus in the Council reappeared the eternal problem which mankind will perhaps never be able to solve, through lack or insufficiency of spiritual understanding in the constitution of its mind. The problem had arisen in Europe in the first days of the Church; it had formed the basis of the duel between St. Augustine and Pelagius; around it the scholasticism of the Middle Ages had continually woven its subtleties, texts, and sophisms without advancing a single step. The two opinions are mutually exclusive and opposed when they are expressed in precise and logical formulas, certainly incompatible with the character of matters which are transcendental; but it cannot be doubted that the solution of the Jesuits (apart from its derivative abuses and perversions) is the true one, seeing that it is the only solution practically possible. Justification by grace, the independent justification through the merits of Christ, condemns man and man's activity, his will, the very springs of life; and this condemnation of man condemns the world, transforms reality, and leads to the abyss of a transcendental enslavement. On the other hand, divine justification revealed in the works of men, in their faith and conscience, makes man and the world divine. This was the Greek solution of the fourth century, it was that of the Gnostics, and that which, despite contrary crises, was always defended by Cathocism in the form of religious dogma. It is the symbolical definition of the theory of Immanence; and that is its chief glory.

The Spanish genius was thus, on the eloquent lips of Laynez and Salmerón, still the champion of humanist culture; and, bold and paradoxical as this may at first appear, it was the individualism of the Peninsula which saved Europe from the slippery slope of predestination. The Latin genius would naturally react against this, but after what struggles and tremendous catastrophes we may easily imagine if we remember that the seed of Anabaptism was sown all over Europe, in France, in the Switzerland of Calvin, in Italy, even in Spain, where the mysticism of the Alumbrados, so far as it is known to us, suggests deep analogies with that spirit which absorbed all things in a Nirvana substantially the same as that of the Buddhists. The mysticism of pre-destination which, with the pantheistic genius of the Germanic peoples, maintains itself in that cloudy atmo-sphere of vague ideas in which they delight, must carry the more logical and lively genius of the Western peoples into the absurd exaggerations of Nihilism.

We cannot further develop here this apology of the renewal of Catholicism by the genius of Spain. From the moment when St. Ignatius finds in the word obedience the solution of the crisis of his conscience he ceases to tread in the spirit of the Peninsula. The phenomenon is the mysterious fruit of an individual soul, a particular, not a collective thing; and the trend of the solutions of the Jesuits in the Council of Trent is also due to general or European causes and is not derived directly from the genius of the Spanish people. To the moral obedience of the saint corresponds in the Council the argument of the theologians when they oppose Contarini's proposal on the ground that it is an innova-tion. This immobility of dogma and this inalterable fixity of belief, an irrational attitude denied by the very history of Catholicism, were indeed the spiritual version of the rule of unconditional obedience to the Papacy, the fundamental doctrine of the Company which was to be the new basis of the edifice of the Church.

The victory of the Spanish in the Council of Trent entails the victory of Spanish mysticism in the soul of the Emperor. The Protestants in their strength sacked his very palace. In the chances of war Maurice of Saxe surprised him at Innspruck in 1552 without an army and racked by gout. The great Emperor, without money or soldiers, fled, carried on a litter as a cripple, a lonely fugitive across the mountains: a true likeness of Catholicism, which was also fleeing from the world, since it had embraced the moral doctrine of obedience. In the soul of the Emperor that moment of humiliation and his cruel sufferings opened new horizons in which he could at last see how chimerical were his great plans, although too late to avoid disaster. And the Church, blind so long, awoke too late for repentance. A tomb awaits both the Emperor and Catholicism, the tomb of obedience, the tomb of Yuste. Buried at Yuste, the Emperor, we are told, hears two masses daily, attends his own funeral service, makes clocks, and amuses himself with gardening; it was too late for the worldly old man to become a saint. Loyola, for his part, the Machiavelli of Catholicism, teaches the Popes, his disciples and instruments, the code (differing in form but substantially the same) of all the princes of Europe. It was then that our Archbishop Bartholomeu dos Martyres said ironically at Rome: 'I think the most illustrious cardinals are in need of a most illustrious and reverend reformation.' This reformation was already made in the testament of Loyola: 'Let us be as a dead body without movement of its own, or as a staff in the hands of a blind man.' Prophetic words! For if the faithful are to be the staff, it is because the Pope has become blind.

Spain, separated from the Empire after the abdication of Charles V, flowed back like a wave upon itself, after having overrun Europe with her soldiers and dominated men's conscience with her doctrine. In their warfare in Europe the rough Spanish captains offer to the observer illuminating contrasts: the hardened warrior was unable to adapt himself like the mystics in order to fuse the soldier's adventurous spirit with the enlightened spirit of the faithful into a new and original product like St. Ignatius. The Duke of Alba, at war with that Paul IV who hated the Spanish so fiercely, is afraid of entering Rome in 1555; the half of his mind which the brutalities of war left free is filled with scruples. He crosses himself and prays; he goes timorously to kiss the Pope's foot, when the Pope finally permits him to enter Rome. The Pope fills him with respect, with fear and trembling. Such also was the temperament of the Conquistadores, whom we will now study, turning to the discovery of the New World after describing the conquest of the Old. At the head of the latter enterprise stood St. Ignatius, at the head of the former we shall find Columbus.

V. THE DISCOVERY OF THE INDIES

COLUMBUS was Genoese by descent but a Spaniard by adoption. The eminent place he holds in the epic of discovery has bound up his name for ever with the history of the Peninsula. A man's birthplace may be a slight factor in the development of his genius, since it is undoubted that to the outward fact of becoming denationalized may correspond a spiritual change in a man's mind. This had occurred in the case of many Spaniards whom we cannot now distinguish from natives of Rome: as statesmen or writers they are only separated from Italians by learned biographers who have inquired into the place of their birth. So it was with Columbus. Among the sailors and merchants of Genoa he is an extraordinary figure, without parallels before or after; connected by descent with Genoa, morally he belongs to the Peninsula. Neither the adventurous daring nor the mystic illumination which impel him were learnt in Italy. He came from Italy a pilot and merchant; Spain transformed him into a hero. Of him it may be said, as Trajan said of a Spanish writer that he was the greatest of the Romans, that the Genoese Columbus was the greatest of Spaniards.

His voyages take him to Madeira, where the papers and charts of a Portuguese navigator are bequeathed to him. Thence he goes to Lisbon to propose to the

King of Portugal the enterprise of the discovery of the Indies. His offer is refused, and he goes to Castille. During his residence at the court of Queen Isabella he is present at the greatest act of that brilliant reign: the conquest of Granada in 1492. He watches the dictatorship of Ximenes, and breathes the hot atmosphere of religious enthusiasm, which then still had a creative force. He sees the silver cross planted victoriously on the towers of the Alhambra. In that moment he was nationalized a Spaniard. The language which he speaks and in which he writes his letters and private papers is not Italian but Spanish. His ambition is to obtain from the discovery money to equip an army of ten thousand horse and a hundred thousand infantry to conquer Jerusalem. Lope de Vega shows him resisting the advice of his comrades to go to lay the enterprise of the discovery before the King of England: let Bartholomew go to England, he will go to

> Castille, for 'tis a land
> That I have learnt to love.

To him the discovery is only a means to an end, the conquest of Jerusalem, the same object that St. Ignatius had proposed to himself in his abasement. Mysticism is the principle which prompts and impels both these heroes; both find in the depth of their soul a burning faith which exceeds any human strength. Ignatius left Barcelona in rags, without money, lacking knowledge of languages or any other means to effect his object. The results of the two adventures were different, but the mental state of the two men was the same, although clothed in intuitions of a different kind. Columbus is a seaman, he takes with him instruments and charts, observes the stars and currents; but the mainspring of his action is faith: 'I have already said that in the discovery of the Indies reason and mathematics and maps of the world availed me not, but the prophecy of Isaiah was fulfilled.'

And indeed during his voyage God appeared to him in the midst of the tempest. In his imagination, excited by the raging storm, he saw visions like those which St. Ignatius had seen in the cave at Manresa. God revealed to him the intimate secrets of things and unrolled before his eyes the map of the whole world. He read the names of the different countries, and in his exalted faith there is something sublime in the very extravagance of his ingenuous geographical statements. 'The Orinoco rises in the earthly paradise, to which none can penetrate save by the will of God.'

The voyage of Columbus has often been described; but it is always worth while to recall the principal moments of an adventure which was in itself extraordinary and was also remarkable for the good fortune which attended the daring of the navigators. Such examples of what man can do, when he rises above the unconscious enslavement in which he is held by worldly conventions, the dictates of self-interest and a lack of independent and lofty thought, are never vain. Belief in their own strength is the chief cause of the great actions of men. Obscure heroes have performed deeds as great as that of Columbus, and, if history records a few and forgets many, that is because history has to measure actions by their results. Every man is a potential hero, and as soon as he is convinced of this and frees himself from the slavery of his surroundings he realizes how easy and simple great actions are, how ample a meaning they give to existence; how incomparably harder, sadder and more painful is a life enslaved by imaginary comforts and delights than a life of toil which fills the spirit with unspeakable consolation.

What the historians call by the high-sounding name of ships really corresponded in size to our present yachts and trawlers. The *Niña* and *Pinta* of Columbus's fleet were vessels in which no one would now dare to cross the Atlantic. It was on August 3, 1492, that the little fleet of three ships left the harbour of Palos. This voyage was entirely different from the coasting voyages of the ancients and from those of the Portuguese who gradually sailed round Africa until Vasco da Gama made bold to cross the Indian Ocean. Modern historical and geographical studies have demonstrated that a series of frustrated attempts led up to Columbus's success; and since men were convinced of the existence of a great continent in the West, tenacity and time or some chance were certain sooner or later to attain the discovery effected by the daring of Columbus. The voyages of fishermen of Northern Europe had extended, it seems, as far as Canada, and Cabral, by chance or plan, had reached the shores of South America; but this does not detract from the historical importance of Columbus's enterprise. We might apply here the anecdote of the egg attributed to the audacious navigator.

From Palos the fleet sailed to the Canaries, which were reached on September 6. There it takes in provisions and sets out. Whither? Westward. They make for no particular harbour or country but for something vague and indefinite, that western land which stretched from pole to pole, from Canada to Tierra del Fuego. Their westward course would in fact carry them necessarily to some point in America because that continent extends from north to south like an unbroken wall. We know that now, but neither Columbus nor Pinzon knew it. And had that continent, where it narrows in the isthmus of Panama, yielded in the course of ages to the erosive action of the sea and produced two Americas with a huge channel between them, the westward voyage might have brought them to India, leaving on either side a whole world in their wake.

Nine days of easterly winds allow them to sail on in the direction 'indicated by the prophet Isaiah'. Pinzón believes that he sees land. They sound in vain and find no bottom even at a hundred fathoms. The seamen become impatient. On the 21st of the month the wind changes, and the crews see in this an order from heaven to return to Spain; but a sudden storm and the toil of all hands in it quells the mutiny. Columbus, like an augur of old, observes the stars and the flight of birds. On the 1st of October they reckon that they have sailed seven hundred leagues from the Canaries: land cannot be far off. Often there is a joyous cry of 'Land', made by some in hope, by others in despair, and by the pilots as a device to restrain the crew; but it is always a false report. Leaning against the sides of the ships, these few dozen men, lost in the ocean of waves, examine the sky with the same fervour with which the penitent monk contemplated the heavens and prayed God for enlightenment. Columbus, standing at the prow of the admiral ship, converses with the Eternal Father, and during these long nights of bitter anxiety is supported by a faith which suffers him not to doubt. Ten days later the prophecy of Isaiah was fulfilled, and the *Pinta*, all beflagged, fired a salute in honour of the new world. On the 11th they landed; they planted a cross in the earth, called the country San Salvador and sang a Te Deum.

Of the three ships only the *Niña* and the *Pinta* returned to Spain; and of these a storm threw on the Cantabrian coast the *Niña*, commanded by Pinzón, who died a few days after landing. Columbus reached Palos on the 16th of March: seven months had sufficed for the discovery of America and the occupation of the Antilles, San Salvador, Concepcion, Fernandina, Isabella, Hispaniola, and Cuba. Turning to those who remained in America, it is difficult for us to realize the courage required to see the ships depart and to remain on those unknown shores, wholly different from Europe, in groups of four or six among a crowd of savage Indians. What fate was in store for these Robinson Crusoes? Could the daring voyage ever be repeated?

Columbus's reception in Spain carries us back to the Middle Ages. It was as though a general of Alexander were returning to Greece laden with the spoils of India. Every one rushed to see the amazing novelties. Utopia had become a splendid reality, and the people were seized with an enthusiasm which made their faith still more fervent. Then did the bells peel from the church-towers and with wild clamour of rejoicing called the peasants to come and see the men of strange colour whom the navigator had brought home, wretched men who had no knowledge of God and had never been baptized. Magistrates in their official robes came bowing gravely to salute the hero; the roads from Palos to Barcelona, where the Court then was, were crowded with people anxious to have sight of him; the fortresses thundered out their salutes; mothers lifted up their children to show them Columbus, and the children, their eyes fixed on the Indians in his train, felt strange impressions and ambitions awake within them. The men thought of the millions of souls to be won for God; of the mountains of gold to be brought home; of long battles and vast kingdoms to be conquered; every one had a dim vision of crosses and orders, riches, military commands, and glory. And this golden rain of potential wealth fell on a people at the height of its strength and vigour and gifted with a fervent faith. All the future captains of India were born in that hour. Columbus reversed the current of the national genius and directed it towards the new world that he had discovered.

The news of the discovery of America, when it reached Lisbon, revived the zest for sea-voyages which had tended to die down. Since in the beginning of the fifteenth century Prince Henry the Navigator had begun to encourage the voyages of discovery, the enterprise had been prosecuted with varying zeal. The death of the prince in 1460 discouraged it. In 1443 the Portuguese had rounded Cape Bojador and Pope Eugenius IV had granted to Portugal the exclusive right to all territories to be discovered from the Cape of Good Hope to India. King João II, called the Perfect Prince, and who holds a high place in the history of the nation, gave a fresh impetus to the voyages. It is not for us here to record the successive stages of the exploration until the moment when Vasco da Gama reached India. The quiet courage, the tenacity, and greatness of our navigators achieved deeds which may be less dramatic but are certainly not smaller than those of our neighbours and comrades in adventure. Later on we shall attempt to discern in what way the overseas captains of Spain differ from those of Portugal, and to show that these differences are mere aspects which do not invalidate that unity of thought, character, and action that make the Peninsula one country, despite the fact that its modern history has divided it politically into two parts.

The crews and pilots of Vasco da Gama likewise mutinied when they found themselves between sea and sky, far from any shore, crossing the Indian Ocean from Mombasa to Calicut. The noble captain summoned a council of pilots on board his own ship. On the deck on one side of him were the charts and nonii,[1] on the other a heap of fetters. He took the instruments and charts and threw them into the sea, and, pointing in the direction of India, said: 'Yonder lies the way, the pilot is God'. The fetters were for those who had lost faith and were to be clapped into the ship's hold.

Columbus set out for the West, Gama for the East; and one day of the year 1521 Magalhães, a Portuguese 'in fact, but not in loyalty', crossed the wall of America by the strait which preserves his name, and with amazement the Portuguese found in the Pacific a ship sailing under the flag of Castille. Starting from the

[1] The *nonius* was so named after the Portuguese inventor Pedro Nunes, who lived during the first three-quarters of the sixteenth century. (Translator's note.)

same point, by different ways, Spaniards and Portuguese met again on the other side of the world. At this unique and sublime moment of modern history all Europe bowed its head and celebrated the genius of the Iberian civilization. The unity of this civilization, with its political dualism, appears especially evident at this moment, when its energies attain their culminating point. Magalhães, a Portuguese sailing under the Spanish flag, by his discovery unites the conquest of Portugal in the East with the conquests of Spain in the West: between them they embrace the whole of the new world which the heroic Peninsula had torn from out the mystery of the sea.

But the observer also sees in this moment the results of the separate, although parallel, development of the two countries and the character of each strongly marked in their overseas enterprises. The necessary expansion of energies for which their European boundaries proved too narrow, a fervent desire to spread the faith, and an instinctive impulse to win riches, these were the common factors in the discoveries and conquests of both Spaniards and Portuguese. In his play entitled 'The New World' Lope de Vega places on the lips of the Devil the lines

> No Christian fervour makes them bold,
> But only greed and lust for gold.

One of the first impressions of the companions of Columbus left in San Salvador is that of the rings and ear-rings worn by the Indians. They inquire of them where the gold comes from and take them aboard as pilots to guide them to the enchanted land concerning which such extravagant legends were in vogue in Europe. It is the Indians who direct the Spanish to Cuba. The same desires incited the Portuguese in India, whither they had gone in the ambition to wrest from Venice her monopoly of trade with the East.

Cortés and Pizarro, Castro and Albuquerque: these are the four great names of the epic of conquest. It is not part of our task to recount the annals of a history which soon filled whole libraries: those campaigns, the description of unknown regions, of new races and customs, were valued as something absolutely new. Cortés reached America just after the Spanish had returned from a first visit to Mexico. The conquest of that region was entrusted to him, and he set out with six hundred Spaniards, eighteen horses, and a few cannon, and with these he subdued the empire of Montezuma in the year 1519. Disembarking at Vera Cruz, he appointed himself captain-general of the colony, burnt his ten ships, and marched into the interior. It is a question of death or victory. The first encounter is picturesque enough, for Montezuma sent against the invaders an army of sorcerers. Their enchantments failed to frighten the Spanish, who entered the capital and seized the person of the emperor. Pizarro for his part tended swine at Trujillo before he set out for America to conquer the empire of the Incas. Like the Duke of Alba in Europe, the Spanish Conquistadores combined an implacable fierceness with extreme devotion: we have already given an explanation of this fact. Cortés never spoke to a priest except with bowed knee and uncovered head, although the chronicler informs us that the object of this piety was to set the Mexicans an example. Whether it was due to artifice or to sincere conviction, the fact remains that these Spanish captains considered themselves apostles, a strange kind of apostles indeed. Spain's mission in their eyes is chiefly religious, and this conviction combined with their natural magnificence and military education to produce documents of a singular extravagance:

I, Alfonso Ojeda, servant of the most high and powerful Kings of Leon, conquerors of the barbarous nations, hereby solemnly inform you that our Lord, the only and eternal God, created the heavens and the earth, and a man and woman, from whom you and I and all men who have ever existed and shall ever exist in the world do descend.

This was Ojeda's address to the natives of the Antilles in 1509. It is in our history overseas, a vast field which gave free rein to the development of character, that all the extravagance and magnificence of the Peninsular temperament is most clearly seen. The Castilian drama, at once tragic and grotesque, is both charming and terrible; a drama in which smiles and blood, Toledo tongues of steel (as Lope de Vega has it), the flowers worn by the women in their hair, sacrilege and piety, blasphemies and cilices, every antithesis and every contrast, jostle one another in a strange confusion; this drama is to be witnessed daily on the brilliant stage of the India of the West.

In the East is played the Portuguese tragedy. The epic figure of Afonso de Albuquerque dominates the scene. In 1503 he had gone out as Governor to India,[1] and it was during his term of office that the greatest conquests were made: Goa and the whole of Malabar, Ceylon and the other islands of the Gulf of Mexico, Ormuz and the peninsula of Malacca, beyond which, through the tributary kingdoms of Pegu and Siam, the Portuguese empire extended to the frontiers of China. The King of Persia, as sovereign of Ormuz, sent to demand tribute from the Portuguese; but Albuquerque showed the ambassadors a pile of cannon-balls and a bundle of swords and made answer, 'That is the coin in which the King of Portugal pays his tribute'. He intended to conquer Egypt in order to seize Suez and thence dominate the Red Sea and aim a thrust at the heart of Mecca, the Jerusalem of Islam; and with this object

[1] That is, with the appointment in his pocket: he did not actually become governor till 1509 and the great conquests were crowded into the six years before his death in 1515. (Translator's note.)

he had thoughts of altering the course of the Nile where it rises in Ethiopia.

The Portuguese heroes have a grave and noble bearing—severe, almost gloomy; it were vain to look for dramatic contrasts in these figures standing out on the tragic scene. Both nations of the Peninsula have the same motives for their actions, but each develops these motives with the resources peculiar to its temperament. Which of them excels the other? Put thus, it is an idle question; yet essentially it is a question worth pondering over. Each of the peoples of the Peninsula develops the resources of its own genius, and from an objective and historical point of view these resources are equivalent: an excess of daring on the one side corresponds to a lack of justice on the other. The faculties of the Portuguese are better balanced, as was natural in their less emphatic temperament; and that is why the Portuguese scene beyond the seas is tragic whereas the Spanish is a comedy—a play as it were by Lope de Vega or Calderón, ending in the bitter smile of Cervantes.

VI. CAMÕES

IT was at this unique creative moment that the Portuguese produced the greatest poem of modern times, a book which is Spain's testament. Portugal had the honour then to become the interpreter of Spain's civilization to the world. This book, the escutcheon as it were of the history of the whole of Spain, and the undying testimony of our national existence, is the poem of Camões, *The Lusiads*. In it we find clearly and marvellously defined what we may call the essence of the genius of the Peninsula. In its first rough expression this genius is represented by the characters of soldiers, whose mysticism finds vent in external, formal devotion; and, without becoming completely fused into the energy of heroic action, gives us men of a dramatic cast, such as the Duke of Alba, trembling before the Pope after victoriously entering Rome, and the majority of the Spanish captains, who combined naturalism with a truly popular piety. The second stage in the development of this genius is represented by the Spanish saints: mysticism in intimate conjunction with the spirit of chivalry produced types such as Santa Teresa and St. Ignatius and literature such as that of Lope de Vega and Calderon, persons and literature in which one sees natural passions and feelings divinized to form strong and original but hybrid characters, unnatural, and therefore without an ideal consistency. The significance of Camões' poem is that it forms the third and definitive stage in the development of this religious sentiment. Camões is not an isolated phenomenon in the Portuguese life of his time because his poem sprang from the essence of its most intimate thought, revealed in that special character which in the sixteenth century distinguishes the Portuguese heroes, such as Albuquerque and Castro, from a Cortés or Pizarro. We can here only lightly sketch the features of Portuguese heroism, described with the pen of genius in *The Lusiads*. The religious enthusiasm which the Spanish saints brought to the sphere of natural sentiment was as it were a naturalization of God, and religion took on that character of mystic naturalism which is evident both in men's lives and in the works of literature and art. As we have remarked, the mysticism of the Peninsula in this way avoided nihilist ecstasy; but on the other hand so paradoxical a solution transformed the world into a pandemonium, since God and the Devil, the saints of heaven and the saints of hell, joined with men to represent those extravagant comedies which the Spanish applauded in the churches and *patios*[1] and acted in real life on the stage of the world.

[1] The *comedias* were at first acted in the courts of houses. It was not till the year 1579 that the first permanent theatre was inaugurated at Madrid. (Translator's note.)

We have said that action in Spain was dramatic, and in Portugal tragic; we can define this idea more clearly by referring to the different kinds of drama. The action of the Portuguese is tragic because what constitutes tragedy, that noble creation of the Greek genius, is the luminous and serene understanding of a dogma. The Spanish dogma which the Jesuit theologians had caused to prevail in the Council of Trent was that of the revelation of universal order in men's minds and of the existence of an absolute justice expressed through men's acts and virtues. Only peoples so constituted that they can thus define the relations of the infinite and the finite can have an epic history, and in the life of Europe after the Greeks, those pioneers of our civilization, come the Italians and the Spanish. Our thought is perhaps now quite clear, especially if we remember the three moments in which, with gradually increasing clearness, the religious soul of the Peninsula displays its essential character. What we may call the humanization of God is in the hearts of the Spanish soldiers but a misty intuition which they cannot reconcile with their personal activity; in the heart of the mystics the two are reconciled but in a paradoxical way, with so real and living a devotion that characters become unnatural and the boundaries between the eternal and the transitory, the essential and the incidental, are confused. Finally, in the heart of the great men, the saintly warriors of Portugal, throbs a feeling which Camões could describe, a soul which he could sing in his immortal poem.

We cannot here comment upon the poem of Camões nor study in detail the antecedent facts which caused Portugal to be privileged to make her voice thus heard in the culminating moment of the history of the Peninsula. But in this sublime book the religious senti‐ment is not merely Portuguese but general, peninsular, Spanish. It causes the poet to inveigh against the Germans, 'stiffnecked herd rebellious against the suc-

cessor of St. Peter', and against 'the Gaul'; to condemn
criminal alliances with the Turks and propose that all
Christian nations should join in the redemption of the
Holy Sepulchre. And if the religion of the poem is
Spanish or peninsular, national pride, never more
fervent than in the days of the greatest mystic extravagance, prompts the poet to write those lines which
represent the historic 'No' of Aragon, the Castilian
protest of Padilla, and the revolt of the Master of Avis
in Portugal:

> It will accept no king's authority
> Unless more excellent than all he be.

The ideas of the absolute truth of Catholicism and of
national pride constitute the basis of the poet's thought.
The manly pride which he describes in its political or
civic aspect is an indispensable element in the construction of the edifice of religion; the other materials are
provided by naturalism. The poet had had personal
experience of the new worlds and strange vast seas: he
had seen tornadoes and tempests; and Adamastor
appeared to him, as to some Greek sailor of old, and
spoke to him as he rounded the dreadful cape between
the mountainous crests of waves and mountains of
leaden-hued clouds. The forging together of these
materials forms his poem, and it is of the same feelings
that the body of his religious ideas consists. God and
the world do not appear to him in irreconcilable
antinomy, nor for him does their reconciliation consist
in bringing heaven down to the earth and transforming
the world, turning reality into chaos and thought into
rapture. 'God', he says, 'envelops this round world: He
is a truth in things and dwells in the visible and in-
visible.' The imagination of the poet gives life to stones;
he endows them with tears, and the harsh outline of
the terrible cape is gifted with the voice of eloquence.
If that were all, we should have a pantheistic, Italian
Camões, with very little originality, however great his

merit as a poet and an artist. But it is just here that the genius of the civilization of which he is the supreme expression gives him a special character. We have seen that mysticism, a not unusual form of religious thought, had in the Peninsula received a peculiar unprecedented cast; and the same thing happened to Camões. In the depths of the soul of the Peninsula exists a principle which transforms and dominates everything else, and this is the independence, the moral and social sovereignty of man. The exceptional variety and adaptability of our racial elements perhaps causes us to understand and embrace all forms of thought, but all these forms, once they have been placed in the crucible of that individualism which may be lulled asleep but never becomes extinct, are transformed and assume a very different shape. Thus it was with mysticism; thus it was with the pantheism of Camões. The universal soul which gives everything a new life is merely the sentiment of freedom and justice, and no abstract sentiment but that which is definitely in the heart of each one of us. Nature was idealized, but the empyrean is only scaled by 'the steep and thorny path of virtue'. Virtue, however, is not identified with natural and universal beauty or holiness, since it expresses individually the particular or personal manner by which each of us becomes an harmonious instrument of the whole, and all of us together the expression of the Absolute

We must here insist on a remark already made by us. We consider it undoubted that, without study of these intimate sentiments which ultimately move and guide the soul of a people, it is impossible to understand either its collective character or its history. The study of the external organs and functions of a collective body is likewise indispensable; but, once the system of its institutions has moulded a people into unity, the principal part in the drama of history belongs to the sentiments which move this body that has now reached the stage of complete organic development. Thus in a sense the evolution of a civilization falls into three great cycles: in the first, phenomena of a natural order predominate—movements of races, formation of languages, of legal symbols, of religious myths; in the second, the chief part is played by phenomena of a social nature, the development of institutions, the clash and strife of classes; finally, in the third, the phenomena of a moral order prevail—that is to say, the conscious definition of the ideas to which all forms of intellectual activity must be subordinated, and out of which legal and economic theories are built up. That will explain why we have described at considerable length the system of Spain's ideas. We have not studied the character of her writers because we supposed it necessary that religion and poetry must be essential elements in the gradual development of a society, but because in such moral aspects we see the intimate force and very soul of civilization in its maturity. We have traced the roots in the past which led to the flowering of Spanish mysticism in the sixteenth century; we have seen how this mysticism prepared and actually achieved that extraordinary movement of overseas discovery and conquest, and how it imposed itself on the rest of Europe. It remains for us to remark that, of the two nations of the Peninsula, it was Portugal which was moved by the impression produced by those new worlds and that new adventure to progress on the path of religious evolution. Spain continued to act the ancient mystic drama. There is nothing in Spanish literature that can be compared—we do not say from an aesthetic point of view but in moral value—to *The Lusiads*. But in Portugal this blaze of genius was of short duration. The soul of Camões was no solitary exception, for Barros, Goes, Couto and other sixteenth-century writers are moved by the same spirit; but after the sixteenth

century the two nations of the Peninsula, which had
shown themselves different from one another when at
the height of their glory and power, become again
morally one, although separated politically as before.
Both were affected in an equal degree by the fatal consequences of that heroic enterprise.

VII. CAUSES OF SPAIN'S DECADENCE

BEFORE considering the immediate causes of the
decadence of the nations of the Peninsula, we must
emphasize the character of that explosion of genius
which we have been examining in its various aspects
and sum up its international consequences in Europe.
On the one hand we find Spain intervening in the
religion and politics of Europe with such an irresistible
energy that we may say that Europe is momentarily
subjected to Spain's hegemony. On the other hand we
find that all this is not enough for the energies of that
nation, and that it throws itself into the enterprise of
discovery and conquest beyond the seas. At first this
second undertaking assists the first, and the gold of the
new world maintains Spain's armies in the old; but
in the course of time it causes the two nations of the
Peninsula to abandon their European interests and give
themselves up exclusively to exploit their overseas
possessions. It is therefore permissible to consider how
different the history of Europe might have been. If
we imagine for a moment that Spain had not discovered
and conquered the Indies, we must believe that in this
case her tenacious effort to subject Europe to her
genius would have been less dramatic and more lasting.
It might not be so, but it is at least a legitimate
inference from the results of her momentary dominion.
We believe that the two branches of European nations
which we call Germanic and Latin would have become
even more sharply isolated, that the wars of religion

would have lasted longer, and that at the end of this fatal struggle Europe would have become one, either under a victorious Protestant Germany or under a victorious Catholic Spain. But farther than this in the sphere of conjecture it is not permissible to venture.

The chief result of history taking such a course as we have conjectured would have been to prevent the existence of seventeenth-century France as the centre or axis of the balance of power in Europe, a kind of neutral country, neither Catholic nor Protestant, or both at once, where the fierceness of religious disputes was countered by the frank laughter and materialistic good sense of the Gaul. This practical, eclectic France established a new form of government suited to her genius and excellently calculated to elude religious problems: a secular monarchy based on the principle of a sovereignty independent of religious authority. A practical spirit, secular monarchy, and the balance of power: these were the three marked features of the situation in Europe after the Peace of Westphalia in 1648—the Peace which put an end to the wars of religion and to the hegemony of Spain in Europe, and inaugurated the reign of the French spirit.

By discovering the new world, the Spanish were the involuntary cause of this change in the history of Europe. The progress in scientific knowledge was not in itself due to the discoveries, but it received a powerful impulse from them; and as a result an increasing number of minds continually drew away from religious questions and coldly considered them as injurious to the progress of humanity. On the other hand the discoveries, by giving an unprecedented scope to commercial activity and exceptional importance to banking and credit, did not invent, since they already existed, but brought to the front two forms of commercial activity fraught with grave social consequences: those of banking and speculation.

The great overseas business under the form of commercial speculation and the influx of gold from America to Europe gave rise to the banking system and invested the old world with a character of an unprecedented kind. Hitherto Europe had lived by exploiting its own wealth and had developed normally. The discoveries deflected this natural course of development, and since then Europe resembles ancient Rome or Carthage, being a centre or focus from which radiates a dominating, exploiting power; and instead of being a nation or group of nations has become the mother-country of the world. New phenomena accompanied this change. From the moment that Europe has to exploit vast uninhabited regions she finds slavery necessary, and that fatal condition of the ancient world reappears in the modern world, although it had been long since morally condemned. Moreover, commerce and banking originated a class which was then new but had been well known at Carthage and Rome and had never died out at Venice, that Carthage of the Middle Ages—the class of the rich, the aristocracy of wealth. This new form of power ousts the decadent military power and crushes the normal development of society and the gradual building up of classes on a basis of labour. And lastly the discoveries, by fostering commercial activity, so foreign to the genius of Spain that her fatal attempt to engage in it killed her, gave the predominating influence in Europe to the Protestant nations, by their nature more fitted for the utilitarian methods which the world now valued. This influence, however, was not religious but merely commercial; and if at first sight it seems that the discoveries were the cause of the final victory of Protestantism, on closer examination we find that it was the commercial, not the religious genius of the Protestant nations that won the victory. The reappearance of slavery, the growth of a moneyed aristocracy without historical or moral traditions, the predominance of utilitarian or egoistic tendencies, which were finally avowed abjectly and openly as a plausible doctrine, the impossibility of a normal development of the social classes, and as it were a paralysation of history: these were the general and fatal consequences for Europe of the discovery of the new world. In pointing them out, describing and condemning them, we do not for an instant mean to imply that they were due to human errors and thus avoidable. Such a reading of history would be absurd. It was inevitable that Europe should complete the discovery and subjection of the surface of the globe, and it was equally inevitable that disturbing consequences must ensue. Not only were these evils necessary but they are (for we still suffer from them) in a sense even beneficial, since we were able through them to extend the sphere of our knowledge and learn the use of a system of credit, a weapon by means of which we shall perhaps be able to resolve problems of political economy which are the same as those that destroyed the ancient world and are now threatening us.

Another, less direct, result of the discoveries was the growth of modern monarchies, or rather the new support to which monarchies now turned. The principle of the divine right of kings had made it independent of the Papacy, and with the gold from the new world and the assistance of the new, less noble and less exacting aristocracy of commerce, it was able to overthrow the old nobility, which had already yielded to the growing strength of the people in the towns. The nations were therefore now governed exclusively by the kings, who from the seventeenth century onward were really absolute. The Church no longer overshadowed them, because indifference in matters of faith had impaired the strength of the Papacy. The military nobility had died out with the last warlike struggles of feudalism in the fifteenth century. The citizens of the towns for their part do not dare to make their support conditional, since their thoughts are rather of riches than of the liberties of which they are gradually deprived. The throne changed from iron to gold; on its steps are to be seen, instead of soldiers, rich merchants dressed in silk, full of servility towards the king, like the upstarts they are, and, in order to compensate themselves for the satire which they have to endure at court, they treat with ferocious cruelty the slaves and poor peasantry on the land which continually falls into their hands. But we must not look forward: these matters belong to a later stage of our history.

Yet in this first decadence of monarchy all the future characteristics are outlined. Our Viceroys in India are the commercial agents of the King, who personally contracts for all the pepper of India; and the Courts of the Peninsula, like that of Carthage, are commercial exchanges of a perfectly systematic kind. This new feature disorganizes everything; and as Spain, corrupted by the gold of the new world, descends slowly into the tomb, she perhaps feels the voices of ancient ages awake in her soul, the blood of some primitive race boil again in her veins, and in her heart spring up once more the barbarous genius of some people come originally from Africa. This is the age of Philip II and of João III, whom we have called two Pharaohs.

Repulsed by Europe, Spain withdrew into the intimate recesses of her genius, and in the darkness of decadence that genius loses the plasticity and life of the days of its expansion. Yet the Spain of Philip II is the same as that of Ximenes, the Portugal of João III is the same as that of João II. Sentiments and ambitions are the same; but there is added the shadow of old age, weariness after a great achievement, and the fatal consequences of that achievement. Baulked energy always festers, and Spain, besides suffering from the general disorganizing consequences of the discoveries, suffered also from the perversion of that spirit which had nobly and enthusiastically subjected Europe. Spain was now undermined by Jesuitism, ravaged by intolerance. The gold of the new world had filled her with rottenness and corruption. But even in her fall Spain is heroic, and as, with ferocious cruelty and a mad exaltation, she applauds her own suicide, she displays the extraordinary vigour of men who, not even as they approach the grave, are capable of exclaiming contritely that they have sinned. The warnings of Cil Vicente and of Cervantes were not understood. Spain only saw in Don Quixote the type of the knights of old and applauded a satire which, if it had no other meaning, would be merely a learned trifle. The figure of Amadis belonged already to a remote past; but the knight-errants whom Cervantes condemned were also those of a divine kind. His butt is the mad obstinacy of a heroism which no longer had a meaning or significance. Cervantes himself had been attacked by this mania; and now, old and disillusioned, he revived the old humour of the clowns of the Spanish drama and produced a work of genius. He too had dreamed of redeeming the divine captive, and as a captive at Algiers had devised means not so much of attaining his own freedom as of wresting the whole region from the hands of the Moor. Free at last but unfortunate, he becomes instead of a hero a clown, wrapped in his tattered cloak, through the holes of which the sun can still shine merrily for him. The dualism of Spain's dramatic history is reproduced vividly in the life of this writer, who ends by condemning utterly the nation whose life was reflected in his own. It is not the Amadises who provoke his disdainful smile and mordant irony: beneath this literary fiction lies the truth concerning the society of his time:

> What would you have me infer, Sancho, from all you have been saying, quoth Don Quixote. I would infer, said Sancho,

that we had better turn saints immediately, and we shall then soon attain to that renown we aim at. And pray take notice, sir, that yesterday or t'other day (for it is so little a while ago that I may so speak) a couple of poor barefooted friars were beatified or canonized, whose iron chains, wherewith they girded and disciplined themselves, people now reckon it a great happiness to touch and kiss; and they are now held in greater veneration than Orlando's sword in the armoury of our lord the king. So that, master of mine, it is better being a poor friar of the meanest order than the valiantest knight-errant whatever; for a couple of dozen of penitential lashes are more esteemed in the sight of God than two thousand tilts with a lance.[1]

A fanatical king rules supreme over this monk-ridden country. In the diocese of Calahorra alone there are 17,000 priests, so unruly that, according to Cabrera, the post of keeper of the episcopal prison was worth 1,500 ducats a year. According to a census taken in 1570, during the reign of Philip II, a quarter of the entire adult population was clerical: there were 312,000 priests, besides 200,000 who had taken minor orders, and there were 400,000 monks. The vigour of the national institutions, exhausted by those years of mighty enterprises, was a thing of the past; and Spain lay like a corpse oppressed by an insatiable monarchy. Gil Vicente remarked that

> Soon there will be no peasants left,
> For all are King's officials now.[2]

The population of Spain during the reign of Philip II was reduced by one-fifth—from ten to eight million inhabitants. The necessity of waging interminable wars had caused Charles V to adopt financial devices which deprived the productive industries of the nation

[1] *Don Quixote*, Part II, chapter viii. Eng. Trans., Charles Jervas, in the World's Classics, vol. ii, pp. 67–8.

[2] Gil Vicente, *Farsa dos Almocreves*, 1. 299 (Cambridge, 1920 ed., p. 44).

of most of their capital. The imperial exchequer being
empty, the troops were obliged to live by plundering
the towns. Forced loans and billeting of soldiers were
followed by debasement of the coinage, monopolies and
extravagant taxation, the surest way to paralyse the
sources of commercial wealth. During the reign of
Philip II the finances were in the hands of the 'arbitris-
tas', or inventors of financial devices: one of them
would propose that there should be a general fast-day
once a month, the money thus saved to go to the King;
another discovered a marvellous powder, an ounce of
which, mixed with six ounces of quicksilver, produced
real silver. And the King listened to and paid for all
these devices, in permanent expectation of a miracle.
He was nearly crazy with delight when they brought
him the news that one of his captains had discovered
in the Moluccas an island the soil and subsoil of which
was pure gold. When the treasures of the natives of
America were exhausted, the Spanish set themselves to
fervent exploitation of the mines. The mountains of
silver which came to Spain and all the gold and dia-
monds which came to Portugal only impoverished the
Peninsula. By this influx of gold and silver from
America the coinage became depreciated, salaries were
raised, prices rose, and the most ancient industry of
exploiting the mines of the Peninsula was abandoned.
In 1574 the exploitation of quicksilver was given up
because the supply of American cinnabar from Guan-
cavelica sufficed for the requirements of Potosi. Technical skill became rarer; the mines of Guadalcanal were
ruined because inefficient engineers allowed them to
be flooded. Philip II, moreover, ordered the mines of
Spain to be closed in order not to diminish the value
of the gold and silver from America; the precious stores
at home could be exploited at any time. And there
was more political economy of the same kind. King
Sebastian, who reigned from 1557 to 1578, forbade

interest on loans with an energy which might have
more than satisfied the most earnest moralist; the penalty
was a heavy one, only short of death, and included
confiscation and deportation. Capital ceased to be
productive, the country groaned under heavy taxation,
industry was ruined. In the reign of Charles there
were at Seville sixteen thousand looms for the manu-
facture of silk and wool; at the death of Philip III
(1621) there were only four hundred. The Mesta, an
association of Andalusian stockbreeders, possessed seven
million sheep when Philip II ascended the throne
(1556); when he died (1598) it possessed only two
million. The Cortes besought the King to expel all
bankers from Spain as the most dangerous of plagues,
ruining and destroying the nation.

Men who had set themselves the avowed object to
wreck a nation would scarcely have acted otherwise.
In less than a quarter of a century after the discovery
of India Portugal could no longer maintain her possessions in North Africa. Before King Manuel died (1521)
foreign merchants who used to come to Lisbon for
cargoes of wheat were bringing us food in exchange for
the spices of India. Before entering on the history of
the Jews, which sets the crowning touch to the folly
which possessed the Peninsula, let us remark that it
shows little insight to dwell on the consequences without pointing out their causes and recognizing that they
were inevitable. The economic errors in administration
were due to the erroneous ideas then generally accepted
and to the immense problems which suddenly confronted
those who were not trained to meet them. No one in
Europe at that time possessed this training; and it was
precisely the results of our mistakes which opened the
eyes of the foreigners who succeeded us in overseas
empire: the Dutch and the English.

But it was not to this cause alone that the ruin of
the Peninsula was due. It was prepared by ignorance;

it was completed by intolerance. Yet how should we expect the tolerant spirit of Dutch merchants in the heirs of the heroes who in the purity of their faith and in the enthusiasm which it awoke in their hearts had found strength for their mighty undertakings? Let us lay aside modern prejudices and attempt to place ourselves in the moral atmosphere of that time; it is only thus that we can understand history. Traditions could not so soon be extinguished; the echo of those great deeds was still ringing in men's ears. How demand prudence of men exalted by great achievements in which they saw miracles and the gracious intervention of the God whom they worshipped with a reverent devotion? That would be to judge them by our own cold reasoning, based on a knowledge which they did not possess. How shall we, who throw away large sums on a caprice and all that we have for a question of honour, cast a slur on those who let the Jews and industrial wealth go in the interests of their faith? To consider history in this way is not only absurd, it is intolerant; for in so doing we judge by our criterion actions which obeyed a totally different criterion. We live in the age of science, they lived in the age of faith; we obey the dictates of utility, they obeyed the dictates of religion. Besides, we have knowledge which they lacked. The method of the Jesuits, although not rigidly exclusive, had a deadening influence—it crept into education and cut off anything that rose above mediocrity. Salamanca, where the number of students had attained 14,000, could only boast half that number at the end of the sixteenth century.[1] Spaniards were forbidden to study in foreign universities. Books were submitted to the censure of the Holy Office; authors, printers, publishers, sellers, and even readers of forbidden

[1] The number of students *increased* during the first half of the century: it rose from 5150 in 1546 to 7832 in 1566, falling gradually after that year to 5093 in 1629. (Translator's note.)

books, were subjected to the penalty of excommunication and death. The Jesuits mutilated knowledge; the inquisitors, wielding the sceptre of their dread monarchy, hurled their thunderbolts against the impious. Torquemada, like Mansur at Córdoba, burnt six thousand volumes in one day at Seville. The first Index is published in 1546, the second in 1550. In this rage to eradicate every faintest expression of anything that might run counter to the purity of the faith, the monarchy, clergy and people acted in complete accord. They did not know that they were committing suicide; but had they known it, did not their faith embolden them to face martyrdom? The propagation of the faith had been the first act of the religious drama of Spain; its purification was the second. We will study this in some detail in view of its importance for the modern history of the Peninsula. In doing so we are obliged to err against chronology, since the division between the propagation and purification of the faith is purely logical. The results of the two are different, the scene and character in each case are also different. The scene of the one is the world; the scene of the other is limited to the Peninsula and its dominions. The one is intimately connected with European politics and the discovery of India, and its consequences are those which we have described; the other, apart from these general motives, furnishes us with the special causes of the decadence of the Peninsula. Yet the two are contemporary. The establishment of the Inquisition in 1483 in Castille and the expulsion of the Jews in 1492 both fall within the reign of Ferdinand and Isabella.

To the expulsion of the Jews we give the last place in the manifestations of the genius of the Peninsula because it is the most characteristic and not because it is the last in point of time. Intrinsically it is the last because it resembles the finishing thrust given to the bull when it lies on the sand, struck down by the sword of the *matador*. The Jewish question in the Peninsula is the clearest proof of the Catholic character of its civilization, although one must recognize that the expulsion obeyed social as well as religious causes. All the documents and historical accounts, whatever may have been their purpose, give us the impression that the Kings of Spain only ceased to interpret the popular will when in a spirit of toleration or a desire for good administration they favoured the Jews. The policy of King Manuel in Portugal is a proof of this and provoked tumults throughout his realm. This hatred of the Jews was general in Europe in the Middle Ages; the people saw in them the men who had crucified Christ, and to this was added the tyranny of their underhand oppression of the people as usurers. Moreover there was the natural envy of wealth and the revolt in men's minds at the sight of these wicked men dandled by fortune, protected by kings, frequently to be seen in the courts of princes, and favoured by the Pope himself. In its rough instinctive logic the people could not understand, much less approve, these contradictions, and victims of extortion found many a concrete fact—a house ruined, shops bought up, the savings of a lifetime devoured by a Jewish usurer in a year of famine—to support their reasoning. The situation in the Peninsula was graver than elsewhere because, taking advantage of the Moorish invasion, the number of Jews in the Peninsula was extraordinarily large.

> And being greatly favoured, said Barros,[1] they possess the fat of the land, and live there in greater prosperity than the natives; for they do not till or sow the land nor build nor fight nor engage in any honest labour. And withal, being thus idle, they enjoy power, honour, favour and riches; they do not risk their lives nor imperil their dignity, and without

[1] The historian João de Barros (1496 ?–1570), author of the *Decadas da India* (1552–63). (Translator's note.)

corporal toil but merely through their incessant machinations they carry off the fruits of every man's labour.

In these words he sums up the position of the Jews and echoes the reasonable complaints of the people. It was a problem of a social and economic character, or merely a question of revenue (as it remains to-day, despite the expulsion) which the government was unable to solve. Hence the various aspects of the story of the Jews, which hovers between religious persecution and anti-social protection. The religious side of the question at this time had thrown into the shade the economic side; and in the exaltation of the Catholic spirit the monarchs were obliged to settle it in a religious sense if they were truly to interpret the will of the people, often against their own feelings. It was the second time that the Jewish question had been raised in Spain. The Visigothic monarchy, which the Moorish invasion destroyed, had not been able to complete the extermination of the Jews; and after eight centuries of warfare the traditions of the Goths were linked with the present time, now that after the conquest of Granada the last refuge of the Moors in Spain had fallen. As of old, the King at the head of the Church, which for its part represents the spirit of the nation, is the Grand Inquisitor; and we shall see in the course of this history how unjust it is to make the Papacy responsible for his acts. The Church at Rome was then too profligate to be fervent in the faith and too avaricious to be intolerant. Enthusiasm and intolerance were to be found only among the Spanish; and the action of the Papacy consisted in modifying the fury of those apostles, in view of money received by the Papacy from the Jews, or from a wish to defend its threatened authority or from humanity natural to children of that golden Italy of the Renaissance.

Such was the zeal of the Catholic Sovereigns to complete the religious unity of Spain that as early as

1478, several years before the date of the Bull of Sixtus IV, Torquemada, Prior of the Dominican convent at Segovia, had been appointed General Inquisitor. The King at last ruled over the whole of Spain and could reduce all his subjects to the true faith, and in presiding over the general assemblies of the Inquisition he resembles the ancient Gothic kings at the head of their councils. The first assembly was held at Seville, and as in the ancient assemblies of the clergy the nobles took part in it. In this assembly it was resolved to complete the unification of the faith. In 1498 eight hundred Jews in a body abandon Spain, preferring this sorrowful exile to renounce their religion:

> Ah my belovèd Spain, for lost is Sion!
> Spain too is lost, our comfort and our refuge.

As in the case of the councils in the time of the Goths, the Inquisition serves in the King's hands as a weapon to subdue the half-feudal nobility created by the reconquest, since in matters of faith there are no privileges and no one is sheltered from the wrath of the terrible tribunal. Its action is so absolute and its devotion so tremendous that it becomes more Catholic than the Pope, usurps his authority, opposes his Bulls and gives to the Church in the Peninsula a national character, with the King at its head, a pope with the Grand Inquisitor as his ruling prelate.

After the expulsion of the Jews there was still some winnowing to be done. There remained the Moors, scattered over the centre of Spain or refugees in the mountains of western Andalusia, to which they had been driven by the raids and persecutions of Cardinal Ximenes. These Moors, captive in Spain after the reconquest, lived at the mercy of waves of intolerance and of the actions and reactions of politics and religion. Historians give their numbers as a total varying between three hundred thousand and nine hundred thousand.

Dwelling isolated from the Christian inhabitants in their *aljamas* or *mourarias*, as the Jews in their ghettos, they formed a group apart. Being industrious and humble, they did not, however, incur the hatred or envy of the people; indeed their business placed them in contact with the common people, and in such a way as was neither irksome to the pride nor injurious to the interests of the Christians. They were gardeners in the country, small shopkeepers in the towns; they followed the humble trades of tinkers, smiths, cobblers, soap-manufacturers, muleteers. As was natural in a completely isolated colony, they were bound closely together by the narrow ties of a common origin and a common lot. There were no beggars among them. If any of them became destitute he received assistance from the rest. They were silent and patient, but necessity rendered them vindictive; and an offence to one of them was considered an offence to all. If one of them committed a crime justice pursued the criminal in vain; they all stood by one another. Conflicts and bloody disputes necessarily ensued, such as those which disturbed Toledo in 1467 and Valladolid in 1470. Individually these Moors were inoffensive, and were often held in esteem, yet they were a source of perpetual disquiet. The nearness of the Moors of Granada and in Morocco across the Straits caused the new Goths to fear a second invasion, in which the Moors in Spain would repeat the part played by the Jews eight centuries before. Thus the Moors in Castille and León were not permitted to go to Granada and must give bail before leaving for Aragon, Valencia or Portugal. The Cortes of the year 1592 at Madrid demanded that they should be distributed over all the provinces of Spain, that they should not be allowed to go more than five leagues from their *aljama*, and that in war they should be given posts of danger, the sooner to end this anomaly. Philip III in 1609 adopted a more drastic method and expelled them in a body. This radical measure, as in the case of the Jews, satisfied both social needs and the demands of conscience. A scrupulous man, by dint of seeing in everything cases of conscience and causes of sin, may gradually destroy all the sources of moral life until he finds himself living in peace and quiet in the foolish emptiness of his brain; and Spain in the same way, being full of scruples, gradually expelled from her midst all the causes of sin until she found herself in a state of purity represented by depopulation, ruin, and that kind of peace which men and nations enjoy in the grave.

The Moors were compelled to cross the Straits and take refuge in Morocco. The Jews earlier had partly taken refuge in Portugal, where the administration had not yet succumbed to the religious fervour which soon afterwards inspired it likewise. Not that the Portuguese people was less ardent in the faith, but King João II in his wisdom was not in agreement with the nation. As early as the year 1481, at Evora, the Cortes had complained of the wealth and ostentation of the Jews. Over twenty thousand families of Spanish Jews fled to Portugal: King João II received them on payment of eight crusados a head, on condition that they should become slaves if they did not leave the country within eight months. These harsh conditions were not carried out, but towards the end of the reign of the Perfect Prince feeling ran so high that it was proposed to colonize the island of S. Thomé with the children of these Jews. A tolerant policy came in with King Manuel, but his marriage to a daughter of the Catholic King occasioned a change in Portuguese policy, and as a wedding present to her King Manuel in 1496 issued an order for the expulsion of all Jews and free Moors, either natives or immigrants, unless they accepted baptism. Death and confiscation of goods was the penalty fixed for those who refused to become exiles or be converted. It seems that the majority of the

Jews chose the latter course, which was certainly the easier, especially as they were determined to make baptism a mockery. The proof of this is that they asked and were granted that their beliefs should not be inquired into for the next twenty years. This dangerous and in a sense absurd solution irritated the fanaticism of the people without giving the Jews the peace they longed for. The faithful at once perceived the mockery, and the fearful sacrilege increased their hatred of the freedom, wealth, and influence of the Jews. The baptisms were sacrilegious, and continually so the use of the sacraments, which the Jews under the guise of Christians received in the hope of bettering their fortunes. This was the beginning of the terrible comedy of blood and shame which was ushered in by King Manuel's decree. The massacre at Lisbon in 1506 found an echo throughout the country, and its repetition was only with difficulty prevented by main force. The old hatred of the Jews had new material to feed upon, and the unpunished acts of sacrilege filled the hearts of the faithful with righteous indignation. This indignation found expression in barbarous acts of assassination, the tragic side of the play in which the shameful part is presented by the miserable hypocrisy of the Jews. The people tumultuously and at random held a permanent court of inquiry into the beliefs of the New Christians; and frequently, in the same tumultuous fashion, arrogated to itself the right to act as executioner of ecclesiastical justice. A kind of informal Inquisition preceded the establishment of the tribunal of the faith. King João III, true embodiment of the fanaticism of the people, understood this because he felt it, and history must see in this the essential motive of the really passionate way in which he succeeded in founding the tribunal against the wish of Rome. Given the situation created by King Manuel and the impossibility of settling it in a tolerant way, as it might be settled in our time, one must admit that the organization of a tribunal of the faith was to be preferred to the anarchical existence of such a tribunal, with the office of judges entrusted to a mob fanaticized by a second mob of raving friars. The King shared the passion of his people, but we must recognize that even from the point of view of sound administration and of justice and order the foundation of the Inquisition was to be desired. Public motives of this kind influenced the monarch, and in private he shared with the rest of Spain an ardent enthusiasm for the purification of the faith. In eighteen years Torquemada had tried a hundred thousand persons; from six to seven thousand had been burnt in effigy; and nine thousand[1] had been burnt in person, like the victims daily offered up in ancient Carthage to Baal in flames.

The same fire burnt in the spirit of King João III, whom a prejudiced modern historian has called 'a fanatic, a knave, and a fool'. To condemn the king without condemning the general tendency is to falsify history and to apply to it a wrong criterion. This historian, of a character as noble as his learning was great and his industry remarkable, has left us an account of the negotiations which led up to the establishment of the Inquisition in Portugal.[2] In his wish to disparage the king, whose crime, if he was guilty, was shared by the whole nation; in his wish to condemn a man of the sixteenth century for what his strong modern spirit rightly condemned, he does not spare quips and insults, and almost exults when he can show us King João III ordering the murder of a man who thwarted the royal plans. Yet who is ignorant of the mad crimes occasioned by reasons of State? Is there any prince of the sixteenth century, or of any century, whose robes are not stained with blood, and in

[1] See Introduction, p. xviii.
[2] Alexandre Herculano, *Da Origem e Estabelecimento da Inquisição em Portugal*, 3 vols (1854-9).

the depths of whose conscience there is not some bitter subject of remorse? And in spite of everything one has this strong impression: King João III might be foolish and fanatical, but he was sincere in his belief; Rome might be corrupt and vile, but its corruption and vileness in this instance served the interests of humanity. As to the Jews, they were real martyrs, but they do not deserve the lyrical applause of blind philanthropists, for love of men rests essentially on love of human dignity, and this was unknown to these martyrs, who abjectly entrusted their whole cause to bribery, and basely submitted to practise the rites of a religion which they loathed. This is made perfectly plain by the story of these negotiations. The Jews treat with Rome as in an open market, and by sheer bribery obtain from successive Popes an attitude opposed to the wishes of the King. In the Bulls which protected the Jews humanity and the papal rights were the phrases which covered the sums received. The correspondence between the Portuguese ambassador and his King is eloquent:

> All the pressure brought to bear on Clement to issue this Brief when he was dying was that of his confessor, who, at the instigation of the New Christians, told him that, since he had had their money, he ought as a matter of conscience to give them their money's worth. That is the truth, as Cardinal Santiquatro [1] related it to Pope Paul in my presence.

In another passage we find that Santiquatro, perceiving that the Jews in Rome obtain whatever they wish by means of bribery, proposes a division of the spoils:

> Santiquatro suggests that the Jews should not have it all their own way. He proposes to mulct them in twenty or thirty thousand crusados, or whatever sum your Highness may decide, and that you should share this sum with the Pope.

[1] The cardinal who defended the interests of the Portuguese Crown.

The Portuguese ambassadors, as politicians untroubled by scruples in the corrupt Italy of that day, insist on this point:

All the negotiations of your Highness with this Pope (Paul III) must be on the basis of his interests; you can obtain anything from him provided it does not adversely affect his interests. It were best for your Highness to go shares with him.

But King João III was obstinate and refused to accept or yield. He was a Catholic, not a politician. Should we wonder if he had imitated the Pope, or are we to expect him to act according to our idea of what becomes great men in the nineteenth century? We consider that his greatness consists precisely in this religious exaltation, which we now condemn in theory but which we may not condemn historically without applying to former times the criterion of principles then unknown. The religious fervour of King João III was such that he wrote to his ambassador in Rome that 'if the post of Grand Inquisitor were a civil post, I would gladly accept it'. At last, in 1536, he obtained for Portugal the establishment of the Inquisition, and henceforth the work of purifying the faith went on in Portugal with the ardour which had long since been the custom in the neighbouring kingdom.

Those who have studied the history of the Papacy during the Renaissance are aware that the state of Christianity at that time could not meet the needs of the truly religious. This is the ultimate cause of those parallel movements of reform which broke out in Spain and Germany and had for their result the Inquisition and Protestantism. The real explanation of these phenomena is that they were rendered necessary by the requirements of historical evolution and of the national character in the Peninsula. If now we study them abstractedly, that is absolutely and apart from the chain of circumstances to which they were subjected, we must admit that in a comparison between the mysticism of the Germans, the naturalism of the Italians, and the idealism of the Peninsula; between the attitude which led to the antics of the Anabaptists, that which led to the monstrous aberrations of the Borgias, and that which led to a company of heroes who dominated the old world and discovered the new, the palm must be awarded to the last, despite its fatal consequences. Excessive toil wears out men's bodies, and excessive thought wears out their brains; and so it is with nations who have carried through some mighty achievement or have lived for some fervent idea. Yet what else truly noble and great is there in the life of individuals or of nations? We do not exist merely to produce and consume and return to the earth from which we came; let us not therefore condemn the harsh consequences of heroism. With the exception of ancient Greece, they were never so cruel as in Spain:

> The unquiet time sails on with rudder lost,
> Whirled forward by a mighty rushing wind.

It was this mighty wind which scattered the Great Armada in 1588, that last effort of the Spanish nation in its duel against Protestantism; it was the same wind that blew clouds of burning sand into the face of King Sebastian, blinding his eyes in death, at the battle of Alcacer Kebir, which in 1578 put an end to the enterprise of redeeming the Holy Places. After wearing themselves out in their fight against the Moors and against the Protestants, those soldiers of God fell vanquished to the ground. They were not defeated by the Moors nor by the Protestants but by that modern spirit which they themselves had fostered when at the Council of Trent they championed the dignity of human reason, and when they discovered unknown worlds in the East and in the West. The fruits of our achievement turned against us, and these mortal blows finally assured the inevitable triumph of the modern spirit which we with our old-fashioned ways and unwieldy strength could now only impede. When the two nations of the Peninsula, exhausted and defeated, embraced like two corpses in a graveyard, in 1580, the hopes of those who looked for this union to produce new strength were in vain. This union had long existed in men's minds. Despite the political division between the two countries, Europe always saw in Castille and Portugal one body animated by one spirit. But now their union was merely formal, for Nature cannot plastically give life to two corpses. This temporary union lasted but half a century and was barren. After their separation the two nations again moved on parallel lines in the seventeenth and eighteenth centuries, and it is this history which we will now rapidly examine.

BOOK V

THE RUINS

I. THE PENINSULA IN THE SEVENTEENTH AND EIGHTEENTH CENTURIES

THE combination of causes which we have pointed out reduced the two nations of the Peninsula to a silence of death after their separation in 1640. Since we do not propose to write the history of these nations, we are now almost at the end of our task. The civilizing influence of the Peninsula ends with the sixteenth century and has left a valuable legacy to the world; from that time onwards it remains for us only to chronicle the facts relating to its internal decay and incidents which are so many fruitless attempts to galvanize a dead organism; we refer to the dictatorships of Aranda and Pombal. Finally we have to relate a collective agitation of an obscure and indefinite character which, as in the Middle Ages, is ushering in the birth of a new collective state of mind, corresponding to Catholicism of old.

We will here quote the words of an illustrious Portuguese writer. The main idea of his treatise[1] seems to us incomplete or untenable in the light of history, but he presents in vivid and eloquent colours the picture of our decadence in the sixteenth and seventeenth centuries:

To a generation of philosophers, learned men and creative artists succeeds the common crowd of men of uncritical learning and of academic and imitative talent. Leaving the society of living men in the open air, we enter a narrow place, close almost as the grave, where the air is thick with the dust of old folios—a place inhabited by learned spectres. Poetry, after the barren, false and artificial exaltation of Góngora and the affectation of conceits which only served to show the lack of thought, falls into the servile and unintelligent imitation of Latin poetry of the dull and monkish school called

[1] Anthero de Quental, *Causas da decadencia dos povos peninsulares.*

classical, which was the very opposite of true inspiration and feeling. A poem is now composed learnedly, like a theological treatise. To translate is considered the ideal; to invent is held to be dangerous and a sign of inferior talent; and a poetical work is judged according to the number of lines it contains translated from Horace and Ovid. Tragedy, Pindaric odes and burlesque poems flourish, indicating the affectation and degradation of true poetry. As to human truth, popular or national sentiment, it was completely disregarded. Invention and originality in this lamentable period consist in cynically merry descriptions of the sordid intrigues and devices of common life. In the picaresque novels of Spain and the popular plays of Portugal that profoundly demoralized age, almost ingenuously innocent in its vices, stands self-accused. Apart from this mordant realism, literature limited itself to official and court spheres, academic discourses, a funeral oration, a panegyric to order, artificial and puerile kinds, and moreover deadly dull. What could be expected from art in such an atmosphere ? We have only to raise our eyes to the gloomy masses of stone which go by the name of the Escorial and the convent of Mafra to see that the same lack of feeling and invention which led to the dull and insipid taste of Classicism likewise produced those heavy masses of Jesuit architecture, coldly correct and wholly devoid of character. How sad is the contrast between these mountains of marble, in which monstrous size was mistaken for greatness, and the delicate, soaring, well-proportioned, and so to say spiritual structure of the Hieronymite convent at Belem, the church of Batalha, the cathedral of Burgos! The depraved spirit of society was reflected with a terrible faithfulness in works of art, which will remain a lasting witness against that period of real moral death. This period pervaded not only feeling, imagination, taste, but also, and especially, men's intelligence. During the last two centuries the Peninsula has not produced a single great man who can be compared with the mighty creators of modern science; not one of the great intellectual discoveries, which are the chief glory and achievement of the modern mind, has come from the Peninsula. During two centuries of fruitful development Europe has revised the ancient sciences and created six or seven new ones: anatomy, physiology, chemistry, celestial mechanics, the differential calculus, historical criticism, geology; it has produced Newton, Descartes, Bacon, Leibniz, Harvey, Buffon, Ducange, Lavoisier, Vico. Where among these real heroes of the epic of thought is there a Spanish or a Portuguese name? What Spanish or Portuguese name is connected with the discovery of a great scientific law, a system, an essential fact? Cultivated Europe has risen to a great and noble position through science mainly; and it is mainly through the lack of science that we sank into nullity and degradation. Our soul was completely dead. Ignorance, oppression and penury lead naturally and fatally to moral degradation; and this is what happened. Among the great there was the sumptuous corruption of court life, with the kings giving the example of vice, brutality, and adultery: Afonso VI, João V, Philip V, Charles IV. Among the people there was the corruption of hypocrisy, and the families of the poor were at the mercy of the vices of the noble and powerful. It was the age of mistresses and bastards. The temptations to which the gold of the nobles subjected the women of the people may be seen in the scandalous case of the nullity of marriage of King Afonso VI and in the *Memoirs* of the Cavalheiro de Oliveira. The trade of pimp was openly recognized and was practised with profit even at Court. Religion ceased to be a living faith and became an unintelligent mechanical formula. We all know what the monks were: their picaresque and ignoble habits still live in the Decameron of popular tradition. And these tonsured buffoons were bloodthirsty. The Inquisition weighed on men's conscience like the vault of a prison. Public spirit gradually sank under the pressure of terror, while vice, becoming more and more refined, placidly occupied the empty place in men's souls left by the absence of dignity, morality, and strong will, which had been crushed and destroyed by fear. The casuists of the seventeenth and eighteenth centuries have left us a shameful monument of the bestial refinement of every kind of vice, depraved imagination, intimate corruption of family life, and general immorality which undermined society in that lamentable time. And on the other hand the casuists show us to what moral degradation the priests had sunk: we see them continually digging in the mud and with zest, almost one might say

as a labour of love, turning over that nauseous heap of in-
famies. All this corruption was reflected in literature. The
corruption in public life in the seventeenth century is por-
trayed with all the emphasis of a sarcastic and implacable pen
in Antonio Vieira's *Art of Thieving* [1]; the corruption of private
life is recorded in Dom Francisco Manuel de Mello's *Guide to
Marriage*,[2] in the popular farces in Portugal, and in the
picaresque romances in Spain. Morality in the Peninsula had
sunk gradually to the lowest depravation.

If we would sum up in a few words the causes of
disorganization in the Peninsula we find the key of the
problem in three causes—individualism, the Jesuits, and
the oversea conquests. All three had become debased
forms of a great idea which had become an anachronism,
and the true and only source of corruption consists in
the fact of the former greatness. Individualism had
produced great men; now it only produces wretches
whose greatness takes the form of unbridled luxury and
who believe that gold and immorality suffice to create
and maintain an aristocracy. Jesuitism, or rather the
mystic tendency from which it sprang, had been the
pith and mainspring of the energy of the Peninsula,
and now it is but a religion of obedience, a school of
methodical perversion. The conquests had been the
enterprise encouraged by those two characteristics—
individualism and mysticism—and now they are but a
source of corruption, flooding the Peninsula with the
taint of gold, the stigma of slavery, syphilis, love of
idleness, and immorality. A Belgian professor, travelling
in the Peninsula, had remarked that 'The cult of Venus
in Spain is exactly like that in ancient Thebes'. A negro
Venus from Guinea and Kaffraria stood on the altars
by the side of Venus Anadyomene. The pimp and the

---

[1] The *Arte de Furtar* (1652) is still anonymous. It was certainly not
written by the great Jesuit preacher Vieira. (Translator's note.)

[2] There is an excellent modern edition of the *Carta de Guia de
Casados*, by Professor Edgar Prestage, Porto 1916; second ed. Porto
1923. (Translator's note.)

picaroon were now the true heirs of the hero and soldier,
whose men 'wise in command and brave in battle',
as the *Chronicle of Don Alvaro de Luna* calls them.
The multiplication of beggars in this country flooded
with gold is shown in a new literary *genre*, the picaresque
novel, dealing with beggars and thieves, which took
the place of the Amadis romances. *Lazarillo de Tormes*
dates from 1520.[1] What was a mercenary to do on his
return from the European and colonial wars, worn out
by many a campaign, hardened by sacks and massacres,
rendered restless by the tumultuous life he had led?
He enlisted as a pandar among the bodyservants of a
nobleman or installed himself as a parasite in the house
of a courtesan. With his waxed moustache, his broad-
brimmed hat jauntily worn on one side, his leathern
doublet, his coloured stockings, a bow of ribands at
the knee, his boast is that he is as noble as the King
except that he has no money. He is a beggar. Money
he obtains from his mistress or from the nobleman who
pays him for murder and assault. The Princess of
Eboli once dismissed one of these men from her service
on the charge of laziness: he had only once committed
a murder. Such were the 'idle, swaggering, brawling,
gambling men' who, in the words of Hurtado de
Mendoza in his *Guerra de Granada*,[2] in their greed for
good living made a private profit out of the life of
courtesans. Such was the people whose literature
displays a character at once tragic and grotesque, mystic
and blasphemous, heroic and squalid, that dramatic
character in which it later appeared in the eyes of
Europe, when Europe no longer ended with the
Pyrenees—a Europe still ignorant of the beauty of the
edifice of which it now saw but the ruins and decay.
The decadence of all idealistic peoples has been of the

[1] The first extant editions of this anonymous little masterpiece are of
the year 1554, but it was doubtless written earlier. (Translator's note.)
[2] First published in 1627, fifty-two years after the author's death.

same kind; such were the Greeks, sunk in piracy and the lowest vice; such the Italians, given over to brigandage. The heroic active Spaniard in his decay transformed this heroism into the practical good sense of Sancho, as a stepping-stone to the 'wisdom' of the picaroon. New precepts replaced the ancient proverbs: Conceive of the air and you will bring forth wind; Vainglory's flower is followed by no fruit; In the presence of the King be silent or speak pleasant words; Better an old woman with money than a girl without a dowry; When bread is scarce help yourself first. But in this very vileness there is so much wit, so much fire and nobility, although a perverted nobility, such a horror of what is common, so elegant an expression, that, even as one pities, one has to confess that the Spaniard remains noble even in his degradation. The inhabitant of the Peninsula reacts against his squalor, not with irony or spleen, but with a frank laughter which has in it a suspicion of satanism, but is not gloomy like the despair of the Italian.

From all this we infer that the causes of the decadence of the Peninsula are not a series of definite facts leading to disorganization and to be contrasted with the former prosperity and glory. Such a dualism does not belong to history nor to nature. The initial causes of life and death are identical; the one entails the other; the beginning of the former supplies the reason for the existence of the latter. The limbs which are eaten away in the darkness of the grave are the same limbs that moved in their strength in the light of the sun. They died and are decomposed because of the exhaustion of that mysterious source of life which gave them unity and a soul. The decadence of nations and the death of individuals are both necessary conditions of their greatness, nay, of their very existence; and the facts or symptoms of collective decay, like the decay of animal organisms, are merely the perversion of the principle of life—a principle which in itself entails death. To say, therefore, that Spain died of this or that cause is simply to indicate what form her death, which was inevitable, assumed. It is the part of the historian to point out and to assign them their exact value. But the primary cause of this decay is so difficult to observe that all the alleged causes seem to us, when thoroughly examined, to be merely necessary consequences. Such are the riches from the New World, the corruption of manners, the gloomy and ferocious religious stupidity, the ridiculous insipidity of the education given. Of all these symptoms the last is that which brought the gravest and most fatal consequences. Scientific education had become in Europe what religious education had been in the past: the basis for the development of the spirit of a nation. The measure of the knowledge of a people was already in the seventeenth century, and more and more afterwards the measure of that people's culture. But the University of Salamanca opposed the reforms of Charles III, declaring that 'Newton's teaching does not produce good logicians or metaphysicians, and Gassendi and Descartes show less agreement than Aristotle with the truth of Holy Writ'.

II. ABSOLUTISM. CHARLES III AND JOSEPH I

THE Marqués de la Ensenada, in insisting with Ferdinand VI on the necessity of reforming education, wrote:

> So far as I am aware we have not a single Chair of Law, Experimental Physics, Anatomy. There are no accurate maps of Spain and its provinces, and no one capable of making them. We have only the inferior ones which come from France and Holland. We are thus ignorant of the true position of the towns and villages and of their distance from one another. It is disgraceful.

It was disgraceful. This feeling of the ministers of Ferdinand VI and Charles III is likewise that of

Pombal. Contact with the nations of Europe had formed in the Peninsula an élite of modern men in whom the national tradition was dead. They saw the prosperity of the powerful monarchy in France, supported by those institutions of absolutism, a standing army, diplomacy, a system of economic protection, and sought to introduce a copy of all this into the Peninsula. But just as, centuries before, the Visigothic monarchy had been a mere episode and fruitless attempt at preservation in the history of Roman Spain's decay, so absolutism was in the history of Spain's modern decadence. At that time Christianity was the element of a future reorganization, as young shoots often spring from the decayed trunks of trees. And even now, by the side of the ephemeral attempts of Aranda and Pombal, the trunk of old Spain showed one or two signs of the advent of science or of the spirit which makes it possible.

It is not for us here to value or judge pure absolutism —that system which really springs from the history of French civilization, although copied more or less faithfully by other nations of Europe. We will study it incidentally and rapidly when occasion arises. What is characteristically ours in the movement to which the names of Joseph I and Charles III are linked is the destruction of the past, not the reconstruction of the present. A sign of energy still left in the dying country is the rage with which it condemns itself, tears off its shroud and gesticulates violently in the grave, a violence in which the critic may see a proof of lack of real strength. One need never believe in one who attacks with fury; it is always a proof of his slight confidence in his own courage. Where there is true energy it is serene and simple as life itself; and régimes of terror, such as those of Pombal, Cromwell, Robespierre or Dom Miguel, give proof of their essential weakness and are their own condemnation, as things of an exceptional and monstrous character, and for that very reason destined to be of but brief duration. They represent a crisis and not a normal movement. Sometimes they are a revolution speeding up an organic development; sometimes, as in our case, they are a revolution attempting violently to stay the irresistible energy of inevitable decay. The immediate causes or, better, the symptoms of this decay were as clear to the ministers of Charles III and Joseph I as they are to us to-day. And the proof is in the excellence of their aim. Their first and heaviest blow fell on the Jesuits. The Company, whose birth we witnessed, had become the most extravagant and hybrid thing ever produced by the brain of man. The product of national mysticism perverted owing to the European education of its founder, it was an attempt to form a divine romance of chivalry without any visions and ecstasies to correspond to the profane enterprises and tourneys; it was a mixture of mystical and practical spirit, of heroism and cunning; it sought to win the world for God by earthly, not by heavenly weapons, not by preaching and example but by political craft. It was a worldly institution which renounced the old apostolic methods as though it would deny its sacred character in order to strengthen its profane importance; and yet essentially it denied the latter since its work was really not of this world, which it sought to pervert in order to dominate and convert it, undermining the authority of kings, undermining the real strength and truth of education, although it professed ostensibly to defend the former and to encourage the latter. The Company in the civil society of that time was like those insects which in the dark slowly and surely eat away the foundations of a building. They were termites of heaven, and their teeth were therefore the sharper, their hold more tenacious, their destruction swift and incessant. Their rule of obedience made them anonymous, and their mystic fervour made them heroic.

Nothing was capable of resisting them in their legions. In a century or less they had won celebrity as saints in their oversea missions, and on the strength of this celebrity they were able to rule in the name of the kings of all the thrones of Europe, not as Ximenes or Richelieu ruled, but as humble confessors, directors of souls and of public education. But one cannot with impunity thus attack the order of things and human nature. At the end of a century the nations began to feel the whole building tremble, and on examining the woodwork found that it was all eaten away by the pertinacious animals and threatened to fall in ruins. That was precisely what the Jesuits wished. If they bowed humbly before the world, it was in order to ruin or gain it. Their policy was a means, their end that indicated by St. Ignatius: to rule in a graveyard. That would be the kingdom of heaven on earth. So monstrous a system could not have existed in the Middle Ages with their ingenuous faith; it was a product of the Renaissance, when religion and positivism, revelation and science, Christianity and humanism were clearly opposed to one another. To this opposition of ideas corresponds the education of men; and Jesuitism, a society of learned men, proposed to use learning as a weapon with which to stab science. They represented a conservative reaction against the inevitable trend of civilization, and are accordingly accused by science and condemned by the modern spirit of Europe. We said just now that one cannot thus attack human nature and the nature of things; and indeed the nations of Europe, realizing the danger, resolved to crush the destructive insect. It was already abundantly clear to what extent so monstrous a system had perverted the very men who put it in practice. The system of compromises between the individual conscience and the religious reason of State was a slippery path, in which men found it difficult to keep their balance. This need not surprise us; and if anything may be said in favour of the Jesuits it is the perfection, from a technical and aesthetic, not from a moral, point of view of an education capable of turning out men to rival the most daring acrobats and sublime rope-dancers of the mind. But all acrobats have falls, and the question of Paraguay was a disaster. Voltaire is certainly not an authority in whose ideas we should implicitly trust; but there is a sentence of his so penetrating in its caustic humour that it will stand as a sentence without appeal and the synthesis of all that has been written on the subject:

> I was a pupil in the College of Assumption, says Cacambo to Candide in America; and I know the government of those fathers as intimately as I know the streets of Cadiz. An admirable government indeed. Their country is already three hundred leagues across and is divided into thirty provinces. The fathers own everything, the peoples nothing: a masterpiece of reason and justice. I consider nothing so divine as these fathers, who here wage war on the Kings of Spain and Portugal and in Europe are their confessors; who here kill the Spanish and in Madrid send them to heaven. It is charming. I assure you you are going to be the happiest of mortals. What a joy for the fathers when they learn that their ranks are to be swelled by a captain of the Bulgarian army.

In Paraguay the attempt was in fact made to set up a Jesuit government, a pure theocracy, no new thing but an absurdity in the middle of the eighteenth century. The fathers hoped to turn the whole world into a Paraguay. We cannot agree with the cold caustic Frenchman that this aim was prompted merely by greed, but undoubtedly greed entered into the medley of motives which guided the thought of the Company. Paraguay was exploited industrially, and this and other traffic swelled the revenue of the Company; and considering that it proposed to destroy profane society with its own weapons, it was natural that it should not renounce wealth. Historically, therefore, we must see in this rather a necessary consequence of a monstrous system than a proof of greed or immorality on the part of individual Jesuits. The historical fact is that, when Spain gave Paraguay to Portugal in exchange for the colony of Sacramento in 1750, the Jesuits in America opposed what they considered an act of spoliation, and Pombal took the opportunity to expel them from Portugal in 1759. The first blow was given, and when eight years later the minister of Charles III expelled them in turn from Spain this daring action of the Peninsular nations surprised Europe, and history may well wonder at the intricate chain of events. How could St. Ignatius have imagined that from Spain, its cradle, would come the Company's deathblow two centuries later? Europe, recovering from its astonishment, followed the energetic example of dead Spain. The Jesuits were expelled fron Naples and Parma and finally from France, and, abandoned by the Pope himself, were forced to seek a refuge among those very Protestant nations which it was the mission of their Company to undermine. For a moment the resistance of Clement XIII during the years 1758 to 1769 suggested to Pombal the idea of making the Portuguese Church independent; but the Pope died in tears, still refusing to abolish the Company, and Ganganelli (1769–1775) was elected in order to perform the act demanded by Aranda, Pombal, Tanucci and Choiseul; by France, Spain and Italy, and Portugal—that is to say, by the concert of Catholic nations. To exterminate the Company, which in fact then represented the Papacy, was to restore the former independence of the national Churches and re-establish the traditional relations between Church and State, between Rome and the Catholic Courts. Such was the immediate result of the expulsion of the Jesuits from the Peninsula, a result manifest in the Concordats which were then made. This relative independence enabled the minister of King Joseph I to check the judicial encroachments of the clergy, to see that the laws concerning mortmain were obeyed, to forbid legacies on behalf of one's soul, and to limit those for pious purposes, chapels and prayers for the dead, and to correct in favour of absolutism that tendency of the mystic spirit to invade the national economy in Spain and Portugal. To exterminate the Company was, further, to free education from a sterilizing control and give science the place which the modern spirit of Europe demanded. Thus the Universities were re-formed, the administration of justice was renewed, and the Jesuit colleges were closed.

But it was not Jesuitism alone that represented that ancient spirit of the Peninsula which had now become debased. Catholic mysticism had created the Inquisi-tion, and its tremendous power, which at first had been fostered by the monarchs, had become their rival now that monarchy was or wished to be modern. The Inquisition, whose ferocity formerly represented the fervent faith of the people, was now but faintly ap-plauded or was even actually condemned by a nation which had become decadent and discouraged and was made irresolute by observing its own condition and comparing it with that of the rest of Europe. At the last *auto de fe* at Seville in 1781 a poor witch was the last victim offered up by Castille to the Catholic Baal. In Portugal the all-powerful Minister burnt Jesuitism in the person of Father Malagrida, and as an offering to the Baal of monarchy the Tavoras and other nobles at Belem. Thus a monarchical terror replaced the religious terror, and Spain, struggling in vain to emerge from the path of inevitable ruin, attempted fruitlessly to implant in its midst the principles of a new civiliza-tion which in a different atmosphere humanism and science had been developing in Europe.

Absolute monarchy was a personal policy of the Ministers. It corresponded to no feeling or consciously essential requirements of the nation; a régime of terror was therefore necessary to carry it through, and for this very reason it was ephemeral. This vain attempt, this incident on the road to ruin, left but one fact behind it, and this fact brought the ruin nearer. The resistance of the aristocracy was broken by the iron despotism of the throne; and when the chimera of a monarchy based on civil law fell to the ground, the nation was henceforth represented merely by its devout kings who had now become omnipotent. The monarchical terror and the religious terror join hands, the two Baals embrace, and the people observe and applaud the orgies of a Charles IV and a Dom Miguel. And, history repeating itself in every detail, foreign invaders set foot on Spanish soil. But let us not forestall events but rather consider the constructive efforts of the epoch of Charles III and Joseph I, since we have witnessed how successful it was in destruction.

The idea that the power of kings is 'a lofty and independent sovereignty which they derive from God and by virtue of which in their wisdom and absolute power they rule and direct their subjects', as the expression was in the schools, had been developed in central Europe, together with the development of classical studies, on which the idea had first been based. Dante's famous treatise, the 'De Monarchia', marks an epoch in the formation of this imperialist theory which was now decking out with Christian words and ideas the old divinization of the Caesars. But the doctrine was not advanced by learning alone. Society was moving intellectually and economically towards a condition or age corresponding to that of Rome under her first emperors; but it was also true that the decay of the power of the Papacy and of the theocratic ideas of the Middle Ages represented the weakening of Christian fervour in the soul of the people and in the minds of the learned; and this decay of the power of the Papacy was a powerful support for a doctrine implanted in Europe in a soil thoroughly well prepared for it. The Jesuits, always acute and well aware of what were the best means to employ against the humanist movement which they sought radically to destroy, appear in the seventeenth century as champions of democracy and theocracy—that is to say, of the ideas of personal and local independence, and of the supreme authority of the Church; in a word, of the ideas of the Middle Ages as opposed to the classical imperialism or absolutism which was a theory in the sixteenth century and became a fact in the seventeenth. It was a Spaniard, Padre Mariana, who in his celebrated book, the *De Rege*, openly and in the light of day attacked the usurpation of monarchy and pointed out to the people the old right of revolt which naturally belonged to it, including in these rights even that of regicide when a monarch abused his usurped power. Openly thus to attack the exceptional power of kings in that age was to run the risk of incurring the penalty imposed upon Mariana, that of death.[1]

Had we to analyse and examine the principles of absolutism we should have to point out the anomaly of its existence in the midst of a religion which was common to nations in themselves independent and at the same time owning the sovereignty of the Pope who was independent of their monarchs. Empire consists in the union of religious and political power; and a monarch can only be absolute when the nation sees in him the representative of a political power sanctioned by a religious authority of which he is the only representative. Such were the emperors in the East and in Rome. Modern absolutism, in inventing two parallel revelations, that of the popes and that of the kings, two simultaneous sovereignties in permanent conflict, sows in the mind of society a disorder marked by open feuds and only mitigated by the system of concordats. The

[1] See Introduction, pp. xiv–xv.

faithful see and will always see in the Pope their true king by divine right; and for them not to obey a foreign authority it were necessary for their king to be at the same time their spiritual head. This essential defect of absolutism, a political and religious system transferred from other ages into the heart of Christian society, was the chief cause of its short duration; and nowhere was this more evident than in the Peninsula, because nowhere else in Europe was the strength of Catholic ideas so great. The absolute monarchies of Charles III and Joseph I ended with those monarchs and have a merely personal value in the history of Spain. They did not spring out of a natural development of the living strength or weakness of the nation. A reaction was immediately apparent in the reigns of Maria I and Charles IV, and the increase in the power of the throne merely strengthened the clergy, who now again reigned in fact, basing their power on the influence which they exercised over rulers and ruled alike.

From another point of view also the system of absolutism carried with it the germ of its own ruin. In claiming divine right for the Crown by virtue of a revelation and a consecration independent of those of the Papacy, it based its origin in the humanist and classical movement, in the traditions of antiquity and in the Græco-Latin civilization. It thus reconstructed a social system on the foundation of a natural right, which, when pushed to its logical conclusion, was destined to overthrow the thrones of Europe at the end of the eighteenth century. The Marques de Pombal, in his reform of the whole of the civil law, abolished the former supremacy of Roman and Canon law, in which the law of modern Europe found its historical expression, and based law on the principles of natural right, while he at the same time restored national law so far as it was compatible with natural law.

This brings us to the third point which we consider

it essential to note in this rapid sketch. The restoration of national law in the monarchies of the eighteenth century represented the idea on which their economic legislation was based. Each nation considered itself an independent whole in Europe, complete in itself and opposed, although not hostile, to the other nations. In the Middle Ages Christian Europe had been a federation under the leadership of Germany or France or Spain, with the Pope as its president. This religious and military headship was now cast off and the federation broken up, and the several nations with their monarchs at their head were now so many independent bodies, socially, politically, and in religion. The unity of European civilization was not lost, but the idea of the collective interests of the nations of Europe was forgotten. A nation that formed an independent whole would naturally abandon the traditions of Roman and Canon law which represented the unity of ancient Europe and of Christian Europe; it would naturally revert to the tradition of national law, in an instinctive need on the part of the nations to base the reason for their existence in the reality of their previous organic development. This, as we have said, brings us to the third point of our study, economic legislation. It is in this that the historian may see the complete expression of the independence of the nations of Europe in the eighteenth century. In that system of absolutism, in which we noticed the opposition between natural and divine right, we must also notice the equally essential antagonism between the naturalism prevailing in ideas and the protection or prohibition expressed in facts through the laws which received the name of the commercial system. Now that the French Revolution has passed over it, we can see that the naturalism of the eighteenth century must of logical necessity lead to an affirmation which would completely destroy divine right and systematic protection.

The essential character of the commercial system is well known: it consisted in giving direct protection to the development of a nation's wealth by declaring war on the wealth of other nations. 'The surest means of enriching a country,' said Sully, 'is to sell every year to foreigners more products than we buy from them.' In this false economic aphorism the monarchs of the Peninsula, and those of contemporary Europe, framed that indispensable need of protection which is felt by economic organisms, as by all natural organisms, if it is to develop and grow. Thus, by the side of chimerical attempts to create exotic industries, of absurd decrees regulating dress, food, and other intimate details of private life; by the side of tyrannical legislation in monetary questions, we find in the time of Charles III and Joseph I an improvement in colonial administration and an attempt to foster the development of national wealth, an attempt partly successful, since the protection granted to exotic industries embraced the natural industries as well. But the Peninsula, with its whole life in decay, might tolerate but could not applaud these attempts, which were unnatural in the sense that they ran counter to the inevitable process of complete decay which always precedes periods of rebirth. Catholicism was still fervent, and the institutions which it had founded had been attacked but not destroyed. There were crowds of monks, and the greater part of the land was in the hands of the secular or regular clergy. America, owing to the labour of the negroes, still yielded enough to support the luxury of a dissolute nobility and the idleness of a devout middle class. The profit of most of Spain's produce in Europe went to the English, much of the land held in entail by an ignorant and feckless nobility remained uncultivated; but this seemed comparatively unimportant so long as the money from overseas filled the deficits in the royal treasury and furnished the pensions and charities which the king distributed so lavishly. The people, debased and effeminate, had lost both the habit of toil and the vigour of its intelligence, and was content to live, idle and foolish, a life which it did not understand. The peasants looked with indifference at their fields full of weeds, and humbly bowed their heads as the lord of the land went by or beat their breasts when they saw a troop of fat friars on their glossy mules trotting along paths formed by the winter rains. Their aesthetic feelings were satisfied by the pomp of religious cere-monies; and when famine came there was the soup at the gates of convents; finally, when death came they were content in the hands of the priest to give up a life which was a burden to them, to receive extreme unction, and to request the priest to say many masses for their soul.

III. CONTEMPORARY SPAIN

THE naturalism of the eighteenth century finally showed itself in its true colours and turned against those monarchies of which it had been the chief sup-port. The French Revolution at the end of the century spread and imposed its new formula over the whole of Europe, unconsciously repeating what had occurred previously in a different way, when all the kingdoms of Europe copied the institutions of France. Yet at that time each nation adapted the type as best it could to its special and traditional elements, producing new kinds similar to those which we studied in the Peninsula, the monarchies of Charles III and Joseph I. Now, on the other hand, the radical character of the formula and the violent way in which the generals of the Republic, last of them Napoleon, attempted by war to impose the new régime, ran counter to the institutions and tradi-tions of the nations in which the idea had not originated, and at the same time offended their love of national independence. The Revolution of 1789 and the declaration of the rights of man in which the principles of the revolution were expressed, were the logical outcome of the ideas of French society since the time when, after the end of the wars of religion, France proposed to construct her constitution on a basis of natural law. But they were not the outcome of German nor of Spanish history; and for this reason the resistance to their invasion soon constrained the French to abandon their project of imposing their naturalistic and Jacobin republic on the whole of Europe. It is not for us here to speak of the violent commotions and severe sufferings which this illusion brought upon France; but we must note that the chief cause of this folly consisted in the narrow views of sectarians and doctrinaires flushed with war, who supposed that the human mind had now made its final discoveries, and that human society was now arriving at the goal of its journey through history. And nothing of this was true. The naturalism of the revolution was but a period in the development of the French nation; in general history, which alone can embrace the various nations of Europe, it was but a moment in the development or definition of humanism, which since the Renaissance had been replacing on a scientific basis a decadent religion in men's minds.

Nowhere in Europe was the resistance to the French (not to their invasion of Spain, for that was a piece of treachery against a defenceless country) so serious as in Spain, for nowhere else did the naturalistic impiety of the invaders find Catholicism so fervently alive. In its name, in the name of their outraged country, and especially in the name of that vein of personal independence which is the basis of the Iberian character, the Spanish organized the holy war of independence. The people, debased, corrupted, and abandoned by their kings, still mustered sufficient energy to expel the invaders, whose impious acts of sacrilege filled them with a terrible fury. The war assumed a primitive character, and the veteran battalions of the Empire retreated in dismay before those guerrilleros, who made a fortress of every rock, an ambush of every mountain gully, converting their wells into graves and the streets of their cities into cemeteries.

The invasion acted on the Peninsula like an earthquake. The whole nation trembled and became aware of its existence. A French writer describes in words both picturesque and true that new impression and the commotions which were its consequence:

> Napoleon unconsciously sowed revolution. In the war of independence Spain had saved herself without the help of her kings and had thus realized that she was still capable of great deeds. Those battles, in which the monarchy had no part, revealed to her new strength and life, and, strange to say, in fighting for her king she began to lose her devotion towards the monarchy. To the question, what is the force which agitates Spain? one cannot reply with the name of a Rousseau or a Mirabeau. The cause is mysterious and invisible, and the more irresistible on that account. And the people accepts rather than provokes this strange revolution in the name of God.

These words show how unanimous was the feeling and how incoherent were the opinions, how enthusiastic the will and how vague the idea which inspired the revolutions of 1812 and 1820 and the Cortes of Cadiz and Lisbon. One and the same man was a radical Jacobin and a fervent Catholic, and men of monkish learning were inspired by Liberal ideas. An orator in the Cortes would declaim in phrases learnt from the French orators and then go home and devoutly pray his rosary and feel a pious horror of Freemasons. Another piled up texts and proofs to prove that even in the eleventh and twelfth centuries parliamentary and liberal institutions were familiar to the Spanish and that the revolution was merely restoring the canons of the Councils of Toledo and of the imaginary Cortes of Lamego. Yet

all this chaos was marked by the utmost candour and
good faith. It was the dazed awakening of a sleeping
nation by means of a terrible war. In the crush of new
impressions ideas surged madly through brains weakened
by centuries of atrophy. That is why what caused so
much astonishment seems quite natural to us now:
that, when the kings returned from exile, restored by
the victory of reaction in France, these ingenuous,
imaginative parliaments vanished like dust in the wind,
disappearing like a mere incident unrelated to preceding
or succeeding events, in the midst of the indifference or
devout fervour of a people which saw its old beloved
symbols restored to it. Between a sleep and a sleep the
Peninsula had drowsily waved its arms, and still half
asleep had expelled the French and sown the seeds of
future revolutions. Now it went back to bed, to wait till
the long dark night of its decadence should definitively
come to an end. It was not a question of many hours,
and this last sleep was brief. Overseas the traditions
of patriotism were weaker, and the example of the
United States of America was near at hand.

> When part of the Latin colonies, says a German historian,
> passed into the power of the utilitarian and Protestant
> democracy of the English, a curious phenomenon was to be
> seen: that of a population with more land than it could culti-
> vate being forced to pay high salaries to workmen who soon
> found themselves in a position to acquire landed property
> of their own and in their turn pay out salaries. The liberal
> reward of labour encouraged marriage and increase of the
> population. Thus the United States in less than fifty years
> saw their population increase from one and a half millions to
> fifteen millions; whereas the colonies of South America,
> given over to idleness and undermined by parasitic bodies,
> civil and religious, and by slavery, became more and more
> decadent.

Many in South America wished to follow the example
of the United States and cut the ties which bound them

to a dying mother-country and prevented the full development of that passion for pleasure and wealth and the satisfaction of personal ambitions which had already assumed a character of independence in colonies whose prolonged existence and fixed population gave them the appearance of nations. The crisis of the invasion of the mother-country, coinciding with the radical jacobinism of the French Revolution and with the spread of the utilitarian doctrines of Bentham, gave the Spanish colonies the opportunity to rebel and, apart from their original complaints, to invoke doctrines which gave a legal colour to their rebellion. The same motives, supported by a dynastic quarrel and by the presence of King John VI in Brazil, furnished this Portuguese colony with the means to effect its separation from the mother-country and to found a Portuguese-American empire by the side of the Spanish republics. These events were the chief immediate causes of the sleeper's final awakening. His supplies were cut off; the overseas possessions no longer furnished the means for a life of pleasure and devout idleness; it became necessary to adopt radical measures and set to work in earnest if Spain wished to continue to exist. This cruel state of affairs strengthened the minorities which had been brought up on revolutionary principles and were admirers of utilitarianism. The trouble broke out almost simultaneously in Spain and Portugal, and in both nations the struggle between tradition and revolution took the character of a dynastic war. Don Carlos and Dom Miguel were the heroes acclaimed by a stupid and fanatical people, by an obstinate aristocracy, and by a Church which saw in the victory of Liberal principles the end of a domination which was as old as Spain herself. The nation could not suddenly abandon its ancient tradition nor welcome an order of ideas which were foreign to its history and offensive to its deep and sincere piety. But the force of events was difficult to resist, and many who could not heartily support the new ideas were convinced of the necessity to make a clean sweep of parasitic institutions. It was in this fact much more than in the strength of Liberal ideas that the force of the revolution lay, resulting in the victory of the constitutional dynasties of Queens Isabel and Maria II.

One may confidently assert that the immediate cause of the new social and political régime in the Peninsula was the separation of the colonies; so much so that the history of the Peninsula in the second quarter of the nineteenth century is not that of a people in process of reconstruction but of a people torn between a radicalism copied from France and the ancient national tradition which had been violently severed but not forgotten. An enormous mass of property had been transferred from the clergy to the middle class; the religious orders had been abolished, the privileges of the nobility extinguished, and parliamentary representation of the nation set up. To judge by the legislation, future historians might think that Spain had been suddenly smitten with repentance and entirely converted to new ways. The facts belie this. The hopes of the traditional parties were not dead, and the instability and artificial character of the modern parties allowed these hopes to grow and to find expression in insurrections and long civil wars. A new aristocracy, different from the old, and whose strength lay in wealth and education, still dominated Spain, and the country could not see in the government any expression of the nation's feelings; its representation in parliament was merely a legal device.

During this period the Peninsula presents to the observer the spectacle of two nations racked by suffering, anger, agony; advancing and retreating without method or consistency, like a man lost in the intricate paths of an unknown forest. Strange were the meanings and extravagant the values then attached to the sonorous phrases of the parliamentary doctrinaires. The nation, completely ignorant both of systems and of history, fell with a pious devotion into the arms of those who cynically fostered disorder. Natural instincts awoke in the people and called them to a nomad existence. The fervour with which it followed its generals and guerrilleros, the enthusiasm with which it applauded acts of sedition and pronunciamientos witness to the disorder reigning in its ideas, and at the same time are proof of a vital energy once more spontaneously and fitfully breaking forth, now that the wind of war had blown away the ashes from the smouldering fire. The parliamentary oligarchs could see no advantage, either to their own interests or as a matter of practical politics, in such a state of affairs. Their narrow spirit of learned doctrinaires did not permit them to see in these disturbances the throes of a new life. Tied to their books, in the dust of their libraries, they piled law on law, mountains of manuscript, in an attempt to effect what only slow time and the spontaneous force of life can effect: to create in the soul of the nation a new conscience and a new organism in the social body. The doctrinaires were not concerned exclusively with learning; they were practical men. With their care for the nation went care for themselves, and they created in their own interests posts and sinecures and revenues which were doubly injurious to the work they had in hand, for by so doing they squandered the last remains of the nation's wealth and discredited themselves in the eyes of the nation. This last consequence, which is common to all oligarchies, was aggravated in the middle of the century when the oligarchs, following as usual the example of France, formed themselves into a party. In thus setting themselves up as an aristocracy they founded by their legislation a system of political privileges based on the harsh dominion of riches obtained more or less honestly in the upheaval which ensued upon the fall of the ancient institutions. At this time one of the foremost writers of the age was travelling in Spain and said:

All depends on what you wish to be. If you, Spain and Portugal, only wish to vegetate, you will, by imitating what we French do, attain a mediocrity which will allow you quietly to sink and fall. But if you wish to live, mediocrity will not suffice. Our doctrinaires will teach you to cling inertly to the *status quo*; but what use is the *status quo* to men who are sinking? If we are going to sleep, why should you follow our example? Why need you accompany us even in decadence?

Either the Peninsula listened to the appeal of this noble spirit or (and this is what really happened) its genius reacted violently against the system of the doctrinaires and the greed of the middle class. New revolutions came to prevent the constitution of a Dutch Spain, and in successive revolutions, by importing all the radical institutions of French naturalism, the past was finally destroyed and the Catholic tradition broken. The process of decay was now complete, although in the wilds of remote provinces or in the recesses of a brain here and there some vestiges of the old traditions might remain. Life is marvellously tenacious; it can only develop organically, and in the same way it dies out. We certainly cannot consider the old Spain completely destroyed nor the new Spain formed: naturalism cannot suffice to breathe life into a social body nor is utilitarianism sufficient to govern a system of political organisms. Socially and morally the new Spain is still in process of construction; it is not finished. The main achievement has been one of destruction; but in the closely connected chain of existence destruction necessarily implies reorganization. Just as in the Middle Ages new elements sprang out of the old, so we see now a series of obscure and anonymous collective movements.

That is why there are no great names; that is why social forces in their imposing masses are set against one another, obedient to the voice of a destiny which is to be traced to the very nature of things. However humiliating it may be to our wisdom, the sum of our observations and new knowledge have only succeeded in destroying the old order of ideas; they have not yet succeeded, and it will be a long time before they do, in replacing that order by a new system. Thus we go collectively impelled by fate without sufficient insight to impose ourselves on its obscure workings. Our naturalism is the sign of our moral disorder just as our utilitarianism is the sign of our social disorder. The European movement, humanist, scientific, or whatever we may like to call it, destroyed Christianity and, with Christianity, the old forms and the old balance between the classes. An important result of this fact was the renewal of natural forces which had lain asleep in the heart of a dying system; fresh desires arose, new ideas were discussed, learning was renovated, the sphere of thought enlarged, wealth and well-being increased. But the final question still remains in men's minds: *Quid inde* ? In the impossibility to reply to this question, not only in Spain but in Europe, lies the supreme proof of the blind character of the movements which influence the nations to-day. This is neither new nor extra-ordinary; it has always been thus in periods of organic construction, and we are clearly living in one of these. The lack of a dominating idea or of a collective senti-ment, such as Catholicism was, need not therefore discourage us: all Europe is in the same plight. Where Europe differs from us is in the degree of the develop-ment of knowledge, order, and industry. These three forms of activity belonging to human societies are, we may affirm, likewise the three essential conditions for a future definition of principles. They are essential be-cause of the positivist character of our civilization and because no superior, humanistic or transcendental civilization can exist without them. Whether reason finds in the mind of man the origin and end of all things, or finds this in a God outside humanity and superior to it, it is certain that men cannot normally attain a state of superiority to other created things without first strengthening and fully developing their natural or animal life. There can be no thought without the organs of thought, and a society cannot be morally alive which is not physically prosperous. The constitution of the organ must precede that of the idea, which can only define itself as the collective body grows and prospers. These are no mere rhetorical phrases— they are the strict truth of natural science. Societies obey biological laws which manifest themselves in individuals in a different way but are essentially the same. What we must do if we wish to be numbered among the nations which are rapidly advancing towards a definition of the system of modern ideas is to reconstruct our social body, which more than any other has been undermined and weakened by an illness lasting three centuries. We must increase our scientific knowledge and improve our industries. We must become as wise and as rich as any people in Europe, not because that is the goal of our ambitions, but because without first achieving that we shall never be able to attain them. Finally we must reconstruct our social organism, since the nation which has not set its house in order and attained economic stability will never be in a position to make its voice felt in the councils of humanity. We may find a warning and example in what we know of the long decay of Roman Spain and the gradual organic growth of modern Spain, which ended in the splendid achievement of the sixteenth century. In many ways our history to-day repeats our ancient history, and if we consider that history carefully we may perhaps see in it the proof of the existence of an essential abiding energy which may free us from imitation of foreign models and give to the work of the organic reconstruction of society a native cast, the more solid because it will rest on the character of the race, and the more effective because it will better correspond to the essential requirements of the work of reconstruction.

Spain has always been a democracy. It was so in its tribal phase; it was so under the Roman municipal system. The invasion of the aristocratic Germanic institutions was unable to destroy the existing institutions of Spain nor to form a hereditary caste there as it did in the rest of Europe. This social and historical fact, combined with the character of the race, its nobility, pride, and personal independence, made of the Peninsula a democracy, under a military or ecclesiastic or monarchic or oligarchic government. The foundation had the unchanging character of an igneous rock; the rest was merely accidental, like surface soil liable to be eaten away by torrents; that is, by actions determined by the will of man. To reconstruct our society on a democratic basis is therefore the more solid way. It is more effective because it solves the economic questions which have been raised by the development of riches under the bourgeois régime of central Europe, and which will be raised in Spain more and more as her education and industries advance. These social questions are represented in our time by the conflicts of class interests, the chief problem which a nation has to solve before it can attain a full organic development.

We believe firmly and devoutly (to express in this way our faith in a universal order) in the future organization of the nations of Europe; we therefore believe in a Spain of the future even greater and more noble than she was in the sixteenth century. We likewise believe that we are already set out on the voyage that will lead us to this haven, although the fog obscures our view after losing sight of the coasts of the old world. What part will the Peninsula play, and what will be the character of that future age? History is not prophecy, but study of the past enables us to forecast the future; and when we see through every crisis and in the most adverse atmosphere the heroism and indomitable energy of the Peninsula still victorious, we are inclined to think that we who were the apostles of the old Catholic idea are destined also to be the apostles of the new ideas also. The independent character of individuals and the fine character of the nation as a whole have given to Spain, and will give to her again when her golden age returns, that noble and sovereign air which distinguishes her in the world. The foreigner may love us or hate us, but he cannot be indifferent. Spain has provoked enthusiasm and hatred, but she has never been regarded with contempt or irony.

Centuries hence some historian, when the sun of that future age is setting (for it is only at such a time that history can meditate calmly on the nature of things), will do for that Spain of the future what we have here lovingly done for the Spain of the past.

INDEX